# ADVANCING THE CULTURE
# OF TEACHING ON CAMPUS

Center for Excellence
in Teaching and Learning

UW-Eau Claire

# ADVANCING THE CULTURE OF TEACHING ON CAMPUS

How a Teaching Center Can Make a Difference

*Edited by*

*Constance E. Cook*

*and Matthew Kaplan*

Foreword by Lester P. Monts

1996–2011 15TH ANNIVERSARY

Sty/us

PUBLISHING, LLC.

STERLING, VIRGINIA

Sty/us

Published by Stylus Publishing, LLC
22883 Quicksilver Drive
Sterling, Virginia 20166-2102

**Library of Congress Cataloging-in-Publication Data**
Advancing the culture of teaching on campus : how a
teaching center can make a difference / edited by Constance
E. Cook and Matthew Kaplan ; foreword by Lester P.
Monts.—1st ed.
    p.   cm.
    Includes bibliographical references and index.
    ISBN 978-1-57922-479-0 (cloth : alk. paper)
    ISBN 978-1-57922-480-6 (pbk. : alk. paper)
    ISBN 978-1-57922-723-4 (library networkable e-edition)
    ISBN 978-1-57922-724-1 (consumer e-edition)
    1. Teacher centers—United States.   I. Cook, Constance
Ewing.   II. Kaplan, Matthew (Matthew Lee)
LB1745.A34   2011
378.1′2—dc22                                    2011013126

13-digit ISBN: 978-1-57922-479-0 (cloth)
13-digit ISBN: 978-1-57922-480-6 (paper)
13-digit ISBN: 978-1-57922-723-4 (library networkable
e-edition)
13-digit ISBN: 978-1-57922-724-1 (consumer e-edition)

Printed in the United States of America

All first editions printed on acid-free paper
that meets the American National Standards Institute
Z39-48 Standard.

Bulk Purchases

Quantity discounts are available for use in workshops
and for staff development.
Call 1-800-232-0223

First Edition, 2011

10  9  8  7  6  5  4  3  2

This book is quite timely, as it coincides with the 50th anniversary of the founding of CRLT and, to a large extent, the field of educational development, in 1962. We want to acknowledge the foresight of the University of Michigan faculty who saw the need for a center devoted to teaching, as well as the faculty and graduate students we have worked with and learned from over the years. Michigan is lucky to have a long history of unusually talented teachers on campus, and they are CRLT's partners as we work together to create a culture of teaching.

This book would not have been possible without the wonderful insights of our CRLT colleagues, and we are grateful for both their outstanding work and their willingness to take time from very packed schedules to write the chapters that comprise this volume. One of the joys of working at CRLT is the collaborative spirit, talent, and creativity of our colleagues, which we trust will come through in their writing as it does for us in our daily interactions with them.

We also wish to thank our colleagues at teaching centers across the country who contributed to the concluding chapter. Their descriptions of challenges and the programs they use to overcome them have allowed us to present a much fuller picture of the power of a teaching center than would otherwise have been possible. We would like to thank Mary Deane Sorcinelli, associate provost for academic development at UMass Amherst, and Michele Marincovich, director of the Center for Teaching and Learning at Stanford University, in particular for reading the manuscript so carefully and giving us wise and useful feedback. We would also like to thank Ruby Siddiqui, a graduate student research assistant at CRLT, who brought her attention to detail to the task of proofreading, compiling and editing the reference list and the index, and countless other tasks involved in preparing the final manuscript. Finally, we would like to express our gratitude to Dr. Lester Monts, UM's senior vice provost for academic affairs, who wrote the foreword to this book. As our champion and a tireless voice for teaching excellence on campus for over 15 years, Dr. Monts has been a partner in all that we have been able to accomplish.

*Connie Cook and Matt Kaplan*

# CONTENTS

FOREWORD       *ix*
*Lester P. Monts*


INTRODUCTION       *I*
**CRLT and Its Role at the University of Michigan**
*Constance E. Cook*


**PART ONE: LEADERSHIP AND CORE FUNCTIONS**

1. LEADING A TEACHING CENTER       *19*
    *Constance E. Cook*

2. MEASURING A TEACHING CENTER'S EFFECTIVENESS       *38*
    *Mary C. Wright*

3. FORGING RELATIONSHIPS WITH FACULTY AND
    ACADEMIC ADMINISTRATORS       *50*
    *Constance E. Cook and Deborah S. Meizlish*

4. CONSULTATIONS ON TEACHING       *65*
    **Using Student Feedback for Instructional Improvement**
    *Cynthia J. Finelli, Tershia Pinder-Grover, and Mary C. Wright*

5. GRADUATE PEER TEACHING CONSULTANTS       *80*
    **Expanding the Center's Reach**
    *Tershia Pinder-Grover, Mary C. Wright, and Deborah S. Meizlish*

6. APPROACHES TO PREPARING FUTURE FACULTY
    FOR TEACHING       *97*
    *Chad Hershock, Christopher R. Groscurth, and Stiliana Milkova*

## PART TWO: SPECIAL EMPHASES AT CRLT

7. THE ROLE OF A TEACHING CENTER IN CURRICULAR
   REFORM AND ASSESSMENT     *121*
   *Constance E. Cook, Deborah S. Meizlish, and Mary C. Wright*

8. STRENGTHENING DIVERSITY THROUGH FACULTY
   DEVELOPMENT     *137*
   *Crisca Bierwert*

9. ENGAGING FACULTY IN EFFECTIVE USE OF
   INSTRUCTIONAL TECHNOLOGY     *151*
   *Erping Zhu, Matthew Kaplan, and Charles Dershimer*

10. ACTION RESEARCH FOR INSTRUCTIONAL
    IMPROVEMENT     *167*
    *Chad Hershock, Constance E. Cook, Mary C. Wright, and
    Christopher O'Neal*

11. ROLE-PLAY AND BEYOND     *183*
    **Strategies for Incorporating Theatre Into Faculty Development**
    *Matthew Kaplan and Jeffrey Steiger*

CONCLUSION     *196*
**Responding to Challenges Faced by Teaching Centers at
Research Universities**
*Matthew Kaplan with contributions from:*
   Terry Aladjem, Lori Breslow, Susanna Calkins, Deborah
   DeZure, Robyn Dunbar, Jean C. Florman, Marne Helgesen,
   Alan Kalish, David Langley, Gregory Light, Angela Linse,
   Michele Marincovich, Joan Middendorf, Allison Pingree,
   William C. Rando, Mary Deane Sorcinelli, Kathy Takayama,
   Pratibha Varma-Nelson, Suzanne Weinstein, and Mary-Ann
   Winkelmes

REFERENCES     *213*

ABOUT THE EDITORS AND CONTRIBUTORS     *235*

INDEX     *243*

# FOREWORD

*Lester P. Monts*

I am pleased that members of the Center for Research on Learning and Teaching (CRLT) staff have written this book describing their work and their strategies for doing it effectively. It will be a valuable contribution to the literature on institutional change. CRLT is the premier teaching center in the country, and it has a significant impact on improvements in teaching and learning on the University of Michigan campus. Through my previus role as chair of the College Board's board of trustees and current member of the Board of the Association of American Colleges and Universities, and through my many consultancies around the United States and abroad, I have often heard firsthand from colleagues about the extent to which CRLT serves as an exemplar for other teaching centers and for academic administrators who want to create a culture of teaching excellence on their campuses.

Until recently, college teaching shared the distinction with only a handful of professions for which directed training as a part of graduate education was not systematically provided. I began my career in higher education in the early 1970s as a studio music professor, providing trumpet lessons to undergraduate and graduate students. I had acquired from my former teachers a mixed set of teaching strategies and pedagogies I imparted to my students that resulted in their mastery of the solo, chamber, and orchestral literature for trumpet. I proceeded to teach my students as I had been taught. So much of studio teaching during that era was part of a vast oral tradition that stretched from the conservatories of Europe to the United States and beyond.

Let me advance ten years to the early 1980s when my teaching responsibilities changed dramatically. After completing a doctoral degree in musicology, acquiring a new teaching position at a Research I university, and preparing to lecture to general education students in a high-enrollment world music course, I faced a new teaching dilemma. Although not completely overwhelmed by these new challenges, I sought consultation from instructional development professionals to help me improve my effectiveness in the classroom.

I do not believe that my particular dilemma was unique. Hundreds if not thousands of professors who were trained in advanced degree programs as scholars and researchers are not always fully prepared to perform the role of "teacher" in our colleges and universities successfully. I developed, some would say, to become a good teacher, not only through my own initiative, but also through several means: through my students and colleagues and with the assistance of faculty development professionals. While I am grateful for the contributions of my former students and colleagues, I want to emphasize the importance of faculty development professionals and the Center for Research on Learning and Teaching at the University of Michigan, Ann Arbor.

I arrived at the University of Michigan in 1993, having come from the University of California–Santa Barbara, where I was a professor of music and dean of undergraduate affairs and honors. At Michigan, I became the vice provost for academic and multicultural affairs—and over the years, my title has changed to senior vice provost for academic affairs and senior counselor to the president for the arts, diversity, and undergraduate affairs. While 16 units now report to me, from ROTC to admissions and financial aid, I especially enjoy my work with CRLT. The values that guide the work of CRLT, from improvement in student learning to inclusive teaching for our diverse student body, are values I share.

CRLT had a rich history before I arrived, with luminaries in the field like Professor Wilbert McKeachie giving it an international reputation. Since my arrival, I have joined Executive Director Constance Cook in focusing CRLT's work on service to the University of Michigan community. While CRLT staff are strong scholars who are regularly engaged in research on innovative practices, they prioritize the campus service that has improved student learning. Michigan is a large, decentralized university, so it is a tribute to the CRLT staff that they have been able to customize their work to suit the needs of so many schools and colleges and work closely with the deans to help implement their priorities.

In 1993, CRLT had a staff of 13, only 5 of whom had PhDs. Over the years, CRLT has grown to the point where there are a dozen PhDs on the regular staff as well as several postdoctoral scholars. I have helped CRLT acquire its first coordinator of multicultural teaching and learning, its first evaluation researcher, and its first engineering specialists, among others. I have also promoted the development of a theatre program, the CRLT Players, which has a national reputation for creative use of theatre to improve teaching and learning.

In the lore of American higher education, a distinction is often drawn between *research* and *teaching* universities, implying that for faculty advancement, greater emphasis is placed on one or the other depending on the institution's profile and mission. If faculty members' advancement at research universities depends in large measure on artistic creativity and scholarly inquiry over teaching, are they developing the necessary skills to perform efficiently and effectively in the studio and classroom? Moreover, under this paradigm, how are students, the institutionally acknowledged focal point of our existence, acquiring the knowledge base in the various fields and disciplines they are being taught?

In this regard, I regularly see the impact of CRLT's work. When I meet with the provost and vice provosts about a new initiative on teaching and learning, the first suggestion is to involve CRLT. When I attend meetings of the Information Technology Council or the Undergraduate Deans Group, I hear about CRLT's role in instructional technology or student learning assessment. When I want strong leadership and good ideas for a committee or an initiative on recognizing faculty who make significant contributions to undergraduate education, I involve CRLT staff in leadership roles. CRLT is well known for the high quality of its work, so when the provost's office wants to have something done really well, we often rely on Executive Director Constance Cook and the CRLT professional staff to do it.

Perhaps most important, there has been a real change over the last two decades in the nature of the Michigan casebooks for faculty tenure and promotion. In the past at the New Faculty Orientation, my job was to emphasize pleasantly yet firmly that excellence in teaching would be a major criterion in the awarding of tenure and promotion, and that the programs and services offered by CRLT were available to new faculty. It is now gratifying to read casebooks containing faculty members' statements on teaching or an accompanying letter from the dean acknowledging CRLT's active engagement in faculty members' performance in the classroom, lab, or studio. In the past, tenure and promotion casebooks generally provided only sparse documentation on teaching effectiveness, but now we are presented with convincing evidence that the faculty member has established a record dedicated to teaching excellence.

I am proud to have been associated with these recent developments at CRLT. Over the last two decades, its role to improve teaching and learning at the University of Michigan and beyond has been significant. This book is full of lessons that CRLT has learned through the years. I hope you find it as informative as I do.

# INTRODUCTION

## CRLT and Its Role at the University of Michigan

*Constance E. Cook*

This is a book about running a teaching center. Or, to be more specific, this is a book about the strategies for running a teaching center on the campus of a research university, the University of Michigan (UM) in Ann Arbor. The Center for Research on Learning and Teaching (CRLT) will be marking its 50th anniversary in 2012—the first teaching center ever to reach this milestone! CRLT, established in 1962, is the oldest teaching center in an institution of higher education. We are very proud of our history, and we want to share with university administrators, especially our teaching center colleagues on other campuses, the lessons we have learned along the way.

The purpose of teaching centers like CRLT is faculty development (also called *educational development* or *instructional development for faculty*, with the name of the role varying from one center to another) (Gillespie, Robertson, & Associates, 2010). Teaching centers are a relatively new part of the administrative structure in academe; most have been established in the period from 1990 to 2010. The role of teaching center director was not added by *The Chronicle for Higher Education* to its list of administrator titles (for salary comparison purposes) until 2005 ("Median Salaries of College Administrators," 2005), and a conservative estimate of the proportion of all U.S. postsecondary institutions having a teaching center is only 21% (Kuhlenschmidt, 2011). Centers have been developed at community colleges, liberal arts colleges, comprehensive universities, and specialized institutions such as free-standing law and medical schools, but it is doctoral and research institutions that most often house teaching centers. In fact, three quarters of these institutions have a center now (Kuhlenschmidt, 2011), including all but one of the Big Ten universities and all of the Ivy League. Unfortunately, media coverage of higher education has focused more on the closing of an occasional center than on the establishment of many new centers and the expansion of existing ones (e.g., Bartlett, 2002; Glenn, 2009). As a result, university administrators, even those who have their own teaching center, may not even be aware of the steady growth in such centers on other campuses.

The development of teaching centers has been one way universities have responded to public criticism of higher education. Public concerns, which often focus on student learning outcomes, have come from students, parents, alumni, businesses, and public officials. Criticism began in earnest in the mid-1980s (e.g., Association of American Colleges, 1985; Bennett, 1984; National Institute of Education, 1984) and has gathered considerable momentum since then (e.g., more recently, Bok, 2006; Callan, Jones, Ewell, & Breneman, 2008; Hacker & Dreifus, 2010; Hussey & Smith, 2009; Shavelson, 2010; Smith, 2009; The Secretary of Education's Commission on the Future of Higher Education, 2006).

CRLT, of course, was created before these pressures began, and its experience has been a privileged one. It has always enjoyed funding and political support on the Michigan campus. In fact, almost every new Michigan provost and dean has prioritized teaching more than the one before. But, in spite of the enlightened administration at Michigan and the public's concern about student learning, it is still challenging to run a teaching center at a research university. The university prioritizes research, of course, so the center must try to find ways to highlight and support good teaching on a campus where faculty derive bigger rewards from research success than from teaching effectiveness. Additionally, at a university of the size and complexity of Michigan, communications are difficult: it is hard to publicize new programs and opportunities for faculty, and even when the word is out, our faculty have little discretionary time to devote to professional development. CRLT serves all 19 schools and colleges at UM, so no one size fits all, and it is important to customize and make discipline-specific the programs the center provides. Finally, amid the cacophony of funding requests to the provost for innovative new programs, it is always a challenge to maintain funding for extant programs, no matter how effective. New programs invariably sound sexier.

Nonetheless, CRLT has thrived, and the purpose of this book is to share our strategies for making a teaching center integral to the university's educational mission. Part of the pleasure and challenge of working at a teaching center is that we deal with so many ill-structured problems; there are no right answers. Nonetheless, we have found at CRLT that some approaches work better for us than others.

Some caveats: We are well aware that good fortune has played a significant role in CRLT's success; the stars have been aligned. We also realize that, as with any case study, there are issues of generalizability: our observations do not apply to all research university teaching centers, of course, and often not to the centers on other types of campuses. But we trust that our readers will select from the CRLT story the lessons that apply to their own context and reconstruct the topics presented here so that they are personally useful (Merriam, 2009). We hope that our book will give other faculty developers an occasion to reflect on the management and practices of their centers, and on how best to create a culture of teaching on their campuses.

## CRLT's Changing Roles Over Time

Those of us who currently staff CRLT inherited a center with a strong reputation and name recognition across the country, thanks largely to the efforts of CRLT's first directors. The Center for Research on Learning and Teaching was created in 1962 by the University of Michigan Board of Regents. Eugene Power, a regent who also served on the board of Xerox, asked the university to explore the use of teaching machines and programmed learning. The university appointed a faculty committee to study the issue, namely the Faculty Senate Committee on the Improvement of Instruction. It created an Ad Hoc Committee on Programmed Learning, which recommended in 1962 that the university create a center for research on effective instruction, not just instructional technology. The faculty requested that the center support UM instructors in adopting methods that research had shown to be effective in improving student learning. The center began with a single staff member, Stanford C. Ericksen, professor and chair of psychology at Vanderbilt University, who was a leading figure on human learning and training and was recruited to direct the new center (see Table I.1 for names of CRLT directors and their disciplinary expertise).

After a short interim term led by James Kulik, Psychology Professor Wilbert McKeachie became CRLT's next director. Professor McKeachie became known especially for his authorship of *McKeachie's Teaching Tips*, the most popular book on college teaching ever published, which is currently in its 13th edition and is now co-authored with Marilla Svinicki (Svinicki &

**TABLE I.1**
**CRLT Directors, 1962–2010**

| Name | Years as Director | Field of Expertise |
|------|-------------------|--------------------|
| Stanford Ericksen | 1962–1973 | Psychology |
| James Kulik (interim director) | 1973–1975 | Psychology |
| Wilbert McKeachie | 1975–1983 | Psychology |
| Donald Brown | 1983–1993 | Psychology |
| Constance E. Cook | 1993–Present | Political Science |

McKeachie, 2011). In 1983, Donald Brown became the CRLT's director, and he was also a psychology professor. He was instrumental in planning the UM Residential College, one of the longest-running undergraduate living-learning programs in the United States. I became director of CRLT in 1993 and currently serve in that role. With the exception of James Kulik, each of the directors has served for an extended period, which probably has contributed to the center's stability and good fortune.

CRLT has always been known for its research and publications. In 1963, Ericksen began publishing *Memo to the Faculty*, a newsletter that announced and analyzed new research and practices related to instruction. Six times a year, CRLT sent the *Memo* to all UM faculty and to subscribers across the country and around the world. The *Memo* ended when Ericksen retired from CRLT in 1982, and it was replaced in 1987 by *CRLT Occasional Papers*, which continue to this day (http://www.crlt.umich.edu/publinks/occasional.php).

From CRLT's beginning, its staff regularly published research findings in national journals. In the years 1963–1993, the majority of professional staff were faculty or research scientists (almost always in psychology), so research and publishing were essential for their tenure and promotion, and they focused on it accordingly.

In addition to CRLT's research agenda, its programs and services grew over time. CRLT staff began offering workshops for faculty in 1968, and by 1976, the center was also providing faculty grants for instructional improvement. CRLT hosted the first orientations for new teaching assistants (TAs) and faculty in 1978 and its first workshop for international TAs in 1985. The first CRLT midterm student feedback services (also known as Small Group Instructional Diagnosis, or SGID) began in 1990.

When the UM provost asked me to direct the center in 1993, he said he wanted CRLT to concentrate on more programs and services for the UM campus. As a result, I began hiring staff members who did not have faculty appointments and could focus attention more fully on improving teaching on our campus without having the competing demand to publish for tenure and promotion. Current CRLT professional staff have PhDs in a wide variety of disciplines (currently anthropology, biology, chemistry, comparative literature, engineering [both electrical and mechanical], political science, sociology, and instructional systems technology). These professional staff are scholars who continue to do research and publish broadly, but those activities are not their first priority.

## CRLT's Current Profile

As this book goes to press in fall 2011, CRLT has 24 regular staff members (including 12 PhDs) and a comparable number of part-time graduate student staff each year. While CRLT is one of the largest teaching centers in the country, it is sobering to realize that these 12 professionals with doctorates are serving about 3,300 faculty and more than 2,000 TAs (called graduate student instructors, or GSIs, at Michigan) in UM's 19 schools and colleges. There is much more demand than this small group can possibly satisfy, which is why strategizing about priorities is our continual preoccupation.

CRLT reports to the senior vice provost, who has been a stalwart ally (see this volume's foreword). Our strategy at UM is to enhance the culture of teaching by using two approaches simultaneously: *depth*, that is, multiple ongoing activities for small numbers of faculty, administrators, and TAs; and *breadth*, that is, onetime activities on myriad topics, in diverse ways, that reach as many people on campus as possible. We also prioritize discipline-specific work since faculty have strong connections to their departments and pay special attention to customized programs and services. Over time, we have established a strong presence in most of Michigan's 19 schools and colleges as well as in the provost's office.

It is difficult to describe CRLT succinctly because the services change from year to year, according to need, and so do the priorities. Our best attempt at an overview of CRLT programs and services appears in the appendix to this introduction.

## How CRLT Differs From Other Teaching Centers

In many respects, CRLT mirrors other centers in the nature of the work we do, but our relatively large staff, with lots of part-time graduate students, allows us more opportunities to provide a greater quantity of high-quality programs and services.

Besides our size, CRLT diverges from the norm in other ways. My comments about our differences and similarities grow out of my familiarity with the Ivy League Plus institutions (the Ivy League plus Stanford, MIT, and the University of Chicago) and the CIC (Committee on Institutional Collaboration, which comprises Big Ten universities plus the University of Chicago), as well as with the literature on research university teaching centers (especially Dotson & Bernstein, 2010; Frantz, Beebe, Horvath, Canales, & Swee, 2005; Gillespie et al., 2010; Kuhlenschmidt, Weaver, & Morgan, 2010; Pchenitchnaia & Cole, 2009; Sorcinelli, Austin, Eddy, & Beach, 2006; Wright, 2000).

### *Areas Where CRLT Is Similar to Most Other Centers*

- Like most centers, CRLT has some instructional technology (IT) expertise (two staff members have a background in technology), but we are not the hub of IT activity on campus. Rather, we serve as a clearinghouse (bringing people and ideas together), a funder, and an evaluator, and we try to have a pedagogy voice at the table when campus IT decision making occurs.
- Like most centers, CRLT no longer administers the course evaluation system (we were able to disengage from that responsibility ten years ago), so faculty can view us solely as an office that provides support for them, not evaluation of them.
- Like most other centers, a good deal of CRLT's resources are allocated to individual services to instructors: consultations and midterm student feedback (MSF) (or SGID).

### *Higher-Priority Foci for CRLT, Compared With Some Other Centers*

- Half of CRLT's work is with faculty, half with teaching assistants. We do more work with faculty than do some other research university centers, many of which focus more on graduate students.
- Half of CRLT's work is discipline-specific, which is more customized work than most teaching centers perform. We believe that the work we do in the disciplines may be more effective than our university-wide work, so we prioritize it in our decisions about use of resources.

- CRLT has a special office for the College of Engineering, called CRLT in Engineering. It is staffed by PhDs in engineering, has space at the college, and serves the engineering faculty solely.
- CRLT provides a consultation on teaching to any faculty member or TA who requests one, as is true of most centers. Thanks to the graduate teaching consultants we hire and train, CRLT does an unusually large number of MSFs (or SGIDs).
- CRLT focuses more attention on multicultural teaching and learning than do many centers, which is appropriate at a university that values diversity as much as Michigan does. We believe that multicultural pedagogy and curriculum make teaching better for all students, not just those at the margins. We try to infuse multicultural elements into all aspects of our programs and services, and we engage in professional development to make this work easier for our staff. Our definition of diversity is very broad, and we focus on both retention of underrepresented students and the range of diversity issues that arise in instructional contexts.
- CRLT has a theatre program, the first for audiences of faculty and TAs and run by a university teaching center. Although we have held National Science Foundation (NSF)–funded training programs on interactive theatre for other centers, only a couple have actually developed a theatre program of their own. The primary focus of our theatre work is diversity and how it plays out in both teaching and learning contexts and faculty work life.
- CRLT does a larger amount of assessment and evaluation research than do most other centers, with a research scientist in charge of evaluation and assessment and every professional staff member doing some of that work.
- CRLT is unusual in administering eight grant competitions, which together fund nearly 100 faculty per year.
- CRLT does more applied research and publishing than do most centers, as previously explained, even though it is not our first priority.
- CRLT is fortunate to administer most of the major teaching prizes on campus so its name is associated with those awards and teaching excellence.
- CRLT administers the chair and associate dean training programs for the provost, which gives us special access and visibility to department chairs.

- CRLT has an unusually large number of services for postdoctoral scholars, including a short course to teach them about teaching and prepare them for the faculty job market.
- For several years, CRLT staff have run the Michigan-China University Leadership Forum (a two-week professional development seminar for Chinese university presidents) on behalf of UM's president, and that initiative is now leading to some assistance for Chinese universities on faculty development (see chapter 1). While some teaching center directors are beginning to consult with teaching centers abroad, I am unaware of any centers that are engaging in an international program of the magnitude of the one we are currently embarking on with China.

## *Lower-Priority Foci for CRLT, Compared With Some Other Centers*

- Like most centers, CRLT has a seminar series, but it is not a major focus for us. Rather, it is a way to make the center visible to the entire campus by publicizing a new set of programs every term.
- Like most peer organizations, CRLT serves as a liaison for the university with national initiatives to improve teaching and learning, for example, those initiated by the Carnegie Foundation for the Advancement of Teaching and the Association of American Colleges and Universities (AAC&U)—recruiting faculty participants, organizing related programs, and disseminating information about the national findings. However, these national initiatives are not a primary focus for CRLT, as they are for many other centers.
- While CRLT has some soft money (e.g., NSF grants), we rarely apply directly for those grants, and when we are involved in them, it is usually in the service of a proposal on which a faculty member is the principal investigator (PI). (Staff in CRLT in Engineering, in the College of Engineering, do serve as PIs on federal grants.)

## Overview of Contents

The chapters that follow detail most of the foci listed in this introduction, explaining our thinking as we decide where our priorities will be and what we are trying to achieve. CRLT staff share a strategic approach to their work and a common set of operational principles (see chapter 1). This book is a collaborative effort by all professional members of the CRLT staff, each of whom has written or contributed to one or more chapters. You will see in these chapters the CRLT approach as it plays out in a wide variety of programs and services. We have divided the book into two major parts, the first covering functions common to teaching centers across the country, and the second describing services that are special emphases at CRLT. The conclusion comprises advice from teaching center directors at research universities across the country.

The entire book has been edited by CRLT Managing Director Matthew Kaplan, with my advice. It represents the vision I have brought to CRLT, with modifications and refinements over time from Matt and all of the capable members of CRLT's staff. When people ask me why CRLT has flourished, my answer is easy: it flourishes because my colleagues are, without exception, unusually bright, creative, collaborative, and committed to improving student learning. Every day, I feel lucky and grateful to be working with such remarkable people. A teaching center is only as good as its staff.

## Part One: Leadership and Core Functions

Chapter 1, "Leading a Teaching Center," describes my philosophy of leadership and how I implement it at CRLT, including the role of the director, our budgetary strategies, and my operational principles. It also explains our approach to staff oversight, especially the hiring process for instructional consultants, management of the workload, and professional development opportunities.

Chapter 2, "Measuring a Teaching Center's Effectiveness," by Mary C. Wright (assistant director for evaluation and assistant research scientist), provides an overview of how to design, implement, and use a comprehensive faculty development evaluation system. In this chapter, she also offers strategies for using evaluation to enhance and grow a teaching center.

Deborah S. Meizlish, an assistant director at CRLT, and I co-authored chapter 3, "Forging Relationships With Faculty and Academic Administrators." We discuss strategies for interacting effectively with various center constituencies, especially the faculty, provost, deans, and department chairs, as well as other university offices. By leveraging its relationships, a teaching center can have a more substantial impact and become integral to programming and decision making on campus.

Chapter 4, "Consultations on Teaching: Using Student Feedback for Instructional Improvement," was written by Cynthia J. Finelli, director of

CRLT in Engineering; Tershia Pinder-Grover, an assistant director at CRLT; and Mary C. Wright. They describe their research on the efficacy of various approaches to MSF and identify how other modes of formative student feedback—such as customized student surveys—can be coupled effectively with a consultation. Finally, they highlight the critical role instructional consultants play in helping instructors interpret student feedback and identify strategies for improvement.

Chapter 5, "Graduate Peer Teaching Consultants: Expanding the Center's Reach," has three co-authors: Tershia Pinder-Grover, Mary C. Wright, and Deborah S. Meizlish, all of whom have directed CRLT's peer teaching consultants (PTCs) programs. Through training workshops and ongoing teaching circles, CRLT's professional staff prepare a cohort of graduate students to be consultants. PTCs consult with TAs on numerous pedagogical topics, observe and videotape their classes, and gather feedback from their students. This chapter describes the selection, training, supervision, and evaluation of CRLT's three PTC programs.

Chapter 6, "Approaches to Preparing Future Faculty for Teaching," was written by Chad Hershock, an assistant director at CRLT; Christopher R. Groscurth, a former CRLT consultant; and Stiliana Milkova, an assistant director at CRLT. Nationally, programs for preparing future faculty (PFF) vary greatly in their design, content, and scope. This chapter discusses five complementary, transferable PFF models, focusing on how each program prepares future faculty to teach, the pros and cons of each approach, and strategies for overcoming the challenges of designing programs for a diverse, interdisciplinary clientele. Finally, the authors consider how these approaches promote a culture of teaching excellence among graduate students and postdoctoral scholars as well as faculty and administrators.

### Part Two: Special Emphases at CRLT

Chapter 7, "The Role of a Teaching Center in Curricular Reform and Assessment," has three co-authors: Deborah S. Meizlish, Mary C. Wright, and me. This chapter provides an overview of the strategies CRLT uses to promote curricular reform and assessment university-wide as well as at the college and department levels. It focuses on how CRLT comes to be involved, the range of services CRLT provides, the ways CRLT consultants try to embed assessment activities in curricular reform and make them succeed, and the value to the academic units in having CRLT support.

Chapter 8, "Strengthening Diversity Through Faculty Development," is written by Crisca Bierwert, CRLT's associate director and coordinator of multicultural learning and teaching. It describes how a teaching center contributes to the social and cultural diversity of a university and includes a review of teaching center programs that address key elements of diversity on campus: the success of diverse students, the engagement and retention of diverse faculty members, and the vibrancy of multicultural ideas and practices in academic units and communities. The chapter also discusses strategic approaches, including community building with other units and embedding multiculturalism in programs to appeal to audiences broader than those who prioritize multicultural goals.

Chapter 9, "Engaging Faculty in Effective Use of Instructional Technology," is co-authored by Erping Zhu, assistant director and coordinator of instructional technology; Matthew Kaplan; and Charles Dershimer, a former CRLT IT specialist. This chapter outlines a holistic approach that supports, evaluates, and disseminates best practices in instructional technology across the academic community, from faculty and TAs to staff and administrators. In addition to an overview of approaches used to promote best practices, the chapter extracts general principles that teaching and learning centers can use as a framework for addressing their own campus technology needs.

Chapter 10, "Action Research for Instructional Improvement," is authored by Chad Hershock and includes a reprint of a 2007 article from *To Improve the Academy* by Mary C. Wright, Christopher O'Neal (former CRLT consultant), and me. It presents action research as a powerful tool that teaching centers can use to improve teaching and learning. This chapter describes CRLT action research projects concerning retention and attrition in science gateway courses and mathematics, with particular attention given to the role of teaching assistants. The epilogue outlines the important curricular changes made in UM departments as a result of CRLT's 2003 action research initiative. The chapter concludes with a discussion of principles for teaching center staff who wish to conduct their own action research projects.

Chapter 11, "Role-Play and Beyond: Strategies for Incorporating Theatre Into Faculty Development," was written by Matthew Kaplan and Jeffrey Steiger, artistic director of the CRLT Players. This chapter focuses on creating role-plays and short vignettes designed to surface the often complex dynamics that surround teaching and administrative processes in the academy. Kaplan and Steiger discuss the goals and benefits of theatre; ways to create vignettes using the real-life experience of faculty, staff, and students; preparation of non-actors for performance; and adaptation of the skills of faculty developers to facilitation of vignettes.

## *Conclusion*

The conclusion, "Responding to Challenges Faced by Teaching Centers at Research Universities," is a compendium of advice from colleagues who are part of the CIC and Ivy League Plus teaching center directors groups and experienced practitioners who have a long history of involvement with faculty development. Each of them describes a specific challenge he or she has faced, along with the successful approaches the author used to handle it. The challenges are grouped by topic, providing a rich source of advice and ideas.

# OVERVIEW OF THE CENTER FOR RESEARCH ON LEARNING AND TEACHING (CRLT)

| | |
|---|---|
| **Established** | 1962 |
| **Reporting Line** | Senior Vice Provost for Academic Affairs |
| **CRLT Mission** | • Creating a culture of teaching at UM<br>• Improving teaching and student learning on campus<br>• Fostering a climate in which diverse students can learn and excel<br>• Researching and disseminating findings for better student learning |
| **Services** | • For 19 UM schools and colleges (including 3,300 faculty and 2,100 TAs)<br>• Total of 18,885 services provided by CRLT in 2009–2010<br>  ○ Services to 4,229 UM individuals<br>  ○ Services to 2,408 external individuals<br>  ○ Service on more than 40 UM committees, and collaboration with 30 UM offices |
| **CRLT Staff** | • Executive Director, Managing Director, and Associate Director<br>• 12 PhD Faculty Developers and 3 postdoctoral scholars<br>• Theatre Artistic Director, Theatre Managing Director, and Theatre Administrative Coordinator (plus about 15 part-time actors)<br>• 7 Project Staff (e.g., events, publications/website, grants, budget, technology)<br>• 22 Peer Teaching Consultants (about .10 FTE apiece)<br>• Special office in the College of Engineering, called CRLT in Engineering, staffed by engineers |
| **Distribution of CRLT Work** | • 50% of CRLT work is faculty-related; 50% teaching assistant–related<br>• 50% of CRLT work is university-wide; 50% is discipline-based |

| | |
|---|---|
| **CRLT's Special Emphases** | • Active and collaborative learning<br>• Multicultural teaching and learning<br>• Assessment of student learning<br>• Interdisciplinary teaching and learning<br>• Instructional technology<br>• Preparing Future Faculty<br>• Evaluation research |
| **For Faculty** | • 8 grant competitions to fund instructional innovations (over $300,000 awarded to more than 95 faculty per year)<br>• Discipline-specific orientations, retreats, workshops, and consultations at departmental and school/college request, for example, on curricular reform, climate, evaluation of teaching, technology<br>• New Faculty Orientation for the whole university<br>• Teaching Academy for all new faculty in the principal undergraduate college<br>• Two Provost's Seminars on Teaching each year<br>• Series of seminars/workshops for faculty every semester<br>• Midterm student feedback, especially for new faculty<br>• Individual consultations; videotaping/observations<br>• Professional development for department chairs and associate deans<br>• Website with teaching strategies and UM resources guide<br>• Publications of research on teaching and learning<br>• Administration of teaching prizes: Thurnau Professors, U.S. Professor of the Year, Michigan Distinguished Professor of the Year, and Teaching Innovation Prizes |
| **CRLT Players Theatre Program** | • Performances for faculty, graduate students, and academic administrators<br>• 25 sketches on teaching and learning, faculty work life, diversity, and medical instruction<br>• In 2009–2010, more than 50 performances for audiences of over 2,700 people |
| **For Graduate Students and Postdoctoral Scholars** | • Orientation for new TAs in Fall and Winter terms<br>• Support for departmental TA development<br>• Orientations for international TAs<br>• Seminars/workshops for TAs every semester<br>• Midterm student feedback, individual consultations, videotaping, and observations<br>• Website and publications<br>• Graduate Teacher Certificate<br>• Graduate Teaching Consultants<br>• 4 Preparing Future Faculty programs<br>• Short-course on college teaching for postdoctoral scholars |

| | |
|---|---|
| **Assessment of Student Learning** | • Assessment of student learning in core courses for deans in 14 UM schools and colleges<br>• Assessment website with resources for faculty<br>• Provost's Seminar on approaches to assessing student learning<br>• Assessment Symposium for department chairs and key faculty<br>• Consultations with individual faculty and academic administrators<br>• Facilitation of workshops and retreats focused on assessing learning<br>• Assistance with data collection, including focus groups and surveys<br>• Grants and resources, including Gilbert Whitaker Fund and the Investigating Student Learning grant, both focused on assessment |
| **Diversity Impact** | • Inclusive teaching strategies embedded in all programs<br>• Assessment of student retention and success for underrepresented groups<br>• Workshops and consultations on identity and classroom dynamics<br>• Workshops and consultations on handling classroom controversy and silence<br>• Consultations on multicultural curricular development and course design<br>• Cross-disciplinary faculty seminars on multicultural and inclusive teaching<br>• Provost's Seminar on internationalization<br>• Networking event for international faculty |
| **CRLT's External Initiatives** | • Administration of research projects funded by the Teagle Foundation, Spencer Foundation, and National Science Foundation<br>• Founder of Committee on Institutional Cooperation (CIC) Teaching Center Directors Group<br>• Member of the Ivy League (Plus) Teaching Consortium<br>• Michigan-China University Leadership Forum: two-week program in collaboration with the Ministry of Education for presidents of top-ranked Chinese universities<br>• Faculty Development Institute (for administrators and faculty at top Chinese universities) |
| **CRLT's Research Projects to Improve Student Learning** | • Experiments to Improve Writing and Critical Thinking<br>• Curricular and Extracurricular Activities That Promote Ethical Development<br>• Efficacy of Video Podcasts in Large Lectures<br>• Role of a Teaching Center in Administrative Training<br>• Investigations of the Science of Learning |

- Impact of Meta-Cognitive Strategies on Disciplinary Writing and Thinking
- Using Screencasts Strategically to Help Student Learning
- Investigating Faculty Perceptions of Millennial Student Learning
- Alternative Methods for Gathering Student Feedback
- How Student Learning Differs from UM in Elite Chinese Universities

# PART ONE

## LEADERSHIP AND CORE FUNCTIONS

# LEADING A TEACHING CENTER

*Constance E. Cook*

Much has been written about how to establish a teaching center, set its priorities, and position it to be an effective change agent on campus (e.g., Chism, 1998; Gillespie, 2010; Sorcinelli, 2002). But there is surprisingly little about the internal operation of a teaching center, perhaps because most of them are so small (Sorcinelli, Austin, Eddy, & Beach, 2006). Nonetheless, organizational management is a critical element in success, and many challenges are involved in running a teaching center. Management is a topic that deserves more attention.

This chapter concerns the basic elements of teaching center direction: the role of the director, finding and nurturing staff, a budgetary model, and operational principles. What follows are my personal opinions and practices, so I often use a first-person pronoun to describe them.

## The Role of the Director

I am a political scientist by training, not an educational specialist. My CRLT professional colleagues are the educational specialists who consult with faculty about teaching improvement and run workshops to train instructors. They do those jobs superbly. My own academic expertise concerns political interest groups: how groups mobilize and advocate for public policy goals (see Cook, 1980, 1998). That academic background has stood me in good stead on campus since university politics are not unlike the public policy-making process. I consider myself the chief lobbyist on campus for teaching improvement, and the strategies I use—such as coalition building, data gathering and dissemination, and logrolling—mirror the ones that lobbyists use

in local politics, state capitals, and Washington, D.C. Perhaps the big difference is that money does not change hands in the same way: CRLT runs eight
grant competitions, as well as all the major teaching awards at UM, but we
always rely on faculty peer review to avoid any possible hint of CRLT impro-
priety or favoritism.

## Role on Campus

Sometimes, people in new academic leadership positions at a research university spend much of their time on airplanes. Teaching center directors can
always attend multiple conferences, and senior people have opportunities to
consult on other campuses and serve as speakers. *However, visibility is one of
the critical jobs of a teaching center director.* I believe that there is no way to
lobby effectively on campus without being on campus myself, so I avoid
frequent travel and devote substantial time to the center's needs. That is
especially necessary in a director's first years, but since things move fast on a
university campus (players change frequently, as do their short-term priorities), it is always helpful to be present to understand and respond to new
opportunities and new challenges. Also, on a campus the size of UM, it takes
a long time to develop relations with the dozens of key players. Being available on campus means that a director can make personal connections with
academic leaders across the university and foster collaborations by serving
on key committees and attending university-wide programs and receptions.
It is important to put the director's brand on events the center does in
collaboration with others, and that is best done by being there, being visible,
and often by making brief introductory remarks. Having my name attached
to the center's presence helps to identify it for some faculty; when they see
my name, they understand the teaching center's involvement.

## Role Beyond Campus

Given the reputation of the University of Michigan, CRLT accomplishments tend to be noticed elsewhere even when I am not on the road trumpeting our activities. No doubt, a good website helps (http://www.crlt
.umich.edu), and ours gets a lot of traffic: more than 330,000 unique visits
annually, including hits from people in more than 200 countries and territo-
ries (visit http://www.crlt.umich.edu/aboutcrlt/aboutcrlt.php to view CRLT's
Annual Report).

For me, colleagueship and advice from other center directors has been
invaluable. Experienced directors at other institutions mentored me as I

assumed my CRLT role, and I have tried to "pay it forward" and serve that function for other directors as well. Most important to me have been my meetings with consortia of directors—both the Ivy League (Plus) Teaching Consortium, which Michigan was invited to join, and the Committee on Institutional Cooperation (CIC, or Big Ten plus Chicago), which I created in 2002. Both of these networks have a day-and-a-half-long annual meeting, plus an occasional reunion at a national conference. But the most valuable aspect of the networks has been the willingness of these directors to share information quickly and candidly through e-mail. I can send a question to these two message groups about a current concern at Michigan (e.g., salary scales for new instructional consultants, online course evaluations, or evaluation of teaching center services), and I am likely to have 15–20 well-informed and candid responses in less than 24 hours. My colleagues inform, advise, and commiserate with me, for which I am grateful. Periodically, I consult on other campuses, usually doing program reviews for other teaching centers. These consultations provide good ideas and help me clarify my own thinking about why we do what we do at CRLT.

## Finding and Nurturing Staff

These days, one of the foci of business management literature is new work on positive organizational scholarship. This scholarship describes strategies for creating a positive environment in the workplace by focusing on strengths, rather than weaknesses; fostering mutually supportive relationships; and providing staff with meaning and purpose (Cameron, 2008). What follows is a description of how we try to create that kind of positive environment at CRLT. I say "we" because I share my management responsibilities with CRLT's managing director and associate director. We meet weekly and discuss issues as a group before I make decisions.

### *Hiring the Right People*

In his seminal book on managing colleges and universities, Keller (1983) said, "In my experience, a decisive difference between the noted colleges and universities and the less-noted ones is the attention they pay to the selection of their people" (p. 137). At CRLT, we believe that hiring may well be the most important task we perform. A center's reputation depends on the quality of its staff. Unlike English departments, for example, teaching centers are still relatively new and are not considered integral to a university's identity. Therefore, it is incumbent on us to prove our value by consistently doing excellent work, and in large quantities. We try to hire people who not only are experts at their work but are also highly motivated, energetic, self-starting, innovative, and collegial.

Good hiring takes a lot of effort, and what usually causes us to hire is that we have to replace people who have left. So, by definition, we are often short-staffed when we begin the labor-intensive task of a search. But the axiom "Pay now or pay later" applies here. If we do not conduct the search thoroughly and, instead, settle for someone who is not quite what we need or about whom we do not know enough, we can find ourselves with much more work, as we try to move that person out of the organization over time. Along the way, poor hires can ruin staff morale and erode a center's good reputation on campus.

### Disciplinary Backgrounds

We believe that a teaching center is most effective on a large campus if its professional staff have PhDs from a variety of disciplines. Of course, it is not possible to pair each department with a staff member who has exactly the same expertise; CRLT has 12 PhDs on staff, but the university has 19 schools and colleges and more than 200 different academic departments. Nonetheless, we try for a rough approximation by, for example, assigning consultants with a science background to faculty and departments in the sciences, medicine, and allied health fields. Faculty relate better to consultants whose disciplinary expertise approximates their own.

### Previous Experience

We hire staff who have had some college teaching experience, at least as a teaching assistant if not as a faculty member or an instructor of record. That experience serves consultants well in understanding and empathizing with the problems instructors bring to them. Additionally (and for us, more importantly), we want staff who have had faculty development experience. Staff at CRLT have worked (or interned) at other teaching centers as faculty developers, been faculty members themselves, or served as departmental mentors for their graduate student colleagues before they received their degrees. It is very hard to find these people, and there is competition for them across the country: in a three-month period at the depths of the recession in 2009, the Professional and Organizational Development Network in

Higher Education (POD) posted 58 ads for faculty developers, assistant or associate directors, or directors of teaching centers. The candidate pool is small, and the competition for the best hires is fierce.

*Advertising*

Figuring out where to post ads is often the biggest challenge. Good hiring starts with good advertising geared to the populations from which candidates are likely to come. There is no single good source of faculty developers because they come from many disciplines and with many different kinds of educational and employment experiences, making it difficult to choose the right media for ads. We need a diverse staff to serve our diverse faculty and enrich our center's perspectives, so we advertise in outlets that reach a variety of populations. These include listservs for faculty development professional organizations (POD, Society for Teaching and Learning in Higher Education [STLHE], regional POD groups), the higher education press websites (*The Chronicle of Higher Education*, Inside Higher Ed), venues for diversity and technology (Diverse Issues in Higher Education, EDUCAUSE), and relevant disciplinary associations.

*Criteria and Processes for Decision Making*

The skills and knowledge base we especially value at CRLT are listed in Table 1.1, along with the search process activities that let candidates demonstrate the extent to which they possess these abilities.

To determine the extent to which candidates have these skills, our hiring process is long and involved. After reviewing candidates' CVs, cover letters, and samples of scholarly writing, we often talk with the most promising ones by videoconference, such as Skype, or we do a quick personal interview for those nearby. The candidates who make the cut then go through a series of steps that enable us to know them better and them to know us as well. The first step is homework: we ask them to write one essay about how they would go about organizing one of the large programs CRLT typically runs for faculty and another essay about a success they have had in bringing about institutional change.

After we review their essays, we invite candidates to come in for short individual interviews with all of CRLT's professional staff. Then comes a group interview with the same people. Since faculty developers typically handle ill-structured problems (Tiberius, Tipping, and Smith, 1997), we ask candidates to role-play a CRLT staff member whose clients are bringing her

### TABLE 1.1
**Desired Candidate Skills and Knowledge, and Processes for
Measuring Them During a Search**

| Desired Skills and Knowledge | Measurement Processes |
| --- | --- |
| Public speaking and presentations | Interviews, workshops |
| Writing and research | Scholarly writing sample, cover letter, written essays |
| Interpersonal skills | Interviews |
| Consultation skills and reflectiveness | Role-plays |
| Knowledge of faculty development and disciplinary literature | Interviews and workshop |
| Event planning | Written essay and interviews |
| Experience with effecting institutional change | Written essay and interviews |

authentic, challenging problems that lack easy solutions (see chapter 11). After each role-play, we ask candidates to debrief what went well and what they might have done differently. Finally, candidates present a workshop on a topic of their choice. The workshop is limited to 50 minutes, followed by a half hour of debriefing with the audience about the strengths and weaknesses of the presentation. We hope candidates use their debriefing opportunities (after the role-plays and workshop) to acknowledge gaps in their own knowledge and areas for growth. We prize people's ability to be reflective (Schön, 1983).

The steps just described take a couple of days, which is useful because people's behavior often changes as they become more comfortable in a new environment. Candidates often fall out of the pool partway through, either because they decide they are not truly serious about wanting the job (it is a lot of work to be a candidate for a CRLT position) or because they do not make the cut. Along the way, they learn how seriously CRLT takes its hiring process and how much we insist on attention to detail and quality control. They also learn, especially from the homework and the scenarios, what the nature of the work really will be. And they get to know their prospective new colleagues.

At the end of the search process, the CRLT professional staff discuss the strengths and challenges of each candidate. No candidate is expected to be perfect, of course, but our discussion of challenges is helpful even for candidates who do get hired, because it shapes the professional development opportunities we provide to that person. The choice of a candidate does not have to be unanimous (the director has the final word), but our lengthy vetting process almost always brings the CRLT staff to a consensus.

### Timeline

We are very thorough in our search processes, but we also try to come to closure on each candidate very quickly. Slow, drawn-out searches often sap the enthusiasm of candidates and make it harder to finalize the deal. Hiring is a courtship: we try to show candidates that CRLT is a great place to work—a place where each individual has a varied and frequently changing set of responsibilities and where there is a healthy combination of autonomy and colleague support. We do not assume that candidates understand our work or our environment, so we try to make the search process as informative as possible. Even if we do decide not to hire particular candidates, we want them to be eager to join our workforce and to gain an understanding of and respect for CRLT during the search process.

### Other Staff Hires

At CRLT, there are seven staff (whom we call *project staff*) whose work ranges from computer support to events planning and website management. They are overseen by an office manager who also does research and editing. For project staff positions, like the consultant positions, we craft a search process with written tasks and oral role-plays. Sometimes we are lucky enough to find an excellent long-term hire; however, we often hire new college graduates who have lots of energy and motivation but are new to office work. Typically, we offer training and mentoring in exchange for having these bright employees with us for a year or two before they go on to graduate school. It is hard to do perpetual hiring, socialization, and mentoring, but we enjoy the new faces and fresh ideas inherent in the frequent turnover of project staff.

### Workload

At CRLT we try to encourage what the business management literature describes as job crafting (Berg, Dutton, & Wrzesniewski, 2008). We have highly motivated, capable staff, and they deserve to have real meaning in their careers. To help them achieve it, we encourage them to customize (or craft) their jobs to fit their own interests and abilities. We try to encourage autonomy and discretion whenever possible. Job customization typically includes cognitive crafting, task crafting, and relational crafting (Wellman & Spreitzer, 2010; Wrzesniewski & Dutton, 2001). In other words, we encourage staff to have new learning experiences on a regular basis (cognitive crafting); change the boundaries of their assignments, as needed, by redirecting, reshaping, and expanding or contracting them as long as they still fit CRLT's mission and workload (task crafting); and collaborate with colleagues on the CRLT staff, elsewhere at UM, and at other campuses (relational crafting). We encourage an entrepreneurial spirit among CRLT's faculty developers. Fortunately, there is so much work and such varied work at CRLT that it is not difficult to customize individual workloads and foci.

### Division of Labor (Task Crafting)

CRLT professional staff work is organized as a matrix, with some staff serving specific disciplinary areas (i.e., engineering, sciences and math, social sciences, humanities and arts) and others serving topic areas (e.g., instructional technology, evaluation research, and multicultural teaching and learning). Some professional staff members combine the two approaches (disciplinary specialists who are also skilled in a specific topic), but most people's work is focused on one or the other.

A center as large as CRLT has the luxury of an ever-changing division of labor. Naturally, we try to put those with specific expertise into the roles that suit and interest them. To illustrate, a consultant with a language background probably would work with the language departments. Since we cannot always pair a unit with a disciplinary expert, staff must have the research and interpersonal skills that enable them to learn about an unfamiliar area, both from the research and by talking to faculty in that discipline. For large events, such as the orientation programs for teaching assistants or the Preparing Future Faculty Conference, we rotate some of the responsibility, giving staff members variety and bringing new ideas to the initiatives. The rotation is possible because we have written detailed procedures manuals for each of the large CRLT events so new consultants (and project staff) can take responsibility but have guidance about how to proceed.

### Support for Professional Staff (Relational Crafting)

Given that professional staff are so precious (it is hard to find people with PhDs, college teaching experience, and faculty development experience), and

CRLT is so selective about the hiring process, we try to get the maximum advantage from each person's expertise by providing him or her with a great deal of assistance. CRLT has several administrative assistants who do the logistical work for our large events, plan our travel, and assist with other time-consuming work, like data entry and analysis for tracking and reporting our services. We also have postdoctoral scholars and graduate students who provide research support: they assist with data collection and analysis, help draft articles, and prepare bibliographies. The availability of administrative support and graduate students is intended to free the professional staff to use their own time as efficiently as possible. While we are fortunate to have the funds to pay for this support, smaller teaching centers might consider using internships or work-study students to get the help they need.

### Professional Development for Staff (Cognitive Crafting)

The variety of topics that comes to a teaching center on a campus as large and complex as ours is truly remarkable. There is never a shortage of challenges and new opportunities. Because we are continually responding to interesting new requests for campus programs and services, we all need to develop skills and knowledge to perform well and serve campus needs. We also seek ways to stimulate and infuse new ideas at CRLT. Job crafting includes cognitive development, that is, finding ways to help staff learn and grow. That kind of activity is the norm at CRLT; we are a learning organization (Senge, 1990, 2000).

We have found at CRLT that expertise as a faculty developer is attained through experience, with people at different stages needing different types of training and lots of feedback (Tiberius et al., 1997). Therefore, we enhance the professional growth of our faculty developers in a variety of ways.

### Mentors

At CRLT, we socialize and train new staff by asking them to attend the programs their colleagues present so they can see how we do things. We also have them shadow CRLT colleagues during consultations and midterm student feedback sessions to learn the skills. Every new professional staff member has a staff mentor, a colleague responsible for initiating discussions about progress and answering questions about procedures, people, and the environment. For many activities of our new colleagues, we provide checklists, flowcharts, and procedures manuals, as befits both novice learners and advanced beginners (Tiberius et al., 1997).

## On-Campus Professional Development

At a research university like Michigan, there are many lectures and programs every day. Professional staff are invited to attend them when they concern a topic of interest or one relevant to the faculty population they are trying to serve (e.g., a science consultant meets faculty colleagues and learns about their current interests by attending talks by award-winning science professors). When they can fit these programs into their day, consultants always derive value from the opportunity to meet more faculty. We also pay for on-campus training programs offered by the instructional technology and human resources offices.

## In-House Programs

For consultants who are more experienced, it is helpful to use case studies and role-plays to develop competence first and then proficiency in faculty development (Tiberius et al., 1997). CRLT has a weekly staff meeting at which we often discuss a tough case that a consultant has experienced, or instruction on a new technique, for example, podcasting. Twice a year, CRLT has a staff retreat—one day in the winter and two in the summer—when we engage in real reflection on our work. Some typical agenda items are reports on the results of CRLT research projects, group discussion of a book that gives us a new lens on our work, speakers or consultants on topics to improve our services, and in-depth discussion of our foci so we can come to closure on unresolved issues (e.g., how to structure our PFF programs or what role CRLT should play in IT initiatives on campus). Each retreat also includes a community-building activity with the project staff, for example, touring the art museum, visiting the newest campus buildings, or taking a bus tour of Detroit to inform our service-learning activities.

## Conferences

We also encourage professional staff to attend conferences (e.g., POD, International Society for the Scholarship of Teaching and Learning [ISSOTL], AAC&U, National Conference for Race & Ethnicity in Higher Education [NCORE]) and disciplinary meetings. Each staff member chooses some conferences each year, and CRLT supports him or her to the extent the budget allows. We prefer that staff not attend disciplinary conferences to the exclusion of those with a broader focus, because our work extends well beyond our own disciplines.

## Teaching

For some staff, teaching serves as professional development. Though CRLT staff occasionally teach courses in their own discipline, we prefer that their interest in teaching be satisfied by leading the courses that CRLT offers (see, especially, chapter 6): a 10-session course for 50 grad students each May on Preparing Future Faculty, a course that meets several times each term to teach 10–12 graduate teaching consultants about faculty and TA development, a 7-session course for 35 postdoctoral science scholars, a multisession course for 10 graduate student mentors in the College of Engineering (CoE), a winter and August class for international teaching assistants, and the Teaching Academy for 40 junior faculty in the liberal arts on how to teach well (i.e., two days of orientation, followed by several other sessions throughout the year).

## Research

CRLT staff are encouraged to do research, and in a typical year, most of them do conference presentations and publish journal articles (and occasionally a book) (see publications in the CRLT Annual Report, http://www.crlt.umich.edu/aboutcrlt/aboutcrlt.php). However, there are some caveats: We ask that service always take priority over research because we do not want to miss opportunities to improve teaching and learning on campus. Like teaching in one's own discipline, research is done during work hours when possible, and when impossible, on one's own time after work and on weekends. There is no requirement that CRLT professional staff do research, but most want to. We always highlight and applaud their publications, and we assist with dissemination.

We find that the research of greatest utility is applied research that can inform and enhance CRLT work. For example, one CRLT research project compared multiple types of consultations to find out which was most effective for faculty (see chapter 4), and another surveyed undergraduates about their experiences in introductory science courses (see chapter 10). The former informed the services we offer faculty, and the latter improved TA training and gateway courses in several departments. CRLT staff also help faculty with their own Scholarship of Teaching and Learning (SoTL) projects, showing them how to do research on their own teaching and assisting with data collection and analysis.

## A Different Budget Model

The CRLT budget comes largely from the provost, but we supplement it with funds from academic units (deans, department chairs, other offices) for which we do labor-intensive work. In the 1990s, UM went through a period when it used responsibility-centered management (RCM), and university offices began charging each other for services. While RCM is no longer used at Michigan, many offices still charge each other for some services. As a result, CRLT has been charging for some services for over a decade. About one-third of our annual budget comes from these funds, some one time funds and some ongoing.

### *Fee-for-Service Approach*

CRLT charges for unit-specific work, as opposed to the work we do for the entire university on behalf of the provost (e.g., orientations, seminar series, grants competitions, consultations with individual faculty, website mainte-nance, and publications). For example, we charge for planning and facilitat-ing a departmental retreat, gathering data on assessment of student learning in a major, leading a specialized workshop for faculty in a department, run-ning focus groups as part of a curricular reform process, or designing a TA training program for a school or college.

Our charges do not represent the full cost of a service; we always share costs. Also, when we send an estimate for a service, we always note that if the office or school/college cannot pay us, we will do the work anyway. Units almost never accept our work for free; they generally pay us the entire amount we request. Our charges are not set in stone: If the program is funded by an external grant, we charge more. If we have done very little or no other recent work for a unit, we may not charge at all or very little. And if the unit does not have many resources, we tend to charge less. Since every service is customized, none is exactly comparable, making it unlikely that clients can compare notes on CRLT costs.

Each year, about ten academic units pay us fees. We use the funds for part-time graduate students who assist us with our work and make it possible for our professional staff to use their time more efficiently. Besides these smaller task-specific funds, we receive the funding equivalent of almost four staff positions (two from the liberal arts college and two from the CoE) for continuing, intensive work we do for them. In the liberal arts college, for example, we assist with various aspects of the departmental TA training pro-grams, run a teaching academy (including midterm student feedback) for junior faculty, and participate in a variety of projects assessing general education. Similarly, we have several agreements with the graduate school for programs that we suggest and then organize and staff, with the school's co-sponsorship and funding: three preparing future faculty programs, a multicultural facilitation workshop, a short-course for postdoctoral scholars, and the Graduate Teacher Certificate (see chapter 6). While this funding from the three colleges is not part of CRLT's base budget, it comes annually and is renegotiated infrequently. We count on it.

## Development and Fund-Raising

CRLT does not do development; instead, the deans do their own fund-raising (a major part of their responsibility), and then they come to CRLT for services for which they pay us. That arrangement saves me time as director, and it means I am not competing with the deans for donor money. It also means that the work we do for schools and colleges is what they really need, and it provides the provost with evidence that the units value CRLT services.

## Federal Agency and Foundation Grants

CRLT does not spend much time on grant proposals from federal agencies or private foundations. We sometimes apply in collaboration with another office or faculty member, or at the behest of the provost or a dean. But we rarely seek out grant funding ourselves. The competition for those funds is substantial, so the odds of getting them are often low, not worth the amount of staff time spent drafting the proposal and then, if successful, providing reports on the project. Most important, external funders have a number of foci and constraints that may shape a proposal and dictate aspects of it that make a project less useful in our own university context. It is wiser for us to raise funds from deans who tell us exactly what they need. As with donor funding, external grants can be a distraction from the priorities of campus leaders.

## CRLT in Engineering

An interesting example of CRLT's budget model is the CRLT in Engineering office, the faculty development office for the CoE (http://www.engin.umich.edu/crltnorth/). It has its own director and consultants (with engineering PhDs), as well as support staff, all of whom occupy CoE space. CRLT in Engineering is a branch office of CRLT, and we divide the salaries of those staff members between CRLT and CoE, with both units paying a certain percentage of each position.

CRLT in Engineering was created because CoE wanted consultants with engineering backgrounds and was eager to engage in several major initiatives to improve student learning. Fortunately, the college had sufficient resources to support its intentions. By putting the staff administration in CRLT, not CoE, we were able to offer the college ease of administration; the ability to change the size of the staff without having to do the hiring or the firing; and the support of the regular CRLT office on specialized topics like diversity, instructional technology, and assessment. In other words, the regular CRLT staff supplement the CRLT in Engineering staff whenever needed.

CRLT in Engineering's programs and services include running the TA training program for the college and offering a series of workshops for faculty and TAs, as well as consultations for any engineering instructor who wants one. However, CRLT in Engineering services differ slightly from the others offered by CRLT, especially in regard to external grants. CRLT in Engineering consultants frequently write proposals (especially to the National Science Foundation [NSF]) and devote a larger portion of their time to research and grant administration. That prioritization is an outgrowth of CoE's emphasis on educational research and SoTL, which is also a priority for ABET, the accreditor for engineering programs. Thus, CRLT in Engineering is customizing its work to the culture in which it is located, and the CRLT budget model allows for that customization.

## Operational Principles

Chapter 3, "Forging Relationships With Faculty and Academic Administrators," describes the strategies CRLT uses on campus to further its mission. But as director, it is my role to create an ethos among our staff about how we will operate and what our approach will be. Teaching centers are an interesting and challenging place to be employed because the work is not prescribed or preordained. We have much control over our jobs and can determine for ourselves, at least in large part, how we can improve teaching on campus. A number of principles guide the work we do, including a service orientation, speedy response time, quality control and accountability, using CRLT solutions to solve institutional problems, opportunism, and persistence. All are described next.

### Service Orientation

The first, and probably most important, principle is being service-oriented and responsive. We have many opportunities to initiate new programs and services, but we are most effective when we respond positively to the requests and opportunities that come to us. CRLT initiatives have the most impact when they align with university initiatives, such as those of the provost. Therefore, we need to prioritize those initiatives and allow time for them. This sounds obvious perhaps, but research shows that teaching centers often do not prioritize advancement of the agenda of their campus leaders (Sorcinelli et al., 2006).

Within our sphere of activity, we try to be fully aware of institutional priorities. To help set our agenda, I regularly meet with deans and ask them to suggest projects and programs, which we implement or help them implement. That does not mean we do not craft our own agenda. We can reject others' requests when they do not fit within our mission of enhancing teaching and learning through work with faculty, administrators, and TAs. Mission creep is a problem that we try to avoid. However, even when we decline a request, we try to be helpful by suggesting other offices on campus whose mission is better geared to a particular need.

Creative faculty developers are good at crafting their own interesting new plans in a vacuum, especially in the summer before the demands of the fall semester begin. To have staff available to address the requests that come to us during the academic year, a director should not let staff overschedule themselves with preplanned activities that will make it impossible for them to be responsive to new opportunities. It is the role of the director to stay abreast of the workload and activities of consultants, to help them avoid burnout from overload, to vary the work so they remain challenged by it, and to delegate incoming work to the people who have the time and skills to undertake it. At CRLT, we find handling the workload to be one of our greatest challenges, since we do not always succeed at figuring out how to do innovation by substitution. While our use of extra graduate students or postdocs does help us accomplish our objectives, staff burnout is always a concern.

### Speedy Response Time

Things move fast on the UM campus, so we try to respond very quickly. As requests or opportunities for services arise, we respond while people are still excited about an idea and eager to engage. Delay often means a missed opportunity. Administrators and faculty are busy; their attention gets diverted if we do not seize the moment. However, this often means that we need to be the ones to keep the initiative on their radar screens by following up to make sure initiatives are moving forward.

## Quality Control and Accountability

As director, I am the one who sets the standards for quality and then functions as the quality control officer. I set the bar high, and my colleagues respond accordingly. Our reputation and people's trust in us are only as good as the quality of the work we do. We continually evaluate CRLT services and believe in continuous improvement processes (see chapter 2 for a description of evaluation strategies). On a university campus, it is foolhardy to send memos or e-mails with typos or grammatical errors, or language that is not clear, succinct, and easy to understand. We check and double- and triple-check every communication because our communications indicate to faculty the quality of our program planning, and faculty are more interested in attending carefully planned, well-thought-out programs. It is not unusual for faculty to say they count on CRLT events being well-organized and informative—worthy of their time.

## Using CRLT Solutions to Solve Institutional Problems

As a political scientist, I studied the garbage can model of policy making (Cohen, March, & Olsen, 1972), which theorizes that solutions often emerge independently, and they are there, ready to address a relevant problem when it presents itself. The emergence of a problem prompts people to go through the "garbage" (i.e., the bank of previously generated solutions) and look for one that might be useful in solving the problem. Although we approach the process thoughtfully, this theoretical model often applies to CRLT's operations. We have a general set of programs (e.g., seminars, workshops, roundtables, and theatre sketches) and repertoire of services (e.g., grants, evaluation research, website maintenance, publications) that can be tailored to fit a particular need. We wait for opportunities and openings (problems) before suggesting these programs and services (solutions). We know we can nudge but cannot initiate our solutions independently without strong support from the provost, deans, chairs, or faculty. So, when an administrator or faculty member identifies a problem, a need, or an interest, we respond with a carefully crafted program or service.

For example, when the provost gave a speech saying that she hoped to encourage more interdisciplinary team-taught courses on campus, we redirected grant competition funds and used them for a new grant that would fund those courses. When a department chair expressed concern about climate for his graduate students, our theatre program created a sketch to elicit conversations about climate among the students. When a faculty member expressed an interest in sharing his insights about adapting wikis for classroom use, we organized a workshop at which he demonstrated his methodology to colleagues. We taped him and put the video on our website. And when another faculty member worked on a lecture capture system that seemed promising for campus use, we collected evaluation data so he would have more credibility as he tried to disseminate it. All of the above have been small wins, or low-hanging fruit (Weick, 1984), that over time have accumulated to show the teaching center's value on campus.

## *Opportunism*

Baron (2006) and Schroeder (2010) suggest that teaching centers should be opportunistic in responding to openings as they emerge on campus, and that is exactly what CRLT tries to do, especially in regard to moving forward on its own strategic goals. I usually learn about openings through networking and frequent contact with campus leaders who keep me abreast of opportunities. For example, some of us who direct similar offices reporting to the provost have monthly breakfast meetings to share news, which helps us identify opportunities for action. Chapter 3 offers more information about how CRLT has interacted with campus leaders, faculty, and other administrative offices.

At CRLT, we have often been opportunistic in starting a new service on a small scale, demonstrating that we can do it well, and then asking for the resources to do more of it. Goals achieved through that method include our interactive theatre program, a satellite office in engineering, the Graduate Teacher Certificate Program, and a long menu of PFF programs. In each case, we have been able to do additional hiring to fulfill these functions only after we were able to demonstrate our capability on a small scale with existing staff.

Sometimes we have waged a concerted campaign to gain visibility for work we are already doing. For example, during the university's reaccreditation process, there was discussion about creating a university assessment office. At CRLT, we had always considered ourselves the assessment office, but it became clear that our assessment work lacked sufficient visibility and synergy. During the years leading up to reaccreditation, we were strategic about finding ways to highlight our work, for example, focusing one of CRLT's semiannual Provost's Seminars on assessment, using our contact with deans and chairs to organize a symposium for them with examples of assessment, targeting two of the CRLT grants competitions to assessment so faculty would have an incentive to do more of it (and with our consultants' support), and providing multiple assessment entries in our seminar series. We also created an extensive UM website with definitions of assessment, links to good sites elsewhere, showcases of UM faculty doing assessment, and lists of CRLT's own assessment projects (http://www.crlt.umich.edu/assessment/index.php). We publicized our website to campus administrators and to those coming for the accreditation site visit. The result was that the accreditors reported that the university's self-study had understated the amount of assessment on campus and concluded that assessment projects were numerous across the schools and colleges, specifically praising CRLT's role in these efforts (University of Michigan, 2010a). Consequently, CRLT was finally recognized as the assessment office it had long been—but too quietly.

A current example of CRLT opportunism is our new initiative in China. As this book goes to press, we are beginning to work with the Ministry of Education on faculty development in elite universities, an initiative designed for broad impact on the institutions with which UM faculty typically collaborate and from which our Chinese students come. CRLT's decision to work with China is a strategic one. Michigan prioritizes internationalization (it was the university's reaccreditation focus in 2010), so the university encourages global initiatives. Chinese collaborations are a special priority because close ties between UM and China date back to the 1880s, and UM has an unusually large number of Chinese students. By working on faculty development in China, CRLT contributes to Michigan branding there, which in turn enhances CRLT's stature on campus.

Since 2005, CRLT has led the Michigan-China University Leadership Forum, a two-week professional development program for leaders of elite Chinese universities. We have thus developed expertise on Chinese higher education and formed connections with key leaders. Through this faculty development initiative, we expect to learn to work more effectively with international students and faculty at Michigan and gain greater understanding of cultural differences that affect teaching and learning.

## *Persistence*

It has been satisfying to watch CRLT's influence grow over time because each achievement seems to make the next goal easier to achieve. On a university campus, there is a snowball effect: if your office gains respect, that respect keeps growing. More respect makes it possible to achieve new strategic goals, which, when achieved, garner more respect in a chicken-and-egg fashion.

A teaching center director must be clear about the strategic goals he or she wants to achieve and advocate persistently for the goals of greatest strategic importance. Among the most important CRLT achievements are several that have built slowly and taken many years of persistence to accomplish, for example:

- occupying a campus space nice enough (and centrally located enough) to signify that the university values teaching improvement and big enough to hold the staff needed to do our work;
- offering faculty enough grant money to make a difference on our well-resourced campus;
- creating a professional development program for associate deans and chairs (with the provost's involvement) to have more visibility at that level of the administration;
- divesting CRLT of the student evaluations office because CRLT is more effective with the faculty when viewed as a unit of support, not evaluation;
- running semiannual Provost's Seminars on Teaching to create university-wide dialogue on cutting-edge pedagogical and curricular issues; and
- administering the university's major teaching awards to associate CRLT with the innovations of our excellent teachers.

One word of caution: At CRLT, we have seen that news travels slowly on a large campus, so it takes a long time to gain respect. Once you gain it, it grows quickly. And it takes an equally long time to lose respect. Once a good reputation has been achieved, colleagues tend to forgive occasional errors. It seems to be the overall contribution of the office that people remember. But when respect for a teaching center is eroded, it is a long road back!

# MEASURING A TEACHING CENTER'S EFFECTIVENESS

*Mary C. Wright*

J ust as colleges and universities are facing greater pressures to measure their impact on student learning, teaching centers are increasingly expected to document their impact on outcomes such as student learning, climate, faculty effectiveness, and faculty/student retention. Although calls for teaching centers to better demonstrate their impact are not new (e.g., Centra, 1976), in an era of accountability, the expectations for measuring effectiveness can only be expected to grow. As Sorcinelli et al. (2006) note, "Everyone, from parents to legislators, expects institutions of higher education to assure measurable outcomes" (p. xv), and this expectation extends to faculty development work as well. However, the literature is not replete with models about how teaching centers can evaluate their work and make public the findings to key stakeholders. Here, we offer a model for other faculty development professionals to approach the evaluation of their work as well as strategies for using the findings to enhance and grow a teaching center.

This chapter begins with a review of the literature on evaluation of faculty development work. It then describes how CRLT documents and evaluates its instructional development work and how it uses these inquiries to refine its practice and highlight the value the center brings to the university. Elsewhere (chapter 7), we discuss how CRLT also collaboratively works with departments, schools, and colleges to assist them in their own endeavors to document their effectiveness. Given this focus of our work, it is even more important that CRLT places a priority on examining the outcomes of its own initiatives.

## How Do Teaching Centers Plan and Evaluate Their Work?

The development of "guiding principles, clear goals and assessment procedures" is one of the best practices for creating and sustaining teaching centers (Sorcinelli, 2002, p. 14). Fortunately, the literature about how teaching centers can assess their work has grown since Centra's 1976 report, which indicated that only 14% of faculty development programs in the United States evaluate themselves in any way. However, despite rich pockets about evaluation of specific program types, there is little about how faculty development centers can construct a comprehensive evaluation plan that guides and documents the effectiveness of their work.

The existence of few published models for how a center can evaluate its work comprehensively may be attributable to the fact that relatively few teaching centers are engaged in a holistic evaluation of their programs and initiatives, as is indicated by several nationwide surveys of faculty development professionals (Centra, 1976; Ferren & Mussell, 1987; Frantz et al., 2005; Hines, 2010). Despite the lack of comprehensive models, there are positive indications that specific aspects of faculty development work are being evaluated systematically by individual centers, such as consultations (Jacobson, Wulff, Grooters, Edwards, & Freisem, 2009), grants programs (Ferren & Mussell, 1987), learning communities (Light, Calkins, Luna, & Drane, 2008), workshops (Connolly & Millar, 2006; Way, Carlson, & Piliero, 2002), goals (Young, 1987), and a center's return on investment (Bothell & Henderson, 2004). Needs assessment models are also a particularly rich area of the literature, with many different published approaches to this critical process (Milloy & Brooke, 2004; Sorcinelli, 2002; Sorenson & Bothell, 2004; Travis, Hursh, Lankewicz, & Tang, 1996). However, given the importance of documenting impact in higher education, faculty development professionals need to think holistically about their center's effectiveness, beyond the impact of a singular initiative.

## CRLT's Comprehensive Evaluation Model

To plan the evaluation of CRLT's work, we have developed a matrix that lists the key questions we seek to answer and how we gather information about them. Menges and Svinicki (1989) describe the matrix model's usefulness for program evaluation, as it matches questions with data sources and can serve as an iterative framework for asking questions, collecting data, and enhancing programs. Although the authors present this tool as an approach to guide program evaluations, we find it to be a helpful strategy for thinking holistically about our center's evaluation goals across many programs, ranging from individual consultations to large-scale initiatives like our instructional theatre program. Other examples of teaching centers that use a matrix tool or some other type of integrated approach to evaluation include the University of Minnesota (Langley, 2008) and The Ohio State University (Plank, Kalish, Rohdieck, & Harper, 2005). However, to our knowledge, this is the first publication to describe in detail how a teaching center frames its comprehensive evaluation system, from the central questions it asks of its work through the processes of data collection and dissemination of findings.

## CRLT's Comprehensive Evaluation Matrix

Table 2.1 presents the matrix, and below we describe the key questions and data sources we have found useful to document our work. Our evaluation lens is focused on the following five questions:

1. How many clients does CRLT serve, and what demographic categories do they represent (e.g., rank, department)?
2. What value or usefulness do participants ascribe to CRLT programs and services?
3. What changes do participants intend to make to their teaching as a result of a CRLT program or service? Following up, what changes actually occur in participants' pedagogical knowledge, behaviors, or attitudes?
4. Over the long term, what is the transfer of learning from CRLT initiatives?
5. What needs are there for new initiatives at the university?

These questions emerge from our engagement with the faculty development literature and from the needs we encounter in our work at UM, such as documenting the impact of our initiatives for deans and other administrators. While other centers may choose different questions to ask of their work, these five areas of inquiry provide us with useful formative feedback as well as summative measures that help us communicate our value to key stakeholders. For each question, we look to multiple data sources to get a richer picture of our effectiveness in this area.

# TABLE 2.1
## How CRLT Evaluates Its Own Programs and Services

| | Event sign-ins and service reports from CRLT staff | Website hits | Immediate feedback questionnaires | Follow-up e-mail and online surveys | Participant reports and narratives | Interviews and focus groups | Measurement of teaching outcomes |
|---|---|---|---|---|---|---|---|
| How many clients (administrative, faculty, and graduate students) does CRLT serve? | X (Analyzed by demographics) | X (Analyzed by on- and off-campus hits) | | | | | |
| How valuable/useful do participants find CRLT services? | | | X (e.g., At all workshops, participants rate the overall value of the session) | X (e.g., New Faculty Orientation & Provost's Seminar on Teaching attendees receive an e-mail asking them to rate the overall value of the event) | X (e.g., E-mails and conversations) | X (e.g., Campus Leadership Program participants) | |
| What changes do instructors report they will make or have made in their teaching as a result of a CRLT service/program? | | | X (e.g., Theatre sketch attendees are asked what they learned that will apply to their work with students) | X (e.g., Midterm student feedback clients are asked about changes they made in their course as a result of the service; Pre- and post-test of Teaching Academy participants' sense of preparation for teaching) | X (e.g., Project reports from recipients of larger CRLT grants) | X (e.g., Interviews and focus groups with faculty/administrators about instructional and organizational changes stemming from theatre performances) | X (e.g., Pre- and post-test study of the impact of different feedback services on student ratings; Investigating Student Learning poster analysis) |
| What has been the long-term impact of CRLT services/programs on participants' attitudes/behaviors? | | | | X (e.g., Survey of Graduate Teaching Consultants about impact of the program on their instructional and mentoring work as faculty) | X (e.g., Teaching with Technology Institute and Teagle presentations) | X (e.g., Interviews in China with Michigan-China University Leadership Forum participants) | |
| What needs are there at the University of Michigan for new programs and services? | | | | X (e.g., Surveys of graduate students to assess the need for a Preparing Future Faculty Seminar and information technology training) | X (e.g., Attendees at TA mentoring events asked to suggest new initiatives) | X (e.g., Initial needs assessment for Campus Leadership Forum) | |

### How Many Clients (Administrators, Faculty, and Graduate Students) Does CRLT Serve?

Most faculty development centers keep very good records on the number of people who attend their programs, probably because evidence of participation is necessary to justify the existence of a program (Eble & McKeachie, 1985). As one survey of faculty development practitioners found, "Most programs, no matter what structure or staff size, take record keeping seriously," by keeping track of the *number* of participants who use faculty development services (Chism & Szabó, 1996, p. 120). For similar motivations, CRLT keeps careful records about the people with whom we work.

To document the number of clients, CRLT uses event registration lists, grant recipient names, and staff service reports, which track every consultation, student feedback session, or program planning meeting. Each of these records also includes key demographic information about clients (rank and departmental affiliation) so we can pinpoint our heaviest areas of service. Additionally, CRLT has a very frequently visited website (http://www.crl t.umich.edu), and although we do not record the identities of those who access our online resources, we use Google Analytics to track the number of annual visits (340,000) and page views (650,000) originating from within campus and outside it.

These data are featured prominently in CRLT's Annual Report, which presents tables on the distribution of CRLT services to UM clients, by school/college affiliation and by rank. (For an online summary, see http:// tiny.cc/CRLTreport.) We also list external organizations that receive services, such as other universities that solicit information from CRLT, as well as the amount of funding awarded to faculty through our grants program.

### How Valuable/Useful Do Participants Find CRLT Services?

Ferren and Mussell (1987) write, "If we can make any predictions about the future of faculty development in higher education, formative evaluation on a regular basis will be essential to ensure that programs evolve and remain effective" (p. 114). Participants' data on the usefulness they attribute to CRLT services and programs is a key source of the formative feedback that we gather, and is critical for the ongoing enhancement of our services.

For our workshops and most events, we gather immediate anonymous feedback that involves both participant self-assessment (i.e., perceived learning) and participants' evaluation of the event. Although these forms are often tailored to meet the individual goals of a particular event, common questions that are asked of participants include:

- Please circle your rating of the overall value of this workshop (with a Likert scale, ranging from 1 [*not at all valuable*] to 5 [*very valuable*]).
- What did you expect to gain from this workshop?
- What aspects of the workshop did you find most useful?
- What might you do differently as a result of attending this workshop?
- Do you have any suggestions for how we could make this program more useful?

These evaluation forms are always short (usually one side of one page), and facilitators leave time in the program to encourage participants to complete them. When we are seeking a more holistic evaluation of an event with multiple sessions (such as our New Faculty Orientation and our university-wide gatherings of faculty at Provost's Seminars on Teaching), we instead send an online evaluation the following day.

Participant narratives complement this immediate feedback and are gathered both informally (through e-mails and conversations) and through structured means. Interviews and focus groups are used strategically, because they are more time- and labor-intensive, to follow up with participants when needed. To illustrate, our Campus Leadership Program—an initiative for chairs and associate deans—had been in place for three years, and we decided to check in to assess whether it was still working effectively. Five-minute phone interviews were scheduled with three groups of administrators: frequent attendees at the program, those who participated in a few sessions, and those who never attended. Although deliberately brief to allow busy chairs and associate deans to participate, the calls were invaluable in reminding administrators about the program and soliciting their input about timing and topics for next year's initiative.

### What Changes Do Instructors Make (or Intend to Make) in Their Teaching as a Result of a CRLT Service/Program?

Although many faculty development programs collect satisfaction data immediately, fewer follow up with faculty to determine how instructors made (or plan to make) changes to their teaching (Chism & Szabó, 1997; Plank & Kalish, 2010). Given that one of the key goals for many teaching centers is changing instructors' teaching behaviors to promote more effective student learning (Sorcinelli et al., 2006), it is important to collect data about both intended and actual outcomes.

As described, immediately after an event, workshop attendees are asked about the changes they intend to make in their teaching. We also ask this question in our longer-term, follow-up evaluations. For example, our Graduate Teacher Certificate Program, which promotes reflection and professional development around pedagogy, asks participants at the end of the year to describe how they might change their teaching practices as a result of their experiences in the program. (See chapter 6 for more details.)

In addition to collecting information about prospective changes, we pay careful attention to measuring the impact of our programs on instructional changes made, through both self-reports and teaching outcomes. Three ways in which CRLT assesses its effect on instructional change are narratives and work products written by recipients of our instructional grants, interviews and focus groups with faculty/administrators about instructional and organizational changes stemming from theatre performances, and surveys of new instructors' sense of preparation before and after an orientation to teaching. (A fourth example, described in chapter 4, is the self-reports and student ratings collected from instructors who participate in our formative student feedback processes.) Although some of these use retrospective self-report data, there is evidence that participants' self-assessments are highly correlated with other measures, such as third-party observations, so they can be used reliably to judge program effectiveness (D'Eon, Sadownik, Harrison, & Nation, 2008).

CRLT awards over $300,000 in instructional grants each year, and because of this major investment, we feel it is important to measure the impact of funding on teaching. All grant recipients are asked to complete a short report on the use of the funding (e.g., the number of students affected) as well as plans for continuation and dissemination. For specific grants programs, we also are able to do more detailed process and outcome evaluations. For example, for our Investigating Student Learning grant, which supports the Scholarship of Teaching and Learning (SoTL), we use surveys to assess what grantees have learned during the year they participate in the grant. In addition, we analyze the final product of the grant, a poster about their research, on the basis of criteria established for effective SoTL projects (Wright, Finelli, Meizlish, & Bergom, 2011).

Another evaluation model is the approach used for the CRLT Theatre Program, which evaluates its effectiveness by administering surveys directly after performances (now totaling more than 2,000 instruments collected). Audiences complete a survey that queries, "What was the *most* significant thing that you learned from the performance that you will apply to your teaching/work with students?" and results are analyzed by appointment (e.g., faculty, administration, graduate students). These immediate self-reports are supplemented by additional surveys and focus groups three months to a year after the performances as well as interviews with administrators about the impact of the event on their organizations (Kaplan, Cook, & Steiger, 2006).

Finally, we also occasionally use pre-/postsurvey models to assess gains, such as in student ratings or instructor confidence. For example, in collaboration with the dean's office of our largest college, Literature, Science, & the Arts (LSA), we offer a multiday required orientation for new assistant professors. One way the Teaching Academy program is assessed is through a pre-/postsurvey that asks participants how prepared they feel for 17 different instructional activities, ranging from designing a course to mentoring graduate students. After the course was first offered in fall 2009, it was gratifying to see the statistically significant increases in participants' sense of preparation for their new teaching responsibilities on the topics covered during the Teaching Academy (Meizlish & Kaplan, 2010).

## What Has Been the Long-Term Impact of CRLT Services/ Programs on Participants' Attitudes/Behaviors?

Long-term transfer, or having instructors retain and apply the ideas discussed in faculty development programming, is another key priority for faculty development centers (Way et al., 2002). Three examples of the ways in which CRLT measures long-term impact are surveys of the graduate students who have worked for CRLT, interviews of participants in our Michigan-China University Leadership Forum, and grant recipients' presentations.

CRLT employs about two dozen graduate students each year and trains them to serve as peer consultants for teaching assistants and to participate in a yearlong teaching circle to foster their own professional development. To better understand the impact of this experience on the peer consultant programs, a long-term study surveyed all peer consultants, starting from the program's inception (Meizlish & Wright, 2009; Pinder-Grover, Root, & Cagin, 2008; also described in chapter 5). Through this process, we were able to uncover the former peer consultants' perceptions of the significant impact the program has had on their current work as faculty and higher education administrators.

CRLT also evaluates the long-term transfer of participants in the Michigan-China University Leadership Forum, an initiative that brings Chinese university presidents to UM's campus to learn more about research university leadership. Over a year after participants visited our campus, CRLT staff traveled to China to interview the first cohort of participants. The one-hour interviews addressed the forum topics that were useful and how the presidents used what they had learned, especially to make changes to their own universities. These findings were extraordinarily helpful, not only for shaping future leadership forums, but also for learning more about the evolving shape of Chinese higher education (Cook, 2008).

Finally, for some of our longer cohort-based initiatives, we use participant presentations and demonstrations of participants' work and lessons learned. For example, participants in the Teaching with Technology Institute (TTI), which supports faculty as they develop instructional technology projects, make a presentation about their work several months after direct CRLT support has ended. They are asked to speak to what has worked for them and what challenges remain, and these aggregate comments serve as a useful evaluation tool for CRLT staff. Similar presentations take place in other programs, such as a yearlong Colloquium on the Science of Multicultural Teaching and Learning, funded by the Teagle Foundation.

## What Needs Are There at the University of Michigan for New Programs and Services?

One of the rich areas that does exist in the literature focuses on needs assessments, or data-gathering activities, to help teaching centers strategically plan the initiatives that would best meet the needs of the instructors on their campuses. For example, Sorcinelli (2002) describes an extensive needs assessment for the University of Massachusetts at Amherst's Center for Teaching, which involved interviews, surveys, and focus groups of new, midcareer, senior, and retired faculty, as well as chairs and deans. As she notes, there are multiple key outcomes from such a process, including information about what faculty development initiatives are needed and the development of future allies to support the center's work. Other examples of faculty development needs assessments are described in Travis et al. (1996), Milloy and Brooke (2004), and Sorenson and Bothell (2004); many of these recommend multimethod approaches that combine depth (e.g., focus groups) and breadth (e.g., surveys).

Although CRLT has operated for nearly 50 years, we still find it helpful to assess the need for new services and programs continually, and we often target particular constituencies or programs. For example, when the provost asked CRLT to design a new administrative leadership program, our assessment focused on (1) a benchmarking study of peer institutions; (2) interviews with successful chairs; and (3) a focused survey of new chairs, experienced chairs, faculty, and deans, which asked them to rank topics for a program (Wright, Cook, & O'Neal, 2009). When CRLT first hoped to tailor national PFF initiatives to best meet the needs of UM's campus, a survey was sent to all graduate students asking about possible timing, structure, and content of such a program, which resulted in a streamlined, efficient PFF Seminar that would circumvent concerns about such a program lengthening time to degree (Cook, Kaplan, Nidiffer, & Wright, 2001). Similarly, to plan workshops and resources that might be useful to graduate students in instructional technology, CRLT surveyed over 1,700 teaching assistants about their training needs (Groscurth, Hershock, & Zhu, 2009). Finally, we also use events to poll attendees quickly about new initiatives needed. For example, when we have gatherings for faculty who supervise teaching assistant development in their own departments, we ask what future CRLT events they would like to see and what issues are most pressing in their departments.

## Internal Use and External Communication of Evaluation Data

CRLT staff use all of the aforementioned data to enhance our programs and initiatives and to communicate to others our center's effectiveness. In some cases, an instructional consultant might read through the findings and discuss them with a colleague, such as for our workshop series. However, more frequently, we discuss these findings as a staff team and report on them to external audiences on campus.

### *Internal Discussions*

Frequently, for our larger events, we debrief both the evaluation data and our own observations at a staff meeting. Typically in this process the staff member in charge of the event presents key metrics (e.g., participation counts and immediate usefulness survey results), followed by a round of comments from other staff members in attendance about key strengths of and suggestions for the program. These notes are recorded and stored for future years, when a similar program might be offered again.

Additionally, for our more intensive evaluation efforts, we plan projects or discuss detailed findings as a group. These lengthier discussions typically occur at our semiannual retreats. At these times, we discuss needs for more intensive evaluation efforts, plan and give feedback on ongoing studies, and reflect on the implications of evaluation findings.

## External Communications

Like all teaching centers, CRLT must market its services to administrators and faculty. Our evaluation data are invaluable for that purpose. They show the range of our services and clients and describe our accomplishments in quantitative and qualitative terms. When another unit has supported an initiative financially, we are able to provide program evaluation reports to the dean, which helps us request continued funding. Additionally, we publish some of our evaluation studies, and we use some of our evaluation data, like powerful quotes, on our marketing materials.

However, for discussions with administrators, our annual report is probably the most important tool for documenting the extent of our activities and their impact. As described earlier, we compile an extensive annual report that includes data about the number of clients served and the types of services we provided to UM's schools, colleges, and departments. We provide the report to the provost, and we frequently draw on it for meetings with other high-level administrators. For example, when the deans of the School of Music, Theatre & Dance and the School of Art & Design asked us about the extent of CRLT's work for the arts, we could easily compile several years of data to respond to their query. Additionally, when we talk to a new dean about the work we have done for his or her school or college in the past, we have years of data to present, often backed up by evidence of improvements in teaching practices, student learning, or faculty satisfaction with our programs. These meetings, with evaluation data to detail our contributions, are invaluable for documenting the role CRLT plays on campus.

## Conclusion

Although documenting the impact of teaching and learning centers is critical, the literature provides few comprehensive evaluation models for faculty development professionals to do so. Three possible reasons for the lack of models are expertise, limited time, and methodological difficulty. Expertise is needed to select metrics that will offer good information about the center's key goals and projects, and choosing among these can be a tricky endeavor. The time needed to orchestrate an evaluation can also be a significant drawback, especially given that most faculty development professionals wear many hats. Finally, methodological concerns are not to be underestimated, in terms of the difficulty of obtaining evidence that will be convincing to key stakeholders, especially in an environment where it is difficult or inappropriate to use control/experimental designs (Ferren & Mussell, 1987), where change is complex and often not immediate (Kucsera & Svinicki, 2010), and "when a central goal of the field—student learning—may be at best a tertiary effect" (Plank & Kalish, 2010, p. 136). On some campuses, careful consideration needs to be given to constructing plans that meet institutional review board and human subjects' approval processes.

The matrix, and the processes outlined in it, have helped CRLT address these three challenges. Regarding time and expertise, it has helped us see the overlap in our evaluation endeavors, so we can share tools (e.g., survey items) when asking similar questions of our programs and map out where future efforts are most needed. Generally, we seek to create evaluation processes that are relatively easy to implement and can be used by all of our instructional consultants. However, we supplement this general "culture of evaluation" with select strategic, more time-intensive projects. Regarding methodological precision, we often find that simple is best, and although select projects involve experimental or randomized designs, most of our evaluation processes involve relatively uncomplicated approaches. This not only makes data collection easier, it also assists with communicating findings to key stakeholders, not all of whom are fluent in sophisticated quantitative or qualitative methodologies.

To assist other teaching centers in the important task of evaluation, this chapter offers a matrix-based process, which has guided CRLT's efforts. Teaching center staff interested in using the matrix approach to evaluation can begin by applying a four-step model to their work: (1) developing key questions that align with a center's need for information as well as key issues in the evaluation literature; (2) identifying metrics that will help answer these questions, and then collecting data about them; (3) reflecting internally on the data collected to refine practice; and (4) communicating to external stakeholders, both on campus and to the broader faculty development community, about the effectiveness of their programs.

Although the questions we ask here are directed to an evaluation of CRLT's programs and services, they—and the metrics used to answer them—can be adapted easily to other faculty development programs. For example, in a small teaching center, key priorities might be measuring participation and value, meeting with faculty and administrators to report on these findings, and discovering new ways the teaching center can serve the college or university. However, in any context, "Documenting the impact of teaching and learning centers is more crucial today than ever" (Plank et al., 2005, p. 173). Teaching centers play a key role on campus, and evaluation data can document their contributions most effectively.

# 3

# FORGING RELATIONSHIPS WITH FACULTY AND ACADEMIC ADMINISTRATORS

*Constance E. Cook and Deborah S. Meizlish*

The Professional and Organizational Development Network in Higher Education (POD), the national organization for professional staff who work at teaching centers, has long observed that teaching improvement efforts should extend to all three aspects of our work: faculty development, instructional development, and organizational development. The following are POD definitions of these terms:

> *Faculty development* generally refers to those programs which focus on the individual faculty member. The most common focus for programs of this type is the **faculty member as a teacher.** . . . [This emphasis views] the faculty member as the driving force behind the institution; therefore, assisting that person to be as productive as possible will make the entire institution more productive.
>
> *Instructional development* takes a different approach for the improvement of the institution. These programs have as their focus **the course, the curriculum and student learning**.
>
> *Organizational development* provides a third perspective on maximizing institutional effectiveness. The focus of these programs is **the organizational structure of the institution and its sub components**. The philosophy is that if one can build an organizational structure which will be efficient and effective in supporting the faculty and students, the teaching/learning process will naturally thrive. (http://www.podnetwork.org/faculty_development/definitions.htm)

At a large, decentralized research university like Michigan, we at CRLT try to focus on all three approaches simultaneously. Were we to limit our work to individual faculty members or to a limited set of courses, our potential impact would be constrained. We have learned from many leaders in our field that teaching centers must attend to the broad array of organizational issues and actors that shape an institution's culture (Baron, 2006; Blumberg, 2010; Chism, 1998; Neal & Peed-Neal, 2010; Sorcinelli et al., 2006). As Gillespie (2010) points out, this means careful attention to the cultivation of relationships and awareness of the specific contexts in which those relationships are embedded. Baron notes that "the effectiveness of faculty development . . . [is] dependent to a very large extent on its ability to influence and participate in organizational development outside of its own confines" (Baron, 2006). CRLT agrees with that philosophy, and as a result, we engage in instructional and organizational development to supplement our work with faculty.

To fulfill Diamond's (2005) vision of teaching centers as "institutional change agencies," CRLT assumes what Perlman, Gueths, and Weber (1988) call "intrapreneurial" leadership on the Michigan campus. They write: "Intrapreneurship implies taking an idea and implementing it. Thus intrapreneurship has two critical dimensions. The first is good ideas, the second the ability and interest in making them real" (p. 17).

CRLT has many good ideas about teaching and learning. However, these initiatives will not come to fruition unless we engage in three very basic activities: making the teaching center visible to its constituents, offering incentives and opportunities to these constituents so they will want to use the center's services, and then meeting their needs. As we show in this chapter, those three operational principles apply to all aspects of the work our center does, including faculty, instructional, and organizational development.

In the following sections we discuss several of CRLT's strategies for working with key constituencies: faculty, academic leaders, and other university offices. While our programmatic offerings (like orientations and consultations) are similar to those offered by colleagues on other campuses (e.g., Dotson & Bernstein, 2010; Frantz et al., 2005; Gillespie et al., 2010; Kuhlenschmidt et al., 2010; Pchenitchnaia & Cole, 2009; Sorcinelli et al., 2006; Wright, 2000), our methods for how we seed them effectively throughout a research university may sometimes differ.

## The Faculty

The leaders of a research university can do much to promote faculty use of a teaching center—for example, support for good leadership and enough resources to be responsive to faculty needs, design of a reward system that focuses on teaching as well as research, and repeated promotion of faculty use of the center. But none of that will be enough unless a teaching center also takes the initiative in making itself visible to the faculty, offering them valuable opportunities, and responding to their needs. At CRLT, we try to do those things in ways that seem effective in the context of a research university and that taken together can help support a culture of teaching. In 2009–2010, a typical year at CRLT, we served 1,468 individual faculty members at UM, and the consultations they received, programs they attended, and grants they received were critical to improvement of the educational process.

### *Being Visible to the Faculty*

Teaching centers are a relatively new phenomenon on most campuses, and faculty may not know what they are and do. It often takes time to spread the word and make the center an integral part of the university community. At a research university, faculty are pulled in many directions on campus and off, and for most, their first priority is research, not teaching. They have little or no discretionary time (Wright, 2010), so getting their attention is the first step.

A teaching center should be as visible as possible, showcasing the importance of teaching and familiarizing campus colleagues with what the center can offer. The fact that the administration has funded the center serves as evidence to faculty that the institution values good teaching, and research shows that faculty respond to institutional priorities (Blackburn & Lawrence, 1995). Faculty may pay more attention to their own teaching because they often hear about teaching-related programs and support services on campus, even if they never attend the programs or use the services themselves.

There are many media outlets and opportunities for publicity on our campus, and no one size fits all. We tailor the publicity to the event or service and the relevant audience, and we use multiple forms of communication (e.g., brief in-person presentations, frequent mass e-mails, individual letters or e-mails, brochures, posters). We try to stay in close touch with the university communications staff and use available outlets, such as daily e-mail news updates and the weekly university newspaper. We send all UM instructors

CRLT's *Occasional Papers*, and we maintain a website that provides information about excellent teaching of all types, such as theoretical discussions, tips, exemplars on our campus and elsewhere, and the location of key university resources.

Another way for a teaching center to gain visibility is to seek out or accept opportunities to organize major institutional activities aimed at faculty. These activities are occasions to convince faculty of the value of good teaching, and they allow a teaching center to deliver its messages, highlight its values, and position itself alongside other actors important to faculty. CRLT's role in organizing New Faculty Orientation is a good example of how we put this recommendation into practice.

CRLT has been hosting the university's New Faculty Orientation for decades. It has gone from being a two-hour solo event to a five-hour program in which CRLT involves much of the university. Over the years, we have learned what new faculty need to know as they start their careers on a complex, decentralized campus. To meet their needs, we provide information on a wide range of units, from the vice president for research to the Benefits Office and Parking Services. We also include most of the university's academic leaders so new faculty can meet them.

Our role convening the orientation provides many advantages. As organizers, we are able to feature teaching and learning as a prominent part of the agenda. We offer several pedagogical sessions at the orientation, enabling us to introduce the faculty to CRLT staff and acquaint them with our expertise on multiple aspects of teaching and learning. The provost and the president, as part of their remarks to new faculty, mention the role of CRLT and highlight the university's commitment to good teaching. UM leaders normalize the idea that faculty should use CRLT services—an important message for them as they begin work on our campus. And we use the occasion to explain that midterm student feedback (described in chapter 4) has become an important part of the faculty socialization process at Michigan.

The orientation serves another purpose as well. It puts us in regular contact with 50 key university offices, all of which participate in the resource fair we organize for new faculty. We get credit for taking responsibility for this large event, and it helps ensure that we are visible to other university offices so they consider us an important player on campus.

## Offering Incentives and Opportunities to Faculty

We use two approaches to incentivizing faculty. One is the customary financial incentive of a grant, and the second concerns prestige on campus, that is, the ways CRLT tries to highlight and enhance the stature of good teachers.

Grants are an important way for CRLT to attract and serve UM faculty. At research universities, writing grant proposals is an integral part of academic culture; our faculty are good at applying for grants and eager to do so. Currently, we run eight different grant competitions to improve teaching and student learning (see Table 3.1). Annually, CRLT funds nearly 100 UM faculty to engage in instructional improvement projects.

The grants serve several strategic purposes: they enable us to align ourselves with important university and college initiatives, they help ensure that we are at the table as important initiatives are developed, and they provide an entry point for offering resources and assistance (above and beyond the grants themselves) to faculty and administrators interested in curricular improvement. Additionally, they help us involve faculty colleagues in teaching improvement decisions because all but the smallest of our eight competitions (the Instructional Development Fund, or IDF) are peer-reviewed by faculty.

Faculty value publicity about their accomplishments, and when we publicize effective teachers, good teaching and learning become more valuable. CRLT routinely showcases excellent and innovative teachers through teaching awards and other dissemination tools. We worked with the senior vice provost to have CRLT manage the major university teaching award, the Thurnau Professorships, which come with funding, a lifetime title, and much prestige. In 2008, we also created, in collaboration with others, the Provost's Teaching Innovation Prizes—five annual prizes that generate publicity and funding for their recipients. And we now administer the university process for nominations for the U.S. Professor of the Year and the State of Michigan's Distinguished Professor Award. While we do not make the actual selections, we manage the recruitment process and have helped rationalize the evaluative selection criteria (Chism, 2005). In this way, we have tried to ensure that a fundamental concern with student learning is at the heart of these competitions, and faculty associate CRLT with these awards because ours is the address to which their nominations are sent. We know the literature says that teaching awards do not necessarily incentivize faculty (Chism & Szabó, 1997; Glenn, 2010), but CRLT's job is to create a culture of teaching on campus, and news about good teaching helps us do that.

Other publicity efforts focus on ensuring that the university includes teaching as part of its public face and on identifying and highlighting the work of innovative teachers on campus. At Michigan, we lobbied to have a "teaching" category added to the main university gateway and wrote the text

## TABLE 3.1
## CRLT Grant Competitions

| Grant | Funding | Special Focus |
|---|---|---|
| Faculty Development Fund (FDF) | Awards of up to $6,000 are available for smaller projects, and awards up to $10,000 are available to departments, programs, and groups of faculty for larger projects. | Course and program development or revision |
| Gilbert Whitaker Fund for the Improvement of Teaching | $10,000 (Stage I) $15,000 (Stage II) | Large-scale curriculum and assessment projects (Stage II grants go to successful Stage I grantees) |
| Instructional Development Fund (IDF) | $500 | Small projects; rolling deadline |
| Investigating Student Learning Grant (ISL) | $3,000 (Individuals) $4,000 (Faculty/graduate student/postdoc teams) | Scholarship of Teaching and Learning (SoTL) projects at the course or program level; individual CRLT consultations |
| Lecturers' Professional Development Grant (LPDG) | $2,000 | Professional development in teaching, research, scholarship, or creative endeavors |
| Multimedia Teaching Grant | $1,500 | Incorporation of multimedia materials into large (75+) undergraduate courses; rolling deadline |
| Teaching with Technology Institute | $2,500 | Integration of instructional technology into teaching; individual consultations from CRLT and other IT offices |

for the pages. And CRLT has used several strategies to highlight excellent teachers. We regularly send "story leads" about teaching innovators to university publicity outlets. We launched our own video series to spotlight the instructional practices of faculty who win the university's top teaching award. We also highlight faculty by asking them to give talks, serve on panels, facilitate discussions, and lead workshops as part of the many programs we organize on campus. In addition, we distribute to our faculty what we call *Occasional Papers*, which often feature faculty views, methods, and accomplishments. We also showcase excellent faculty work on the CRLT website, such as the 50 faculty chosen as exemplars of innovative uses of instructional technology (http://www.crlt.umich.edu/inst/tech examples.php).

## *Responding to Faculty Needs*

On the Michigan campus, faculty know that research is their first priority. Therefore, at New Faculty Orientation and elsewhere, CRLT stresses the complementarity of teaching and research (Cook & Marincovich, 2010). We tell faculty that contrary to what they might expect from a teaching center, we do not want them to put excessive amounts of time into their teaching. We say that effective teaching is efficient instruction (Boice, 1991a, 1991b, 2000; Wankat, 2002), a message that is appealing to busy faculty who need to achieve a certain level of scholarly productivity for tenure. We also explain the scholarship of teaching and learning (SoTL), which CRLT promotes and supports (Cook, 2004; see also chapter 7). SoTL engages faculty who seek institutional prestige for their focus on teaching (e.g., NSF funding) while also encouraging research-based instructional practices.

CRLT also serves the Michigan faculty by stressing innovation, not remediation. Our faculty are among the best in the world, and we treat them with the respect they deserve. We tell the junior faculty that good teachers are made, not born, and we can teach them about innovative pedagogies so they get more satisfaction and sense of accomplishment from their teaching, just as they do from their research. While it is important for faculty to be able to come to CRLT for assistance, typical Michigan faculty, like those elsewhere (Blackburn & Lawrence, 1995; Bok, 2006), do not consider themselves poor teachers, nor do their students. At UM, the average course evaluation is more than 4.0 out of a possible 5.0 (Kulik, 2009). Our faculty prefer, therefore, to hear about cutting-edge innovations and emerging issues (e.g., sustainability in the classroom or teaching ethics in the professions), rather than have CRLT focus solely on teaching techniques.

Another key CRLT message concerns diversity, which is an integral part of the value system at UM. Faculty are eager to retain their diverse students and help them achieve their potential. To support faculty in these endeavors,

CRLT programs, consultations, and theatre productions focus on individual differences among learners and the creation of learning environments in which diverse students can learn and excel (more about this topic appears in chapter 8). We draw attention to the perspectives of diverse students, encourage faculty to reflect on the impact of their own practice, and build faculty capacity to employ inclusive pedagogies and use inclusive curricula.

A hallmark of CRLT programs is the opportunity for faculty to network, and faculty always enjoy meeting colleagues. On a campus the size of Michigan, it is not always easy to build a sense of community, but we believe faculty teach better if they feel comfortable in their environment and have colleagues with whom to share ideas and concerns. We even host some programs that are purely social in nature, such as receptions for new faculty or a dinner for international faculty. At CRLT, we are trying to advance the values of a liberal arts college at a large university by building a strong sense of community around teaching and learning. CRLT programs are among the few events where faculty at a large university can come together across disciplines and have discussions about border-crossing issues of mutual interest.

Another way CRLT serves faculty needs is by creating customized programs. At a research university faculty needs are varied. They run from the development and enhancement of basic teaching skills to support for innovative uses of instructional technology, and from teaching first-year seminars to mentoring graduate students. Like other centers, we craft our programs to speak to the different stages of faculty careers (Austin, 2010), and we design programs that concern not only pedagogies in the disciplines ("pedagogical content knowledge" [Shulman, 1986]), but also teaching and professional development issues related to faculty identities and backgrounds (e.g., gender, race, international status) (see chapter 8). We do a great deal of needs assessment to inform our programming decisions (see chapter 2).

We also inform our programming by involving faculty opinion leaders in our planning and implementation (Cook & Sorcinelli, 2005; Eble & McKeachie, 1985; Sorcinelli, 2002; Sorcinelli et al., 2006). Like many teaching centers (Frantz et al., 2005), CRLT has a Faculty Advisory Board to guide our policy and program decisions (http://www.crlt.umich.edu/aboutc rlt/facadvis.php). The board helps us emphasize faculty ownership of teaching improvement; in fact, we give the board complete control over the selection of CRLT grantees so they feel real ownership of the process.

CRLT recruits (sometimes with the advice of the senior vice provost or deans) about a dozen faculty each year for the Advisory Board. We have more board members from the liberal arts and engineering colleges, the two largest undergraduate colleges, but we have several professional schools/colleges represented as well, plus the medical school. The board members we choose are opinion leaders in their units and represent a wide range of disciplines. While we try to include some teaching award winners, we also look beyond the "usual suspects" and invite faculty who are as well known for their research as for their teaching. Members serve for two-year terms, with half rotating off the board each year. We use recruitment to the board as a way to expand our base of informed faculty who can serve as liaisons between our center and the rest of the university community. The good citizens on the faculty who serve on committees like the CRLT Advisory Board often go on to become department chairs, associate deans, or vice provosts. It has been important to CRLT to have these new friends in high places—people who already know us well and value what we do.

But the Advisory Board is not the only place where we initiate collaborations with faculty. We routinely establish ad hoc planning or advisory committees for virtually every major program we launch—whether our semiannual Provost's Seminar on Teaching (a half-day gathering for faculty to consider teaching and learning topics that have been prioritized by the provost) or the launch of a new initiative. In this way, we can capitalize on individuals who are opinion leaders in specific university locations, use their participation as a recruiting tool to entice other faculty to spend their scarce time with us, and benefit from their wisdom to craft programs that will serve the current needs of the faculty.

## Academic Leaders: Provost, Deans, Directors of Other Offices

We turn now to our work with academic leaders, which typically involves a mixture of organizational and instructional development. Often, the two go hand in hand. For it to be effective, a teaching center must be aware of the priorities of the central administration, the leadership of the schools and colleges, and the directors of other university offices. This is no easy task at a large decentralized university. In addition, as Baron (2006) notes, it is important to stay abreast of national and campus "hot button issues" that intersect with the values and priorities of a teaching center (e.g., accreditation or student retention). And just as with faculty development, a teaching center can be effective with administrators only if it takes the initiative in three key areas: making itself visible, offering administrators incentives and opportunities, and then demonstrating that it is responsive to the needs of these campus leaders.

## Being Visible to Administrators

New academic administrators may be unfamiliar with a teaching center or wary that asking for help might be seen as problematic. Whenever we go to meet new deans or chairs, or the directors of other university offices, we take the current CRLT Annual Report, which lists the services we performed for that academic unit during the last year (http://www.crlt.umich.edu/aboutc rlt/AnnualReport10.pdf). Although it varies from year to year because the units' requests and needs change, the list is always extensive, giving new administrators the impression that we are in demand in other units, and encouraging them to use CRLT, too. The annual overview of CRLT work is both evidence of success and important to our efforts at future collaborations around teaching and learning.

At CRLT, we do not rely on word of mouth about our activities. Instead, we work hard to familiarize administrators with our work. We routinely create opportunities for administrators, especially the provost, to speak at CRLT's major programs so they can observe firsthand the strategies we use and the audience we command. Busy administrators are unlikely to remember clearly the information about programs they never experience. Additionally, we carefully evaluate each program and service that CRLT provides and write comprehensive reports for our constituents, documenting our success (see chapter 2). We have already described our resource fair at New Faculty Orientation, which acquaints at least 50 university offices with the work of CRLT. We regularly accept all invitations to showcase CRLT work at campus programs that others run as well, for example, school or college orientations, poster fairs about interesting faculty projects, and conferences held on our campus.

CRLT had long sought more access to department chairs, so we were glad to help a former provost develop the Provost's Campus Leadership Program for chairs and associate deans (http://www.provost.umich.edu/pro grams/faculty_development.html). Faculty live in their own disciplines, and it is their department chairs who most often command their attention (Hativa & Marincovich, 1995). At a research university, chairs typically are driven by their desire to increase the department's national rankings, which depend on research, not teaching. Therefore, chairs are often the most difficult layer of the administration for a teaching center to access. We thought that an opportunity to regularly engage departmental leaders would enhance our efforts at cultural transformation (Gillespie, 2010).

We began the Provost's Campus Leadership Program with a careful benchmarking study and a needs assessment of current officeholders (Wright, Cook, & O'Neal, 2010). Based on the data we collected, we worked with the provost to create a program with a day of orientation for new chairs and academic administrators in the early fall, followed by monthly roundtables for new and experienced ones. While the sessions rarely address teaching and learning issues directly (at Michigan, chairs do not consider them the biggest challenge), the Leadership Program makes CRLT seem like a player to these important administrators, so they are more likely to consider our work an important resource. As one chair noted, "Because of CRLT's very visible role in organizing these [Leadership Program] events, when I needed help with an evaluation of our somewhat controversial and relatively new set of core courses, I enlisted CRLT's help" (D. Allan, personal communication, January 13, 2010).

While we work hard to be as visible as possible on the UM campus, there is a paradox in our approach: We do not always take credit publicly for our contributions in individual units. We often find it wise to give credit to those who have the most responsibility. For example, when the mathematics department instituted a multiyear initiative on calculus reform with a CRLT staff member integral to its implementation, CRLT did not trumpet its role because it was math that deserved the credit. When we helped design the Teaching Academy in our liberal arts college, we were careful to give the credit for it to the dean who had initiated the idea. (Those achievements appeared in the CRLT annual report, but we did no other publicity.) We try to ensure that those who determine appropriations to CRLT always know about our contributions, but as with the two examples, CRLT is likely to fare better if we do not highlight our role over that of the people most responsible (i.e., those whose success is at stake). We know academic leaders will rely on CRLT more readily if they understand that we will not detract from the credit they deserve for their innovations.

## Offering Incentives and Opportunities to Administrators

One of the services CRLT provides to the individual units, and to the provost, is targeted research to help them gather the data they need to address specific issues. As mentioned in chapter 1, we often suggest and then carry out research to provide academic leaders with data relevant to their responsibilities and concerns. For example, when the dean of the liberal arts college had a concern about retention of students in the sciences, CRLT designed a research project on the role of TAs in retention of prospective majors in introductory science and mathematics courses (see chapter 10). When an associate dean in engineering asked which of our various consultation services was most effective in improving teaching in his unit, we designed a study to answer his question (see chapter 4). Through these applied research projects, we have gained the respect of academic leaders on our campus, helped to solve pedagogical problems, and generated additional assignments for ourselves by helping to implement ideas that our research shows are effective.

Another benefit CRLT offers to academic leaders is helping them avoid having to reinvent the wheel. For example, our long history of involvement in TA training (see chapters 5 and 6) means that we can readily provide models and examples of best practices to any new administrator tackling this issue. The same goes for other tricky but perennial issues, such as peer review of teaching.

CRLT offers expertise and infrastructure that can help the provost, deans, and chairs address their priorities, as well as a flexible staffing structure that can be deployed as needed. As new deans are appointed, we routinely meet with them to learn their priorities and familiarize them with the range of CRLT services. At Michigan, our deans have more autonomy than those at most other institutions but vary tremendously in the organizational structures they oversee. Some have large staffs who work in clearly defined areas and spend much of their time on institutional maintenance. For these deans, CRLT's value is that we can help them chart new directions in teaching and learning by devoting attention to ideas they want to explore or doing the targeted research that enables them to argue for change. Other deans have much more limited staff. For them, we can help prioritize a change process and assist with direct implementation through project design, research, and meeting facilitation. Much of this work takes place in curricular reform and assessment efforts, which we detail in more depth in chapter 7.

Regardless of the exact topic or administrative client, several features distinguish our work. First, we provide background and context. Deans want to know how their practices compare to initiatives in other units of the university and at similar institutions across the country, and CRLT does research to answer those questions. Second, when appropriate, we propose solutions for their consideration and explain how such innovations might meet their needs. While it is important that stakeholders in the unit embrace any new innovation, we play an important role in identifying options that might win such approval. Third, we help keep processes moving. We do not wait to be summoned. Instead, we make sure we are on the dean's calendar, and we offer to facilitate certain tasks (like drafting memos or proposals) to help the dean make progress. Fourth, we serve as a sounding board. Much of an administrator's work is dictated by strategic necessities, so the opportunity to puzzle over those strategies with an informed outsider can be a valuable asset.

## Meeting Administrators' Needs

### The Provost

While most teaching centers report to the provost, as we do, research shows that for many centers, the provost's agenda is rarely their agenda (Sorcinelli et al., 2006). This is not true for CRLT. We could not be effective if we did not align ourselves with the provost's agenda. In the last two decades, the average tenure for a UM provost has been three years. As the officeholder has changed, so have the priorities. However, all have wanted to see better teaching and learning and had specific ideas about how to advance that cause. One fostered more and better interdisciplinary teaching, another championed assessment of student learning, and a third tried to improve instructional technology. In each administration there were instructional development roles the teaching center could play, such as researching extant services on campus and informing task force work, funding individual faculty projects that mirrored the provost's priorities, offering programs to showcase innovative teaching in a particular area, and developing web resources to inform the campus community. We considered each new priority to be an opportunity. In every case, CRLT brought in staff with the expertise to focus on the new priorities and an infrastructure to make programmatic collaboration possible. By aligning CRLT with the priorities of the academic leadership, we built its trust in our ability to do good work.

### Deans

The University of Michigan has 19 schools and colleges with 19 very autonomous deans. Across this sprawling university there are more than 200 departments or department equivalents. Half of CRLT's work is what we call *discipline-specific*—that is, instructional development custom designed for a specific unit. We believe, as many in the field increasingly do (Pchenitch-naia & Cole, 2009), that real change can happen only if it is strongly supported in these individual units.

We do not deliver off-the-shelf programs. Rather, we conduct a systematic needs assessment and then work with a small steering committee of faculty within the unit to craft a program that uses disciplinary examples and highlights effective faculty within the unit. For example, when the sociology department asked us to design a workshop on effective instructional strategies in large lectures, we worked with it to identify a group of faculty—drawn from all ranks—to feature at the workshop. We then began the workshop with a conversation in which these faculty discussed their goals and practices in large lecture courses. By using them as exemplars, we could highlight effective practices already in use in the department and identify these faculty as resources for their colleagues to consult as they engaged in similar initiatives.

## Collaborations With Other Offices

We try to engage much of the campus community in collaborations, not only with every school and college, but also with all of the central administration offices that deal with academic issues. In so doing, we split some of the workload and expenses with those offices, thereby serving their needs as well as our own. We find that a relatively small office like CRLT can leverage its influence substantially by collaborating frequently with other offices (Albright, 1988; Sorcinelli, 2002). Therefore, in a typical year, we collaborate with about 30 other offices (http://www.crlt.umich.edu/aboutcrlt/Annual Report10.pdf). For example, we collaborate with the Office of Student Affairs on issues like service learning, with New Student Programs on sending consistent messages about academic integrity, with the Ethics in Public Life faculty about curricular issues, with the Office of International Programs about student learning during study abroad, with the Undergraduate Research Opportunities Program about documenting student learning, with the National Center for Institutional Diversity about hosting programs on multicultural teaching and learning, with the Sweetland Center for Writing about assisting instructors with writing assignments, and with the Digital Media Commons and the Library about instructional technology. Whenever possible, we have staff members on university committees and task forces to make sure there is a voice for student learning (Sorcinelli, 2002). (In a typical year, our staff serve on about 45 standing or ad hoc committees [http://

www.crlt.umich.edu/aboutcrlt/AnnualReport10.pdf].) The more we collaborate and participate, the easier it is to understand how the campus works and find opportunities for teaching and learning initiatives (Chism, 1998). Since information flow is difficult on a large, diverse campus, CRLT often serves as a clearinghouse, connecting key people who care about certain topics and helping to generate a critical mass of people on the issues of concern to CRLT.

Taken together the strategies we have described in this chapter enable us to focus on culture change at the institutional level as well as instructional change at the individual faculty level. We agree with Pat Hutchings (2006) that creating change in academe is akin to moving a large battleship: it takes multiple, coordinated efforts pushing in the same direction over a considerable period of time. However, once the ship begins to turn, it has remarkable momentum. When we sometimes hear people remark, "CRLT is everywhere," we are pleased. That is exactly what we want them to think. As we make CRLT more visible, we are also making the culture of teaching more visible. We are turning the battleship by exercising intra-preneurial leadership.

# 4

# CONSULTATIONS ON TEACHING

## Using Student Feedback for Instructional Improvement

*Cynthia J. Finelli, Tershia Pinder-Grover, and Mary C. Wright*

For several decades, many teaching and learning centers have used formative student feedback to enhance student learning and instructional practice (e.g., Redmond & Clark, 1982; Wulff & Nyquist, 1986). Research indicates that formative student feedback effectively enhances instructional practice and student learning, especially when data are paired with a consultation (Abbott, Wulff, Nyquist, Ropp, & Hess, 1990; Cohen, 1980; Diamond, 2004; Hunt, 2003; Overall & Marsh, 1979; Penny & Coe, 2004; Snooks, Neeley, & Revere, 2007). Small Group Instructional Diagnoses, midterm student feedbacks (MSFs), and Quick Course Diagnoses are some frequently used formative feedback systems, each of which typically begins with small-group student reflection on questions about their learning or satisfaction with a class, followed by a large-group discussion (Black, 1998; Millis, 2004; Redmond & Clark, 1982).

In this chapter, we describe the formative student feedback system used most frequently at CRLT, the MSF. Over the span of a year, CRLT consultants conduct more than 350 MSFs for UM faculty and TAs, which allow more than 15,000 students to offer constructive feedback to their instructors. We describe the process used and the most common strengths and suggestions students raise in MSFs. We also present our research on the impact of different kinds of data on the consultation process and describe ways in which other modes of formative student feedback—such as specially designed student surveys—can provide effective alternatives to MSFs.

## MSF Process Used

Following is a brief description of the general process CRLT consultants use to conduct the MSF. Because this five-step system has been described elsewhere (Black, 1998), we summarize it briefly here.

1. *The consultant and instructor have an initial meeting* to discuss instructional goals, learn about classroom and disciplinary context concerns, and plan out logistical issues.

2. *The consultant observes the instructor's classroom* to record observable data (such as participation patterns). These data can be recorded through detailed notes, a map of classroom activities, a detailed timeline, or a videotape.

3. *The consultant facilitates the student feedback session*, which typically takes place on the same day as the observation. At the end of class, the instructor turns the class over to the consultant, who introduces himself or herself, frames the procedure positively, and then divides the class into groups of four to eight students. Each small group receives a handout with the following two questions:

   a. List the major strengths in this course. (What is helping you learn in the course?) Please explain briefly or give an example for each strength.

   b. List changes that could be made in the course to assist you in learning. Please explain how these suggested changes could be made. After five to seven minutes, groups volunteer responses, which are listed by the consultant (on the chalkboard, overhead projector, or LCD projector). Students are encouraged to comment if they disagree with a particular response, and the consultant might ask for clarification or more specific information.

4. *The consultant writes a report for the instructor* using the observational notes and student feedback forms.

5. *The consultant and instructor have a final meeting*, usually soon after the feedback session. At this meeting, the consultant shares the report and presents the feedback, discusses next steps with the instructor, and strategizes about how to report back to the class any changes that will be made (or not made, but why).

## Common Themes

At CRLT, our professional consultants typically conduct around 180 faculty MSFs, while our graduate peer teaching consultants conduct about the same number of MSFs for TAs. (See chapter 5 for more details about the peer teaching consultant programs.) We ran focus group discussions with both groups of consultants in 2010 to ascertain their perception of the most common themes arising in the MSF sessions. Tables 4.1 and 4.2 list the consultants' perceptions of the strengths and suggestions students cited most frequently. Although elicited only from consultants at UM, these themes may suggest the general instructional approaches students in a research university voice as effective (and ineffective).

Our discussions revealed several instructor strengths that were common for both faculty and TAs, many of which (e.g., enthusiasm, interaction, rapport, and clarity) are related to higher student ratings (Murray, 1985). Some themes did vary by instructor type, with consultants reporting different strengths for faculty than for TAs; other themes varied by discipline (e.g., consultants noted different strengths for instructors teaching engineering, math, or science courses from those for instructors teaching humanities or social science courses). With regard to suggestions, there was less commonality between faculty and TAs, with only two suggestions (providing clearer expectations and better integrating course components) overlapping between the two groups. As was the case for strengths, some of the most commonly cited suggestions for faculty are different from those for TAs, and for both instructor types, the suggestions vary by discipline.

## Faculty Feedback on the MSF Process

To assess the effectiveness of the MSF process, CRLT sends out a survey at the end of each term to faculty who have had an MSF to solicit feedback about the consultant, the MSF, and any changes the faculty made as a result of having the MSF (see the appendix to this chapter). In 2009, 145 surveys were sent to faculty members, with 78 faculty responding (54% response rate). One hundred percent of respondents felt that the CRLT consultant was effective in implementing the process and discussing the feedback. In addition, 99% of respondents felt that the service was valuable. The respondents were asked to select all of the reasons why they felt the service was valuable from a list of options. The most commonly cited reasons of the MSF's value are as follows:

- It enabled me to discuss my teaching with a consultant (noted by 82% of faculty).
- It gave me new insights into my teaching/my students (77%).

- Students appreciated the process (62%).
- It confirmed assumptions I had about my teaching/my students (60%).
- It gave me more confidence in my teaching (50%).
- It gave me specific strategies to improve my teaching/course (46%).
- The atmosphere in my class improved as a result of the service (26%).
- It made me aware of resources and programs relevant to my teaching (24%).

Of those who responded, 90% indicated that they made or were planning to make changes to the course as a result of the MSF. Those who actually described these changes (76% of respondents) were most likely to mention incorporating active or interactive learning strategies (40%), such as building in more time in a lecture for student questions, introducing more group work into their classrooms, or changing how they facilitated discussions. The next most frequently named modification involved assessment processes, such as clarifying expectations, giving feedback more promptly, and helping students better understand the purpose of assignments (25%). Finally, 19% wrote about adding or modifying tools to help students understand lectures better (e.g., providing skeletal notes in advance or improving their handwriting on the board). When asked about changes they planned to make in the future, 60% of faculty responded, and the most common comment (44%) was similar to the following response: "I will implement the [same] changes made this term from the beginning."

## Research on Data Used to Guide Consultations

Student feedback generated during the MSF is one type of data that can guide consultations, but others are also commonly used, such as student ratings and video recordings of the classroom. We conducted a study in the College of Engineering at UM to ascertain which type of data is most effective for promoting instructional improvement. A complete description of the study has been published elsewhere (Finelli et al., 2008), so we highlight only the key aspects of it here.

The project spanned two academic terms, and 49 engineering faculty participated. Those who agreed to participate were randomly divided into various intervention groups in which consultants from CRLT used student ratings data, student feedback from an MSF, or a videotaped class session as the basis of a consultation. We used three different measures to assess the

**TABLE 4.1**
**Most Frequently Named Strengths of Course/Instructor**

| *Faculty* | *Teaching Assistants (TAs)* |
|---|---|
| The faculty member is knowledgeable. | The TA is knowledgeable. |
| The faculty member is approachable/has good rapport with students. | The TA is approachable/has good rapport with students. |
| The faculty member is available (e.g., willing to meet with students). | The TA is available (e.g., willing to meet with students). |
| The faculty member wants students to learn/ understand. | *The TA seems to care about teaching and students. |
| The faculty member is enthusiastic. | †The TA is enthusiastic. |
| The faculty member uses visual aids (e.g., PowerPoint, video clips) and the blackboard well. | †The TA answers questions well. |
| *The faculty member provides a good overview at the beginning of class and revisits it during class. | The TA provides clear explanations and is a good "translator" of the material. |
| *The faculty member includes ample real-world/practical examples. | †The TA is a good discussion facilitator. |
| The faculty member is well prepared. | †The TA has established a good classroom climate. |
| †The faculty member facilitates discussion well, especially providing structure and summary of main threads. | |

Note: Strengths are listed in no particular order.
*Items more frequently named for instructors teaching engineering, math, or science courses.
†Items more frequently named for instructors teaching humanities or social sciences courses.

### TABLE 4.2
### Most Frequently Named Suggestions for Course/Instructor

| *Faculty* | *Teaching Assistants (TAs)* |
| --- | --- |
| The faculty member should provide clearer expectations for assignments and/or exams. | The TA should give greater preparation for exams or other key assessments, including clarification of expectations. |
| †The faculty member should improve his/her use of the readings (e.g., incorporate them better into class, reduce the amount of reading, identify the relevance of a reading). | †The TA should integrate parts of the course better (e.g., lecture and section or readings and section). |
| The faculty member should provide more "big picture" information to contextualize how a concept, lesson, or unit fits into the overall course and/or discipline. | The TA should select more meaningful content and activities in discussion (e.g., more application/real-world examples). |
| The faculty member should provide a daily overview/objectives on the board at the beginning of class. | The TA should provide feedback on student assignments and return them more promptly. |
| The faculty member should provide more concrete examples, hands-on activities, and/or practice problems. | The TA should manage classroom dynamics more effectively (e.g., students who dominate discussions, checking for student understanding and questions). |
| The faculty member should post slides before class. | *The TA should improve on his or her presentation skills (e.g., voice projection, talking to the board, and movement around the room). |
| *The faculty member should improve the PowerPoint presentations (e.g., use less text and more visuals, eliminate typos, and reduce number of densely packed slides). | |

Note: Suggestions are listed in no particular order.
*Items more frequently named for instructors teaching engineering, math, or science courses.
†Items more frequently named for instructors teaching humanities or social sciences courses.

impact of the consultation. First, we analyzed gains on a 17-item student rating of teaching survey. These items, drawn from a professionally designed bank of items that comprise the UM student ratings system, focus on both the research-based traits of effective teaching (Chickering & Gamson, 1987; Sorcinelli, 1991) and classroom behaviors linked to college teaching effectiveness (Murray, 1985). Student surveys were collected at midterm ($N = 2,579$) and again at the end of the term ($N = 2,296$), and for each of the 17 items, we calculated the average normalized gain score (Hake, 1998) for each intervention group. Second, as another measure of the impact of the consultation, we used changes in teaching as reported by the faculty in an open-ended survey completed after the course was over. Third, we assessed faculty perceptions of both the consultation and the consultant.

## Gains in Student Ratings

Every intervention group had positive gains on some of the 17 survey items. The groups that had a consultation informed solely by student ratings of teaching or by a videotape of their class had two and three items, respectively, with a statistically significant positive gain ($p < 0.05$). However, the group that had a consultation guided by student feedback from an MSF demonstrated improvement on five items. Notably, student ratings of "enthusiasm," "teaching in a way to serve students' needs," "use of techniques to foster class participation," "use of class time," and "setting high standards for students" improved more for faculty who had participated in MSF-based consultations than for faculty in all other intervention groups.

## Changes in Teaching Practice

At the conclusion of the project, 27 of the 49 faculty reported changes they had made. The most commonly cited changes (in order of decreasing frequency) were:

- introducing more active learning into the course (noted by 37% of the faculty);
- explaining concepts more clearly (19%);
- managing class time differently (11%);
- giving feedback to students more promptly (7%);
- calling on students by name more often (7%); and
- changing the pace of the class (7%).

The proportion of faculty who reported making changes was greatest in the group that received an MSF-based consultation.

## Faculty Perceptions

Faculty in all intervention groups had highly positive perceptions of both the consultation and the consultant; they agreed that the consultation was helpful in improving teaching. They also reported that, as a result of the consultation, it was easy for them to identify areas on which to work and to design and incorporate changes into their teaching. Faculty agreed that the consultant provided ample suggestions about teaching and encouraged them to reflect on their teaching. Finally, across intervention groups, faculty agreed that it was worth the time it took to complete the consultation, and they would recommend the process to colleagues in their department.

When asked about the most useful aspects of the process, faculty who received an MSF most consistently identified the importance of the instructional consultant's classroom visit for interpreting students' comments and feedback. Similarly, many instructors who viewed a videotape of the class session noted its merit during the consultation. Other highly valued aspects of the project were the consultation itself and the suggestions the instructional consultant provided.

Only half of the faculty responded to a question asking them to describe the *least* helpful aspects of the consultation. Their answers generally involved study design issues (e.g., items listed on the student ratings form) rather than comments about the consultation or its perceived efficacy. However, two main themes did emerge: (1) some faculty commented that the short time horizon between the consultation and the end of the term limited their ability to modify their teaching methods or to assess the effect of making changes, and (2) some faculty noted their dislike of the "learner-based" format of the video-based consultation in which self-reflection, rather than feedback from the students or the instructional consultant, was the primary technique used (as described in Lewis & Povlacs, 2001). This discrepancy is probably the result of faculty preference rather than consultant style.

## Summary

Our research shows that the kind of data used in consultations has a significant influence on their impact. In general, faculty who received MSF-based consultations had greater gains in student ratings, reported more detailed changes in teaching, and rated most aspects of the consultation at least as high as did faculty in other groups. On the other hand, faculty who had video-based consultations did not have uniform gains in student ratings when analyzed in the aggregate, nor did they consistently report making changes in teaching or rate the experience highly. Consultations informed solely by student ratings data resulted in limited improvement.

It is important to note that our study demonstrates that the instructional consultant plays a key role in helping the faculty member interpret the available data *and* identify strategies for improving teaching. Drawing on their experience and professional judgment, instructional consultants had the ability to quickly direct faculty attention to specific teaching practices and avoid overwhelming the instructor with too much information. By way of contrast, faculty in a control group who received feedback data without a consultation did not benefit from a trained, neutral third party, and these faculty showed fewer improvements in teaching than did faculty in the intervention groups.

## Other Ways to Use Student Feedback

In spite of the tremendous value of the MSF, faculty are sometimes hesitant to give up the class time required for the process (Black, 1998; Hunt, 2003). At the same time they desire more tailored feedback than is available from a typical student rating of teaching form. Here we describe two specific ways we have addressed this dilemma at CRLT: (1) using a survey-based alternative to the MSF, and (2) consulting with faculty around student ratings.

### The Two-Survey Method

We developed and assessed a Two-Survey Method (TSM) alternative to the MSF to collect useful student feedback using less class time. Like the MSF, the TSM allows students to provide detailed feedback to faculty and presents the responses as a classroom consensus. However, the TSM requires only up to 10 minutes of in-class time, compared to the 20–30 minutes required for the MSF. In addition, the TSM can be used to help clarify responses from student ratings that may be ambiguous or divergent, especially if the response rates are low.

The TSM is based on the Delphi technique, an approach that uses multiple surveys to obtain consensus from the same cohort of experts (Dalkey & Helmer, 1963). Students are surveyed initially outside of class, and this information is combined with a consultant's observation to develop a second survey. This new survey provides faculty with more focused feedback and allows students to confirm or refute selected items identified from the initial survey. For any areas of improvement, the students' survey responses provide a prioritized list of suggestions the instructor could use to enhance the class.

The TSM is described in detail in Finelli, Wright, and Pinder-Grover (2010), but, in short, the eight-step process works as follows:

1. *The consultant and instructor have an initial meeting* to discuss instructional goals, learn about classroom and disciplinary context concerns, and plan out logistical issues (this may happen after step 2).
2. *Survey #1 is administered (outside of class).* This first survey could take the form of student ratings from an online survey or an end-of-term survey from a previous term for the same class. The instructor shares results with the consultant.
3. *The consultant observes the instructor's classroom* to record observable data (such as participation patterns). Observations of the instructor's behavior or classroom dynamics can aid in interpreting the survey data.
4. *The consultant develops Survey #2* by combining data from Survey #1 with observation notes. The consultant identifies two items from Survey #1 that students rate as strengths and designs items for Survey #2 that ask students to agree or disagree with the assertions and explain why. Then, the consultant identifies two "challenge" areas (low-rated items) and develops a variety of possible strategies the instructor might use to overcome them. For example, in a class where students do not agree that *the instructor uses techniques to foster class participation,* the consultant might suggest strategies such as:

   • having students work in small groups to work with examples presented in lecture (with the understanding that students will be called on randomly to explain their work);
   • having students turn to their neighbors periodically during lecture to discuss ways to relate the lecture material to the real world (with the understanding that students will be selected randomly to report on their ideas);
   • having students work together to address a basic question about a homework problem (e.g., how to set up the problem, what assumptions need to be made and why) in the class period prior to when the homework is due;

   Survey #2 asks students to rank the suggestions in order of importance. Finally, the survey includes open-ended items to allow students to identify other strengths or suggestions the instructor should know.

5. *Survey #2 is revised.* Together, the consultant and instructor review and revise Survey #2. For example, the instructor may want to select alternative strengths or challenge areas from Survey #1 around which to design Survey #2 and/or edit the strategies so they resonate with his or her teaching style and classroom context. *This process is critical because it establishes instructor buy-in and ensures that the instructor is willing to implement the proposed strategies if the students request them.*

6. *The consultant administers Survey #2* in class without the instructor present. It typically takes seven to ten minutes for the consultant to introduce the process and for students to complete the survey.

7. *The consultant writes a report for the instructor* using quantitative data from Survey #2 (e.g., 62% of the students ranked "having students work in small groups to do some of the class examples" as the most important way to foster greater class participation) supplemented with qualitative comments for clarification.

8. *The consultant and instructor have a final meeting*, usually soon after the feedback session. At this meeting, the consultant presents the feedback, discusses next steps with the instructor, and strategizes about how to report back to the class any changes that will be made (or not made, and why).

We tested the TSM in the College of Engineering at UM, with faculty teaching undergraduate students from a wide range of class sizes (13–137 students) and content areas. The faculty reported being "very satisfied," and they noted that the efficiency of the TSM and focused student feedback made the process a successful alternative to the standard MSF (Finelli et al., 2010). They also reported that students appreciated having their voices heard. All faculty who were surveyed indicated that they made (or planned to make) changes to their teaching practice as a result of the TSM.

Because Survey #2 is designed so that specific strategies (agreed upon by the instructor) are integral to feedback provided by the students, faculty are empowered to act on these strategies and can do so knowing the value students place on them. Furthermore, students who previously participated in a standard MSF in a different class indicated that the TSM method was a better use of class time because of its efficiency (Finelli et al., 2010).

## Student Ratings

If instructors are unable to allow a consultant any classroom time to gather feedback, student ratings obtained during the midterm or at the end of the term can also provide valuable insights and suggestions for effective instruction. At UM, student ratings are based on evaluative statements that focus on the course, the instructor, and student learning (e.g., "Overall, the instructor was an excellent teacher," "The instructor treated students with respect," "I developed the ability to solve real problems in this field"), and students rate these statements on a five-point Likert scale ($1 = strongly\ disagree$; $5 = strongly\ agree$). Students also have the option of providing open-ended comments. Instructors receive a summary of the numerical data that includes a comparison with medians from across the university and the school or college as well as a summary of student comments.

Consultants help instructors interpret these numerical ratings, clarify open-ended comments, and provide suggestions on how best to respond to student feedback in the future. For instance, consultants might ask instructors to reflect on the patterns in the data and identify any teaching practices that may inform the numerical scores and open-ended comments. The consultant may also offer his or her observations of the ratings by identifying any items that are rated particularly high or low and note any striking distributions in the student responses (i.e., bimodal distributions or majority of responses rated in a particular category). Consultants help instructors focus on high-impact items on the student ratings, such as clarity of presentations, grading, etc., and provide suggestions for improvement (see also Murray, 1985).

## Conclusion

Consultations to improve teaching can be based on a variety of data. We have found that student feedback from an MSF can have significant impact on instructor teaching practices, as can student ratings of teaching or data collected from a survey-based alternative to the MSF process. Other types of non-student-based data—including classroom observations, course materials such as a syllabus, or conversations with instructors—can also be used effectively to guide consultations, but they were beyond the scope of the studies presented here.

Regardless of the data used to inform consultations, we have identified several principles for their success. First, flexibility is important, as one size does not fit all. The method for collecting student feedback should be tailored to meet the needs, goals, and comfort level of the instructor. Second, the instructional consultant is key to the process, acting as an advocate to help instructors interpret student feedback and identify strategies for improvement. Though CRLT has a staff of more than ten professional consultants, institutions with smaller centers and fewer resources can find ways for other faculty to be trained in consulting. Several handbooks for instructional consultation may be useful for this process (e.g., Brinko & Menges, 1997; Lewis & Povlacs, 2001). Third, a research-based approach can be critical for convincing faculty to participate in and administrators to support the consultation process. As described here, the purposeful integration of student feedback with an instructional consultation has real, demonstrable potential to improve teaching practices on a college campus.

# MSF FEEDBACK FORM

Dear [Name of Client],

Earlier this term, one of CRLT's consultants, [name of consultant], conducted a midterm student feedback session in your course. Would you please complete the following short questionnaire about the feedback session? CRLT is interested in continuing to improve our services and in finding out how this service affects teaching and learning. We welcome your comments and suggestions. The information you provide will be shared with the individual consultant who visited your class. If you prefer to respond by campus mail, just print out the survey, write in your responses, and return to: [CRLT address].

1. Was the CRLT consultant effective in implementing the process and discussing the feedback?

    __ Yes __ No

    Comments/suggestions:

2. Overall, did you feel the service was valuable?

    __ Yes __ No

    If not, please explain:

3. If you felt the service was valuable, what made it so? (Check all that apply.)

        __ It enabled me to discuss my teaching with a consultant
        __ It confirmed assumptions I had about my teaching/my students

___ It gave me new insights into my teaching/my students
___ It gave me specific strategies to improve my teaching/course
___ The atmosphere in my class improved as a result of the service
___ It gave me more confidence in my teaching
___ It made me aware of resources and programs relevant to my teaching
___ Students appreciated the process
___ Other:

4. Did you make any changes in your course/teaching this term as a result of this service?

___ Yes ___ No

Please explain:

5. Do you plan to make changes in future terms as a result of the service?

___ Yes ___ No

Please explain:

6. Would you recommend use of this service for colleagues in your department?

___ Yes ___ No

Why or why not?

Thank you very much for your feedback.

# GRADUATE PEER TEACHING CONSULTANTS

Expanding the Center's Reach

*Tershia Pinder-Grover, Mary C. Wright, and Deborah S. Meizlish*

At CRLT, we train a cohort of graduate students, generally called peer teaching consultants (PTCs), in TA development to extend the center's ability to meet the pedagogical needs of the graduate student community. We do this through three programs: a centralized program employing PTCs from across the university, a program supervised by CRLT but dedicated to unit-specific TA development serving the needs of a particular college, and a new centralized program focused specifically on supporting TA needs in instructional technology. In this chapter, we situate our approach to PTC programs in the context of similar programs nationwide, discuss the institutional considerations that led to the development of these programs, provide an overview of how these programs are run, and present evaluation data regarding the impact these programs have on the TAs and the PTCs themselves. We conclude with some lessons from our experience that may be valuable for others interested in this hybrid approach.

## CRLT's PTC Programs in Context

Centers at a number of research universities have instituted PTC programs to address the teaching needs of graduate and professional students on their campuses (Border & von Hoene, 2010; Huntzinger, McPherron, & Rajagopal, 2011; Horii, 2010). These efforts began with Stanford University's Teaching

Assistant Consultant Program in 1979 (Marincovich, 1997; Marincovich & Gordon, 1991) and have grown substantially since then. A recent taxonomy of lead TA/mentor programs identified 62 such initiatives in the United States (Kalish et al., 2009). The most common PTC structure is a *department-based* program, in which a teaching center provides support to a lead teaching assistant's work within one disciplinary context, such as the University of Georgia's Future Faculty Program, Ohio State's Graduate Teaching Fellows Program, and the University of Colorado–Boulder's Lead Graduate Teacher Network. Where centralized programs exist, they are typically organized as graduate student learning communities, with a focus on teaching, workshops, and professional development, but involving no external consultation work (e.g., the University of Utah's TA Scholars program and Cornell's Master Teaching Assistant Program). We have identified five programs that run *centralized* peer consultant programs to train and support graduate students as they give instructors feedback on classroom teaching, often through cross-disciplinary observations and Small Group Instructional Diagnosis (SGID). Examples include Penn State's Graduate Assistantships at the Schreyer Institute and Brown University's Teaching Consultant Program. Although the teaching center's professional staff organizes many of these efforts, some programs, like the University of California–Davis's teaching assistant consultant program, are managed by lead graduate students (Huntzinger et al., 2011).

Offering both centralized and unit-specific programs allows a teaching center to be responsive to the variety of teaching-related professional development needs of graduate and professional students. Although it can be difficult to establish, this integrated model is a highly effective approach to instructional development, allowing for central coordination as well as discipline-specific initiatives (Lewis, 2010).

## Emergence of CRLT's PTC programs

CRLT's first PTC program, the Graduate Teaching Consultant (GTC) Program, was created in 1997 to better enable the center to meet the growing demand among graduate students for its consultation and midterm student feedback (MSF, the name we use for SGID) services. This increase in requests for services reflected other important developments at the university, including a reorganization of the TA training program in the College of Literature, Science, and the Arts (LSA), UM's largest academic unit, which employs the majority of TAs at the university. In 1996, LSA instituted department-based TA training programs. To support these efforts, the college contracted with CRLT to support and supplement the faculty coordinators and advanced graduate students who ran TA training within each department. The GTC program became one important feature in CRLT's support of LSA's TA training. By hiring a cross-disciplinary set of advanced PhD students to be PTCs, CRLT was positioned to offer credible consultants for the many TAs required or encouraged to seek consultations and MSFs as part of their training (see chapter 4 for more details). CRLT also leveraged the skill-based training developed for PTCs by opening those workshops to LSA's departmental TA trainers (Pinder-Grover, Milkova, & Hershock, in press). In this way, CRLT helped build the capacity of the faculty and graduate students running TA training in the college while making them aware of the resources we had to supplement their efforts. Over the years, the GTC program grew to include consultants from other units across the university as well.

Established in 1999, the PTC program in the College of Engineering (CoE) also reflects CRLT's efforts to support and foster a culture of teaching. Funded by CoE but coordinated and supervised by CRLT staff, the Engineering Graduate Student Mentor (EGSM) program selects and trains advanced engineering graduate students to support new engineering TAs and the ongoing pedagogical development of all engineering TAs (O'Neal & Karlin, 2004). Several factors led to the creation of the unit-based PTC program in engineering. First, beginning in 1999, CoE administrators wanted to establish a mandatory TA training program designed specifically for all new engineering TAs. To do so would require an investment in additional staff who could train and support new TAs, and a PTC program seemed like an ideal way to meet that need. Second, the concurrent development of a new engineering pedagogy course (see Montgomery, 1999), as well as an active student chapter of the American Society for Engineering Education, heightened graduate student interest in and commitment to teaching and pedagogy within the college. Many of these students interested in working on engineering pedagogy formed the initial pool of PTC recruits. These two factors contributed to an environment within the college that was more focused on teaching excellence and more willing to support and engage conversations about teaching. Finally, because CRLT already had a long history of providing TA training and support for CoE, we were able to take advantage of this climate to collaborate with the college to create the PTC program.

In 2009, CRLT established a third PTC program that specifically focuses on the instructional technology needs of TAs, called IT-PTCs (or instructional technology PTCs). The impetus for this program grew out of a TA needs assessment survey CRLT conducted that identified unmet needs for pedagogical support of instructional technology. TAs reported six barriers to using instructional technology: lack of time, access, training, awareness, autonomy, and appropriateness of IT in the disciplinary context (Zhu, Groscurth, Bergom, & Hershock, 2010). To address these issues, this new group of PTCs provides workshops on instructional technology and consults with individual TAs and faculty who have specific IT needs (see chapter 4 for more details).

Today, the central PTC program employs 14 graduate consultants from 13 different UM departments while the engineering PTC adds another 10 consultants from across 12 CoE departments. In addition, the IT-PTC initiative involves three graduate students from three different schools and colleges. These three programs highlight an integrated approach to supporting TA development by creating one unit-based program that specifically addresses the needs of a particular disciplinary culture, a centralized program that provides general teaching support to the campus, and a centralized program that offers targeted support to meet a specific instructional need.

## PTC Program Description

While these programs serve different student populations and teaching cultures, the duties and professional development of the graduate students within each are quite similar. The PTCs observe classes, gather student feedback, consult on a variety of pedagogical topics, and conduct teaching-related workshops based on the needs of the center. New PTCs participate in several TA developmental workshops, including Running Practice Teaching Sessions, Consulting with Graduate Student Instructors, Observing Classes and Conducting MSFs, and Writing Teaching Philosophy Statements (see this chapter's Appendix A; for discussion of training programs at other universities see Horii, 2010; Marincovich, 1997; Marincovich, Clerici-Arias, Denman, & Wright Dunbar, 2007). New PTCs are also mentored by experienced PTCs at the beginning of their tenure in the program. In addition, all PTCs receive ongoing professional development through regularly scheduled teaching circles facilitated by CRLT's professional staff. Appendix B includes the 2009–2010 central PTC program syllabus and highlights the various topics and resources that the PTCs review as a part of their ongoing professional development (see Meizlish, Pinder-Grover, & Wright, in press, for details). During these discussions, PTCs receive training on key topics for graduate and professional student development practitioners (Border & von Hoene, 2010), such as pedagogy, consulting, data collection, and instructional technology. Finally, PTCs bring to CRLT insights into the teaching culture of their home departments.

PTCs are selected based on their previous teaching experience, overall reflection about teaching and learning, and potential to consult effectively with their peers. The program coordinators review application materials, which vary depending on the program, but may include the following: cover letters and resumes, reflective statements about their own student evaluations or their interest in and qualifications for the position, and faculty recommendations (see Appendix C). CRLT's professional staff interview highly qualified applicants to learn more about their background and overall interest in the program and observe the candidates in a consultation role-play (see chapter 11), which provides a glimpse of their potential as peer consultants. (For details about the selection process, see Meizlish et al., in press.)

Each of the PTC program coordinators provides supervision to the program by connecting PTCs with clients, meeting with PTCs in the middle of the term to determine their involvement in the program, providing teaching and consulting resources through a program-specific website or wiki, and collecting evaluation information about the PTC's performance. In the centralized programs, clients contact the coordinator for a particular service via e-mail. The coordinator matches the client with a particular PTC based largely on the latter's availability. In the unit-based program, the coordinator assigns all TAs in the College of Engineering to a PTC. The clients and EGSMs are in regular contact, which allows the EGSM to respond to a particular consultation request as needed. In both cases, the program coordinator sends a follow-up evaluation for services such as a classroom observation and MSFs (see the appendix to chapter 4). In addition, program coordinators seek feedback from the PTCs to improve the professional development sessions and the overall PTC experience.

## Evaluation

PTCs are enormously productive. For example, over the course of one year (2009–2010), GTCs and EGSMs conducted 186 MSF sessions (representing the perspectives of 6,766 students); 39 observations or consultations about videotaped class sessions; and 76 consultations on pedagogy, course design, student ratings, or teaching philosophies, primarily for graduate students and postdoctoral scholars. To put these figures into perspective, during the same period, CRLT full-time staff conducted 202 MSF sessions (representing the perspectives of 8,544 students), 15 observations or videotape consultations, and 1,456 consultations, primarily for faculty. From these data, it is clear that the PTCs enable CRLT to extend its reach considerably, but what is not clear is the impact of the program on individual TAs and on the GTCs and EGSMs themselves. The following two sections present data from clients and findings from extensive long-term evaluation of the two programs. Because the IT-PTC program is very new, long-term evaluation data do not yet exist.

### Client Feedback

All graduate students who receive an MSF from CRLT are surveyed regarding their satisfaction with the process, the changes they have made as a result of the feedback, and whether they would recommend the MSF to others. (See the appendix to chapter 4 for the feedback form, which is distributed by e-mail.) With the rarest of exceptions, all clients report satisfaction with the process, indicate they have made changes to their teaching, and say they would recommend the process to others. For example, during the 2009–2010 academic year, 100% of the 48 TAs who responded to the survey for the Engineering PTC program felt the service was valuable, over 80% made—or planned to make—changes to their teaching, and 98% would recommend the MSF to their peers. In particular, the reasons TAs cited most commonly for why they value the MSF process include the following:

- It enabled me to discuss my teaching with a consultant (noted by 85% of engineering TAs).
- It gave me new insights into my teaching (79%).
- It gave me specific strategies to improve my teaching (79%).
- It gave me more confidence in my teaching (71%).
- It confirmed assumptions I had about my teaching (58%).
- Students appreciated the process (31%).
- The atmosphere in my class improved as a result of the service (27%).
- It made me aware of resources and programs relevant to my teaching (23%).

Typical comments we see regarding TAs' perceptions of their interactions with the consultant include:

> Very professional and helpful service; one that ALL teachers should participate in. I will continue these evaluations every semester I teach! Thanks for providing the service!

> Thank you very much for your service. You have helped me be more thoughtful about my role as an instructor. Initially, I had my anxiety about having someone watch me and give me feedback about my teaching, especially given that this was my first time as an instructor, but this was one of the best experiences for me.

> I think that everything I learned can be used in another step toward becoming a more effective teacher overall. I also would use this evaluation again because I think that students really benefit from it.

These quotes suggest the profoundly positive impact CRLT's peer teaching consultants have had on graduate students' teaching, classroom environment, and professional development.

## Impact of Programs on GTCs and EGSMs

CRLT has also assessed the extended impact that involvement in the GTC and EGSM programs has had on the PTCs themselves. The central questions guiding this evaluation were:

1. How does the training and work of the GTC/EGSM programs benefit the consultants during their tenure in the programs and beyond?
2. How do the programs impact the consultants' teaching practices and mentoring?

An online survey was sent to consultants asking them about their present positions, the perceived influences the program had on their careers and instructional practices, and networking with colleagues around pedagogical and professional development issues. (For the complete GTC survey, see Meizlish and Wright, 2009; for the EGSM survey see Pinder-Grover, Millunchick, and Bierwert, 2008.) The survey was sent to all alumni of the GTC program from its inception in 1997 ($n = 48$), and to all EGSMs who participated in the program from 2001 to 2007 ($n = 52$). Overall, 72 former consultants responded, a 72% return rate.

Although former consultants reported many benefits of participation, we focus on two key effects here. First, participants reported that the programs had a significant impact on their mentorship practices. Nearly all (95%) PTCs indicated that they had taken on a mentorship role, by advising or consulting with coworkers around instructional or professional development issues. Additionally, most (69%) reported sharing resources around instructional issues. Of the former GTCs who responded, 11 indicated that they had a teaching center on their campus, 7 said they worked with the teaching center in some capacity, and 4 specifically indicated that they gave workshops for their centers. These findings suggest that the programs help shape PTCs' future collegial interactions and have a broader impact on teaching and learning at campuses across the country.

Second, the survey findings indicate that participation in the programs has an important impact on former consultants' instructional practices. Despite the fact that the PTCs took a variety of career paths after graduation (ranging from industry to faculty positions), they applied their experiences to the instructional contexts most relevant to their current positions. For example, a respondent from industry summarized the impact of his EGSM training and experiences as follows: "[I] have applied lessons learned from each of these aspects to my current job. . . . I can lead a team better, and I know how to develop and teach a course." In addition to teaching skills, others mentioned attitudinal shifts that the programs helped to foster, such as this former GTC, who noted, "CRLT opened my eyes. It changed my life. I was one of those graduate students on the way to blaming students for the shortcomings of his own courses. . . . I began to see that there were alternatives to 'blaming the students,' specifically ways . . . to promote 'significant learning experiences.'"

In summary, the findings from client surveys and the long-term evaluation of the GTC and EGSM programs suggest that both have a profound impact on graduate student development at the University of Michigan and beyond. The programs help TAs collect and interpret student feedback, and they contribute to the professional development of the GTCs and EGSMs themselves.

## Implications

Training graduate students in TA development helps CRLT fulfill its mission to "promote excellence and innovation in teaching" throughout the university. Whether these graduate students work with a cohort of TAs in their discipline or support TAs from a variety of disciplinary contexts, these programs benefit both TAs and peer teaching consultants. Moreover, PTCs can serve as CRLT's "eyes" and "ears" within the graduate student community, informing us of important needs and developments within the TA population. Finally, given the need to "attract new voices and faces to the field in an intentional way" (McDonald, 2010, p. 38), it is important to note that five former PTCs are currently full-time faculty developers at CRLT or elsewhere.

For centers that wish to leverage these benefits and establish a PTC program, our experience offers four important lessons. First, it is valuable to draw from multiple models as centers work to establish partnerships with administrators around TA training. Our hybrid model enables us to meet the TA training needs of many units simultaneously. Departmental resources wax and wane with changes in leadership and priorities. While one unit emphasizes videotape consultations, others emphasize student feedback. Our PTCs can do both, and they enable us to help each department meet its specific goals. Our unit-based model in engineering puts us in close and continuous contact with the administration of one of our largest colleges on TA training issues. Second, it may be necessary to conduct an assessment to determine whether there are any unmet needs PTCs can fill (such as the IT-GTC program). Third, as described here, it is essential to have rigorous hiring and ongoing training programs to maintain quality work and help PTCs develop as consultants. Finally, it is critical to evaluate the program through multiple metrics, to justify its ongoing existence and to make necessary improvements. In all, graduate peer teaching consultants are uniquely situated to serve the TA population and expand the capacity for the teaching center to promote teaching and learning throughout the university.

# PTC PROGRAM MANDATORY TRAINING WORKSHOP SERIES*

| Workshop | Goals | Activities |
|---|---|---|
| Running Practice Teaching Sessions | • To empathize with the feelings and concerns of new instructors by examining past experiences and teaching a lesson<br>• To provide and solicit constructive feedback<br>• To facilitate a reflective conversation about teaching within a given time constraint | • Reflection on first-time teaching experiences within a small group<br>• Identification of characteristics or qualities of constructive feedback through a large-group conversation<br>• Video demonstration of a practice teaching lesson with a large-group discussion on the facilitation process<br>• Development and delivery of a practice teaching session<br>• Facilitation of a practice teaching lesson with a discussion on the process |
| Consulting With Teaching Assistants | • To discuss issues that can arise in consultations<br>• To practice and reflect on strategies for consulting<br>• To develop a "toolkit" with a range of approaches to consulting<br>• To gain confidence in consulting | • Discussion of the consultation process, including establishing rapport, identifying issues, strategizing with the client, providing resources, and following up with the client<br>• Presentation on interpreting quantitative student ratings<br>• Consultation role-play on student ratings<br>• Discussion and role-play on consultation models such as "product," "prescriptive," "collaborative," etc. (Brinko, 1997) |

| Workshop | Goals | Activities |
|---|---|---|
| Observing Classes and Conducting Midterm Student Feedbacks (MSFs) | • To identify and interpret observable data<br>• To practice taking observation notes<br>• To practice sharing observation notes and student data with clients<br>• To experience an MSF from a student perspective | • Discussion of the consultant's approach to meeting with a client prior to a classroom visit<br>• Discussion of types of observable and objective data<br>• Collection of observation data using video and follow-up consultation<br>• Presentation and participation in the MSF process |
| Writing a Teaching Philosophy Statement | • To discuss the benefits of writing a teaching philosophy<br>• To examine sample philosophies<br>• To reflect on ways participants can represent their teaching experiences in the philosophy statement | • Background presentation on teaching philosophies (why write one, what search committees look for, etc.)<br>• Discussion on teaching philosophy rubric (O'Neal, Meizlish, & Kaplan, 2007)<br>• Critique of sample teaching philosophy statements individually and in small groups<br>• Individual reflection on ways to get started with a teaching philosophy statement |

*For more details, see Pinder-Grover et al., in press.

# FALL 2009–WINTER 2010 GRADUATE TEACHING CONSULTANT (GTC) SYLLABUS

*Mary C. Wright & Stiliana Milkova, CRLT*

*Meetings in the Fall Term focus primarily on professional development for doing the work of a GTC: consulting, gathering student feedback, conveying feedback to clients, reviewing teaching philosophies, and doing workshops. Topics are consistent year to year. In contrast, Winter Term meeting topics change every year and are developed by GTCs, focusing on growing further as a consultant, developing as an instructor, and exploring faculty development as a career option. (The following topics are the ones the 2009–2010 GTC group selected.)*

| Topic (Length) | Meeting Structure and Resources |
|---|---|
| Introductions<br>90-minute meeting | Through interactive presentations and icebreaker activities, this meeting introduces GTCs to CRLT, to each other, and to the GTC program. |
| | CRLT Resources (publications and at CRLT website, http://www.crlt.umich.edu). |
| | See also: GTC CTools site. Available: CTools.umich.edu (GTC Program tab), CRLT GSI Guidebook (available: http://www.crlt.umich.edu/gsis/gsi_guide.php). |
| | POD. "About the POD Network," Available: http://www.podnetwork.org/about.htm |
| | POD. "POD Listserv," Available: http://www.podnetwork.org/listserve.htm |
| | Professional and Organizational Network in Higher Education (POD). "What is faculty development?" Available: http://www.podnetwork.org/faculty_development/definitions.htm |
| | Stanley, 2001. |
| | Tiberius, Tipping, & Smith, 1997. |

| *Topic (Length)* | *Meeting Structure and Resources* |
| --- | --- |
| Consulting with GSIs: Early Feedback and Student Ratings (new GTCs only) 2-hour meeting | New GTCs participate in the consulting GSI workshop (see Appendix A, PTC Program Mandatory Training Workshop Series for more details). |
| Observing Classes and Conducting Midterm Student Feedbacks (new GTCs only) 3-hour meeting | New GTCs participate in this workshop (see Appendix A for more details). After this session, new GTCs are paired with experienced GTCs for one MSF. |
| Videotape consultations, MSF follow-up, and case study about TAs educated abroad 90-minute meeting | This meeting allows new GTCs to ask follow-up questions about the consultation and MSF training, with experienced GTCs answering their inquiries. We then go through the protocol for videotape consultations and examine specific issues of consulting with an international TA through a role-play of a videotape consultation with a client who has been educated abroad. Finelli et al., 2008. |
| Consulting on teaching philosophies (new GTCs only) 70-minute meeting | New GTCs participate in the workshop (see Appendix A for more details). Resources available at PFF Conference site: http://www.crlt.umich.edu/gsis/onedayPFF.php |
| More on consulting about teaching philosophies for the CRLT certificate program (group norming) 90-minute meeting | GTCs examine several teaching philosophies with a rubric, and together, we discuss our ratings of these documents as well as how to provide feedback to the authors effectively. O'Neal, Meizlish, & Kaplan, 2007. |
| Topics on Consulting: Roundtable, POD, and ISSOTL Conference debriefs, Designing workshops 90-minute meeting | At this meeting, we begin a regular feature of the year, the roundtable, where GTCs have an opportunity to discuss consultation challenges with their peers. Following the roundtable, GTCs who have attended the POD or ISSOTL conferences discuss their experiences and share resources with other GTCs. Finally, a GTC with experience in giving workshops discusses his or her process and advice, and CRLT resources on effective workshop design are distributed and discussed. If time allows, GTCs design a mini-workshop on active learning in small groups. |
| Individual 30-minute meetings that take place in mid-fall. | Individual meetings with CRLT professional staff focusing on client feedback, workload, strengths and challenges of the position, and topics the GTC would like to address in Winter Term. |
| Winter Term Planning 90-minute meeting | After the roundtable, the GTCs and CRLT staff co-construct the topics that will be addressed in Winter Term meetings. |

| *Topic (Length)* | *Meeting Structure and Resources* |
| --- | --- |
| Observation reports, Consultation role-play, Active learning, and Classroom Assessment Techniques (CATs) 90-minute meeting | After the roundtable and dissemination of resources on active learning and classroom assessment techniques, this meeting focuses on different ways to convey observational data effectively to clients. GTCs share their classroom observation reports with one another and discuss pros/cons of various presentation strategies. We then role-play a consultation based on selected reports and debrief strategies to work with a "resistant" client. (All reports are anonymous to protect a client's identity.)<br><br>Angelo & Cross, 1993.<br><br>Barkley, Cross, & Major, 2005.<br><br>Bean, 2001.<br><br>O'Neal & Pinder-Grover, in press. |
| Cases on TA and consultant identity 90 minutes | In small groups, GTCs discuss three cases that address how student, TA, and GTC identity shape the dynamic of a consultation. GTCs generate effective strategies for consulting around identity issues. |
| Millennial learners 90 minutes | CRLT staff present on millennial learners. GTCs discuss in small groups how the general guidelines (principles) for teaching millennials could be applied to specific activities in their classrooms. Pinder-Grover & Groscurth, 2009. |
| Science of learning 90 minutes | After the roundtable, CRLT staff present findings of their research on student learning, and GTCs discuss the applications to their work. Examples of research on student learning, which are useful for consulting, are distributed.<br><br>Brandsford, Brown, & Cocking, 2000.<br><br>Brookfield, 1996.<br><br>deWinstanley & Bjork, 2002.<br><br>Dweck, 2002.<br><br>King & Kitchener, 1994.<br><br>Svinicki, 1999. |
| Curriculum assessment and evaluation 90 minutes | After the roundtable, CRLT staff define evaluation and assessment, discuss CRLT work in this area, and highlight several examples of assessment projects at UM. In small groups, GTCs are asked to develop an assessment plan for the GTC program.<br><br>Angelo, 1995.<br><br>Levin-Rozales, 2003.<br><br>Selections from Patton, 2002.<br><br>Rhodes, 2002.<br><br>Smith, 2008. |

| Topic (Length) | Meeting Structure and Resources |
| --- | --- |
| Interdisciplinary course design; End-of-year wrap-up<br>90 minutes | CRLT staff discuss principles of interdisciplinary course design and facilitate an activity where GTC pairs develop a course topic and learning objectives for an interdisciplinary class. GTCs evaluate the GTC program (using ideas generated from the previous meeting and a survey). The group also says good-bye to GTCs who are moving on to other positions, through a roundtable format.<br><br>CRLT Annotated Bibliography for New Faculty Orientation (Books available to check out at CRLT Library)<br><br>CRLT Articles Frequently Used in Consulting (Articles available at CRLT front desk)<br><br>Weimer, 2002.<br><br>Wiggins & McTighe, 1998. |

# EGSM PROGRAM CALL FOR APPLICATIONS

## Call for applications for the Engineering GSI Mentor program (Fall 2009)

The College of Engineering and the Center for Research on Learning and Teaching (CRLT) North are seeking applicants to fill positions in the successful EGSM program. EGSMs have been invaluable by assisting engineering GSIs with their teaching assignments. The details of the job description, including payment, are shown below. **DEADLINE FOR APPLICATIONS IS FRIDAY, APRIL 10, 2009.**

Activities as an EGSM include, but are not limited to, the following:

- **Observe GSIs** and **provide feedback** to them
- **Collect feedback** from GSIs' students
- **Perform one-on-one consultations** with individual GSIs
- **Lead workshops** and **participate** in advanced teaching seminars

EGSMs receive training to support these roles and are expected to participate actively in the Engineering GSI Teacher Training. Graduate students who have served at least one term as a GSI at the University of Michigan, preferably, but not necessarily, in the College of Engineering, are eligible for these positions. EGSMs may be assigned GSIs from outside of their program department.

The EGSM position in the College of Engineering is a paid appointment, and the applicant is required to have other support of at least 25% as a GSI or a GSRA, or must have a fellowship that covers benefits. Proof of this primary appointment must be submitted to be eligible for hiring. The EGSM appointment does not carry any tuition waiver or benefits.

Applicants should submit:

1. A brief personal statement describing your reasons for wanting to be a graduate student mentor
2. A list of courses taught with a description of your responsibilities
3. An application form

For more information about the program, visit: http://www.engin.umich .edu/teaching/crltnorth/

# 6

# APPROACHES TO PREPARING FUTURE FACULTY FOR TEACHING

*Chad Hershock, Christopher R. Groscurth, and Stiliana Milkova*

T eaching centers play an important role in preparing graduate students and postdocs for their future roles as faculty members. The Preparing Future Faculty (PFF) initiative in U.S. higher education is more than 20 years old (for a historical review, see Association of American Colleges and Universities [AAC&U], 2010). Realizing that research training alone is insufficient for preparing graduate students to enter the professoriate, proponents of this initiative sought to introduce graduate students to the full suite of faculty roles and responsibilities (i.e., teaching, research, and service) in a variety of institutional contexts, especially non-research-oriented universities, and to provide opportunities for mentoring, reflection, and feedback on their professional development. Nationally, programs for PFF vary greatly in design, content, scope, and disciplinary focus, but they all share a common goal of not significantly affecting progress toward degrees (Austin, Connolly, & Colbeck, 2008; Cook et al., 2001; Marincovich, Prostko, & Stout, 1998; Smith, 2003). At CRLT, we think about PFF within a broad developmental framework (e.g., see Nyquist & Sprague, 1998), recognizing that individuals develop as instructors at different rates, independent of the stage of their academic career. Thus, we offer an array of programs to support both the early and advanced stages of prefaculty development, helping graduate students and postdocs across campus prepare for teaching and their first faculty positions (http://www.crlt.umich.edu/gsis/pff.php).

This chapter describes several effective, transferable models for PFF implemented by CRLT, all of which prioritize teaching at the classroom, curricular, and institutional levels. These programs include teaching orientations; a ten-session, intensive PFF Seminar; a one-day PFF Conference; an intercampus mentorship program on college teaching; a postdoctoral short-course on college teaching in science and engineering; and a graduate teacher certificate program that documents participants' professional development activities in college-level teaching. These complementary approaches to PFF programming fill a critical gap in graduate student and postdoctoral training by providing interdisciplinary opportunities to (1) learn about, practice, and reflect on effective, research-based teaching methods; (2) discuss U.S. higher education and faculty work life, a topic of special importance for international students educated outside of the United States; and (3) prepare and receive feedback on teaching materials for the academic job market.

This chapter considers the benefits and limitations of each program, including the challenges related to designing PFF programs for a diverse, interdisciplinary clientele. We offer strategies for overcoming those challenges for faculty developers and administrators seeking to implement or enhance PFF programs. We conclude by discussing the implications of these programs for promoting a culture of teaching excellence.

## Teaching Orientations

Many teaching centers at doctoral institutions offer teaching orientations as a core part of their programming for graduate student development. In fact, much has been written about the important role of teaching centers in teaching assistant (TA) development, including various models for TA orientation programs (e.g., Armstrong, Felten, Johnston, & Pingree, 2006; Bellows & Weissinger, 2005; Frantz et al., 2005; Smith, 2003). Given the typically early timing of TA training in a graduate student's career, one might not necessarily consider it to be PFF programming. However, CRLT's teaching orientations are often the first PFF experience for graduate students who are new to teaching at an institution like UM, laying the foundation on which other PFF programs may build. TA training also provides valuable opportunities to engage experienced graduate student and postdoctoral instructors in preparation for teaching activities. For example, CRLT trains advanced graduate student and postdoctoral instructors to be mentors and teaching consultants for novice instructors (see chapter 5 in this volume and Pinder-Grover et al., in press). Teaching orientations provide opportunities for these developmentally advanced instructors to design and facilitate pedagogy workshops and microteaching sessions under the mentorship of teaching center staff. Planning and engaging in these dialogues on teaching and learning with new instructors can serve as capstone experiences for PFF by allowing experienced instructors to reflect on their own practice, teaching philosophy, evolution as instructors, and professional development experiences.

Opportunities for these capstone PFF experiences occur frequently because CRLT offers several TA orientation services annually, including (1) two daylong, campus-wide orientations that serve 400–500 graduate students per year (http://www.crlt.umich.edu/gsis/gsio.php); (2) a daylong training that is mandatory for all TAs in the College of Engineering (http://www.crlt.umich.edu/gsis/egsio.php); (3) three- and ten-week courses for international TAs (ITAs) who completed their undergraduate education in a language other than English (http://www.crlt.umich.edu/gsis/igsicomm.php); (4) customized TA training sessions for individual departments; (5) a seminar series on instructional methods held throughout the fall and winter terms (http://www.crlt.umich.edu/gsis/gsi_seminars.php); and (6) individual consultations on classroom teaching and confidential early evaluation services (e.g., midterm student feedback sessions).

Our orientation events share a common training structure. Initially, we interactively expose participants to research-based principles of college-level teaching and learning while modeling best practices. Then, in subsequent sessions, participants actively engage in synthesizing and applying these principles to their own teaching, with opportunities to practice and receive feedback. For example, we first use interactive lectures and theatre productions (see chapter 11) to identify challenges to and discuss strategies for facilitating student learning. Topics include, but are not limited to, instructor authority and credibility, student diversity, classroom climate, effective classroom communication, the science of learning, and effective student-centered pedagogies. After participants reflect on these issues and strategies, they participate in microteaching sessions. In small groups of five to seven participants, each TA delivers a five- or ten-minute lesson (sometimes with the requirement of incorporating active learning), practicing what he or she has learned and receiving formative feedback on his or her teaching from peers, experienced instructors, and CRLT instructional consultants in a low-stakes, supportive environment (e.g., see Appendix A in Pinder-Grover et al., in press). Then, participants select from a menu of concurrent sessions on teaching methods specific to their instructional roles as TAs, such as grading student writing, grading in quantitative courses, leading discussions, managing group work, teaching one-on-one in studio courses, teaching foreign languages, and using instructional technology effectively. All concurrent sessions are highly interactive with activities to encourage TAs to apply further specific pedagogies to their own specific teaching context.

In the orientation for ITAs, CRLT partners with UM's English Language Institute. This intensive, extended training program contains many sessions on pedagogy as well as classroom English skills, with multiple micro-teaching sessions for practicing and receiving feedback on both skill sets (Wright & Bogart, 2006; Wright & Kaplan, 2007; Wright, Purkiss, O'Neal, & Cook, 2008). Additionally, undergraduate students, trained by CRLT, provide constructive feedback during these microteaching sessions, adding an additional layer of authenticity and perspective for the TAs while providing an intercultural learning experience for both the undergraduates and ITAs (Wright & Bogart, 2006).

There are several advantages and limitations to using experienced TAs and postdocs as facilitators in TA orientations, in addition to providing them with a capstone PFF experience. Advantages include the ability to (1) provide opportunities for practice, reflection, and feedback on teaching in small groups during orientations that serve hundreds of new TAs; (2) offer many specific sessions based on the needs of different disciplines or TA responsibilities; and (3) ensure that facilitators understand the context and challenges of the session topics because they have relevant classroom experience. The major limitation is the perpetually labor-intensive recruitment and training of facilitators. Large orientations may require 40–50 facilitators to provide a single set of simultaneous microteaching sessions for 300–400 new TAs. Furthermore, workshop facilitators turn over rapidly as they graduate or move to other institutions. Therefore, new facilitators must be recruited and trained for discipline-specific workshops each semester. Overcoming these challenges requires continuous and careful planning by teaching center staff, starting as early as nine months before each orientation.

## The PFF Seminar

The purpose of the PFF Seminar, a partnership between the Graduate School and CRLT, is to prepare a select group of advanced graduate students for their first faculty jobs. The seminar meets two days per week for five weeks during May and June. Each day is four and a half hours long. Because of the highly interactive and experiential nature of the seminar, only 51 graduate students who apply from UM's 19 schools and colleges are invited to participate in the annual seminar (typically a 70–80% acceptance rate).

To prepare participants to teach at the college level and succeed as faculty, the seminar has three objectives. First, participants learn about aspects of the higher education enterprise that are most relevant to the careers of future faculty, such as academic freedom, student diversity, tenure, and assessment. To give participants an experiential understanding of diverse institutional types, CRLT has built strategic partnerships with colleges and universities in Michigan, providing those who take part with an opportunity to meet faculty from a range of local colleges and universities. Participants visit and meet with faculty and administrators on one of these campuses. They debrief these visits with one another, which helps them make informed decisions about which teaching and research context best aligns with their professional goals. In addition, participants hear from a panel of community college faculty, and they have several opportunities to interact with UM faculty on a variety of topics. Participants routinely report that the panels, one-on-one meetings, and group discussions with faculty and administrators across different institutions are extremely useful for informing their job search strategies.

Second, participants are introduced to research on selected topics in teaching and learning (e.g., multicultural teaching, instructional technology, active learning) and they participate in activities that require them to apply these principles and practices to a course they plan to teach. In addition, the methods CRLT facilitators use model research-based techniques for promoting student learning, equipping participants with a toolkit of teaching strategies. This approach allows facilitators to explain their teaching methods and share strategies for overcoming the challenges of a learner-centered classroom.

Third, because a focus of the seminar is preparation for the academic job search, participants write a teaching philosophy statement and a syllabus for a course they plan to teach at UM or as a new faculty member at another institution, and they receive feedback on their teaching documents from peers in their discipline and CRLT consultants. The teaching philosophy is assessed using a research-based rubric developed at CRLT (Meizlish & Kaplan, 2008; O'Neal, Meizlish, & Kaplan, 2007), and the syllabus is assessed using the principles of effective course design, such as the alignment of teaching objectives, assessments, and methods (Diamond, 1998; Whetten, 2007). To further prepare for the academic job market, mock interviews with faculty and postdocs are held to prepare participants for the types of questions regarding teaching they will be asked during on-campus interviews.

Differences among participants in disciplinary backgrounds and teaching experience present challenges for designing PFF programs to satisfy everyone's needs. However, in the same way that social diversity is an asset for student learning (Nagda, Gurin, Sorensen, & Zuniga, 2009), our cross-disciplinary seminar benefits from these differences among participants. For instance, participants with little or no teaching experience benefit from dialogues with those who have more experience, and they often question and challenge the assumptions and biases about teaching and learning that more experienced participants take for granted. Similarly, discussions across disciplines foster critical examination of teaching practices while exposing participants to different approaches to and perspectives on teaching and learning. Because these reciprocal exchanges are so valuable, we strive to maximize the diversity of teaching experience and disciplinary background among participants in programs with limited enrollment and competitive selection processes. To accommodate diversity of disciplinary background, we include faculty from a range of disciplines and often group the participants so they hear from faculty in areas most closely aligned with their own.

The PFF Seminar has several limitations that warrant consideration. First, the program is highly selective, benefiting a relatively small number of UM's graduate students each year. Second, given the unique conventions for writing cover letters and research statements across disciplines, the PFF Seminar does not offer instruction on these topics. Instead, we encourage students to use UM's Career Center and seek advice from their advisory committee. Finally, although the seminar lasts only one month, it represents a large time commitment for everyone involved. During the seminar, many of the participants are busy collecting data, writing dissertations, and/or preparing for the impending job search in the fall. In addition, coordinating the seminar requires a great deal of effort from CRLT's staff.

## The PFF Conference

To overcome some of the limitations of the PFF Seminar, CRLT has partnered with the Graduate School and with the Career Center to offer a condensed PFF experience, a half-day conference called "Getting Ready for an Academic Career." The overarching goal of the conference is to provide participants with an overview of the academic job search and the different stages of a faculty career at different types of institutions, together with concrete strategies and resources for succeeding at each stage. The conference also seeks to address the discipline-specific needs of graduate students and postdoctoral scholars in the humanities, social sciences, and STEM (science, technology, engineering, and mathematics) fields. The conference thus presents participants with an overview of the skills and knowledge necessary to embark on and succeed in a faculty career. This just-in-time approach serves the needs of those who are already in the job market and previews the academic career path for those who are about to enter the market in the near future. Although it is a stand-alone experience, the conference also offers an introduction to CRLT's more time-intensive PFF offerings.

The PFF Conference takes place in the early fall and begins with a plenary panel discussion entitled "Life After the PhD: Adjusting to a New Institutional Context," featuring faculty and postdoctoral scholars from different institutions and disciplines who speak about the teaching, research, and institutional culture at their college or university. These panelists also participate in other sessions throughout the day to continue to offer their institutional, disciplinary, and personal perspective.

The plenary session is followed by three sets of 75-minute concurrent sessions featuring four or five interactive workshops and panel discussions. Two implicit tracks inform the programming of the concurrent sessions: (1) succeeding in the academic job search process, and (2) understanding different aspects of faculty work and life in different disciplinary and institutional contexts. Session topics from the first track include developing a teaching philosophy, writing effective cover letters, enhancing one's CV, and interviewing for the academy. The second track includes sessions on strategies for managing dual careers, maintaining faculty work life balance, navigating the tenure-track process, and succeeding as a new faculty member. To address the demands of participants' different disciplinary backgrounds, we offer sessions that target specific fields or divide into breakout sessions by discipline. The conference also offers a session for international graduate students who want to pursue a faculty career in the United States. To increase access, conference materials are posted online the day after the event, and select panel presentations are videotaped and made available online as well.

Since its inception in 2003, an average of 240 participants have attended the conference each year. An obvious limitation of this condensed model is that participants have fewer chances to engage in in-depth dialogues about teaching and to reflect on and develop their own teaching. Nevertheless, feedback indicates that the conference is meeting its goals: participants report that they learn about faculty work life and the tenure-track process at different types of institutions and they regularly report that they received useful advice, practical tools, and resources for launching their careers.

## Intercampus Mentorship Program

A productive relationship with a faculty mentor or advisor is key to the graduate student's socialization into the faculty career (Austin, 2002; Gardner, 2007; Lovitts, 2008). More important, building a network of multiple mentors can maximize the volume and value of resources available to graduate students as they prepare for teaching and research (Johnson & Huwe, 2003; Sorcinelli & Yun, 2007). Neither the PFF Seminar nor the PFF Conference allows for sustained interaction with faculty members at other institutions. That is why CRLT has partnered with the Graduate School to develop the Intercampus Mentorship Program (IMP), which opens a programmatic space for UM graduate students and postdocs to construct a network of mentors. The program facilitates a mentoring relationship between graduate students and faculty at nearby colleges and universities so graduate students can learn about academic life in a different institutional environment.

The program offers two types of experiences: a short-term mentorship that entails one to three meetings or campus visits, and a long-term mentorship that involves three to seven campus visits and provides opportunities for more in-depth or ambitious projects or teaching experiences. The program is structured to allow a flexible mentorship relationship. The partners in both short- and long-term programs are given freedom to decide the nature of the mentorship so they can design the experience to be most beneficial to them. At the same time, participants are encouraged to consider substantive activities such as observing a class, giving guest lectures in a course, developing a syllabus, designing assignments or educational materials, mentoring undergraduates about graduate school in their field, and discussing research.

The program is administered through a website that contains a list of participating faculty mentors (http://sitemaker.umich.edu/rackham-crlt/gsi_introduction). Prospective participants in the short-term program browse the list of faculty mentors, and then contact a faculty member of their choosing for an initial meeting to discuss a possible mentorship plan. Mentees are reimbursed for transportation, meals, and lodging and receive a small stipend if they carry out a teaching-related project. In contrast to the short-term program, which is open to both graduate students and postdoctoral scholars, only graduate students are eligible for long-term mentorship. Interested students submit an online application in which they identify a faculty mentor, describe their goals and plans for the mentorship, and outline an estimated budget. Long-term mentees are reimbursed for their expenses, and mentors receive a small stipend. Follow-up online surveys are sent to both mentor and mentee to assess the participants' experience.

To implement this program, CRLT has built and continues to build a network of volunteer faculty mentors across disciplines and institutions. Recruiting new faculty mentors is key to the program's success, yet it also constitutes one of its logistical challenges. CRLT works with a faculty contact at a participating institution to identify possible new mentors and publicize the program to colleagues. At some institutions, a mass e-mail is sent to all faculty to inform them of this opportunity. At others, there is no recruitment per se; prospective mentees browse the institution's web page to identify a potential mentor, and CRLT then facilitates contact with the faculty. Another way we recruit faculty mentors is through campus visits. For example, during campus visits that are part of the PFF Seminar described previously, CRLT staff members deliver posters and brochures describing the IMP to faculty contacts on that campus, who then publicize the program. Prospective mentors contact the program coordinator, who adds their teaching and research profiles to the IMP's online database of mentors.

Through this PFF model, participants are able to design a flexible mentorship experience that fits their needs, availability, and interests. The flexibility of the program, however, could also be a disadvantage, because the mentoring experience may be construed too broadly. Nevertheless, at the completion of the program, participants report that the IMP enabled them to explore different institutional types for a faculty job, develop useful contacts for the job search, and acquire a better understanding of teaching and students at various institutions. Faculty mentors also benefit from a flexible relationship with young scholars and future colleagues who offer a new perspective on their teaching or research, as well as from the intrinsic rewards of mentorship.

## Postdoctoral Short-Course on College Teaching in Science and Engineering

The UM community includes approximately 1,200 postdocs, most of whom are affiliated with STEM departments. By the time they enter the academic job market, the majority of the STEM postdocs have fewer than two terms of college-level teaching experience, and many have no experience at all. This dearth of teaching experience results in part because graduate studies in science and engineering are often funded by fellowships and research assistantships rather than teaching assistantships. The lack of teaching experience is compounded by postdoctoral mentorship that traditionally focuses on research, with few opportunities for classroom teaching or pedagogical training. Relatively few departments explicitly include teaching in postdoc job descriptions. Furthermore, a large proportion of these postdocs were educated abroad and are unfamiliar with the system of higher education in the United States, the culture of teaching, and the nature and expectations of U.S. students.

To better prepare a select group of advanced postdocs to teach effectively as future faculty and to be more competitive in the job market, CRLT and the Graduate School collaborate to provide the Postdoctoral Short-Course on College Teaching in Science and Engineering (PSC). Postdocs are selected through a competitive application process (~50% acceptance rate). The short-course is designed to provide postdocs from a variety of disciplines with opportunities to (1) develop a toolkit of evidence-based teaching methods, (2) apply the research on teaching and learning to the design of their future courses, (3) practice and receive feedback on their teaching, and (4) reflect on and explain their teaching practices and philosophy.

When we designed this program, the major challenge was the limitations full-time research appointments placed on postdocs. To overcome this challenge, we developed a "hybrid" course format, combining self-paced online learning with three-hour face-to-face seminars. The seminars occur weekly for seven consecutive weeks and follow a similar format, emphasizing advanced preparation, so time in sessions can be devoted to active learning and reflection. Topics include course design, effective lecturing, active learning methods, assessment of student learning, teaching for inclusion and retention of students in STEM, and instructional technology.

For each session, the online components include a video podcast introducing session topics, short research-based readings to support the podcast, and preparatory assignments that are used during the next face-to-face session. Video podcasts include existing video clips used in CRLT's programs, customized screencasts, and video recordings of CRLT presentations and workshops. Because the first exposure to fundamental concepts occurs online, the face-to-face sessions focus exclusively on "hands-on" activities and discussions that allow participants to clarify, synthesize, and apply the material introduced in the online components to their own teaching and course design.

All seven sessions are integrated and build on one another, leading participants to four capstone experiences: (1) a five-minute practice teaching session, in which they explain one concept from their discipline; (2) a 15-minute practice teaching session, including active learning; (3) completion of a syllabus for a course they could teach as a future faculty member; and (4) completion of an inquiry-based lesson plan for a laboratory course activity. During practice teaching sessions, postdocs are assigned to small groups in breakout rooms. Each presenter receives feedback from peers (who role-play students) and an experienced CRLT facilitator. Because 50% of participants are international postdocs, a consultant from the English Language Institute provides feedback on classroom English skills for those who request it. Participants also receive feedback on their syllabi and inquiry-based labs online from their peers and from the CRLT staff. Participants who successfully complete all course requirements receive a certificate of completion.

Virtually all participants report that the short-course hybrid format was an important piece of their postdoctoral mentorship in preparation to be a faculty member and gave them skills and knowledge to enhance their teaching practice. Furthermore, they report that the hybrid course structure was an effective use of their time and preferable to attending lectures.

This approach requires relatively large investments of staff time to create video podcasts, preparatory assignments, and lesson plans for session activities, as well as provide individual feedback on preparatory assignments and capstone experiences. However, once the online materials are created, these resources can be reused in future iterations of the short-course or in other programs. Another potential limitation is the small number of postdocs served (32 per course offering). Due to the amount of individual feedback associated with the capstone assignments, increasing the number of participants would significantly increase the workload for the course directors. However, this PFF model is scalable and certainly could be expanded to accommodate larger numbers, assuming staffing and funding are available.

## UM Graduate Teacher Certificate

Nationally, PFF certificate programs that systematically document and provide institutional recognition for teaching experience and professional development for college-level teaching are increasingly common (von Hoene et al., 2006). As with other PFF models, certificate requirements and activities differ among institutions based on specific professional development contexts and varying beliefs regarding teaching competencies and approaches for developing those competencies.

At Michigan, a large number of professional development opportunities for teaching are available to graduate students across campus, including, but not limited to, disciplinary courses on teaching, department- and college-level teaching orientations, departmental peer mentorship on teaching, and the many CRLT programs and services for TA development described in this chapter and book. However, many graduate students are unaware of the breadth of opportunities, or they experience them in a piecemeal fashion. Consequently, CRLT designed the UM Graduate Teacher Certificate to integrate existing teaching and professional development opportunities into a cohesive PFF experience that parallels one's research training. By completing program requirements, participants develop and refine their teaching skills, reflect and obtain feedback on their teaching, and write and receive feedback on their teaching philosophy statement in preparation for their faculty job search.

The certificate documents one's professional development activities in five areas (see the appendix to this chapter): (1) orientation to college-level teaching and learning; (2) exposure to new teaching strategies through seminars and courses; (3) experience as a TA, including a consultation on classroom teaching; (4) mentorship on teaching from a faculty member; and (5) preparation of a teaching philosophy statement. Participants may submit documentation for activities completed at UM prior to enrolling in the program and may complete the requirements in any order within five years of enrolling. However, we encourage participants to complete the teaching philosophy statement last as a reflective, capstone experience. Trained CRLT consultants review all teaching statements, provide feedback, and offer consultations using a research-based rubric (O'Neal et al., 2007). Participants may revise and resubmit their statements, if necessary, to meet program requirements.

Graduate students who complete all requirements receive a UM Graduate Teacher Certificate. Because the program is free and does not require tuition payment, the certificate does not appear on official UM transcripts, but may be highlighted in one's CV and cover letters for job applications. Certificate recipients also receive an award letter and an official description of the program to provide to job interviewers and faculty search committees.

The certificate is administered entirely online (http://sitemaker.umich .edu/um.gtc). Through the program's interactive website, participants may view requirements, eligibility criteria, and deadlines; enroll in the program; access resources and support for completing requirements; find answers to frequently asked questions; and submit and track the status of documentation for professional development activities.

During the first two years of implementation, 386 graduate students from 18 of UM's 19 schools and colleges enrolled in the certificate program. Ninety-eight students from 43 graduate programs in 13 schools and colleges completed all requirements. Overall, certificate recipients report that completing the requirements increased their skills and knowledge about teaching, increased their confidence in their teaching ability, and positively changed their current or future teaching practices. Additionally, most recipients reported increased confidence in their ability to talk about teaching during job interviews and a greater desire to pursue additional professional development in teaching.

Inclusivity was the major barrier to implementing the certificate program successfully. Within and across UM schools and colleges, the availability, nature, and extent of TA training programs, teaching assistantships, mentorship on teaching, and pedagogy courses vary significantly. Consequently, we worked with the Graduate School, our funder, and designed each requirement to be as flexible as possible, offering multiple options for satisfying certificate criteria (e.g., see the appendix to this chapter). Furthermore, we allow students to petition the program regarding changes to requirements. For instance, because it is difficult for CRLT to monitor offerings of college-level pedagogy courses across campus, students may petition to add courses by submitting a syllabus. Similarly, for some units, two terms of teaching experience is an insurmountable requirement that would exclude all of their graduate students. Students in graduate programs with limited teaching opportunities can petition to replace one term of teaching by completing an additional item from another requirement (e.g., a second pedagogy course or mentorship on teaching). An interdisciplinary faculty advisory committee reviews all petitions. Embedding such flexibility in requirements and administrative procedures facilitates participation and support across campus from faculty, administrators, and students.

## Recommendations for Faculty Developers and Administrators

In previous sections, we offered strategies for overcoming the specific challenges presented by each PFF model. Here, we offer general recommendations for those seeking to adapt any of the PFF models to launch campus-wide programs. Regardless of the PFF model of interest, these approaches have been integral to positioning our programs strategically to satisfy the needs of a diverse clientele on our campus and to prepare future faculty to teach well.

## Leverage the Expertise of Your Teaching Center

PFF programs are most effective when they leverage the expertise of teaching centers regarding research on teaching and learning and academic careers. For example, our faculty, postdoc, and graduate student clients repeatedly report an interest in learning about and applying the research on teaching and learning. However, they are also frequently unfamiliar with or do not have time to explore thoroughly the peer-reviewed literature on teaching and learning in their disciplines. PFF programs present an opportunity to distill and summarize this literature. Consequently, we use research-based evidence as the foundation of PFF program elements. For example, in the PFF Seminar and Conference module, titled "Hit the Ground Running With Your Academic Career," participants discuss strategies for time management and balancing one's teaching and research responsibilities based on research by Boice (1991b). In the PFF Seminar, modules on developing one's teaching philosophy are based on national research examining the criteria search committees use to evaluate teaching effectiveness (Meizlish & Kaplan, 2008). Similarly, in the Postdoc Short-Course, sessions focused on active learning in large lectures are supported by research on peer instruction published in the journal *Science* (Smith et al., 2009), whereas sessions on teaching strategies that increase student retention in science and engineering majors are based on literature reviews (Kendall Brown, Hershock, Finelli, & O'Neal, 2009).

## Identify Needs, Assets, and Barriers

At a large, decentralized institution like UM, it is easy for academic and administrative units to "reinvent the wheel" or create programs that duplicate effort toward a common goal. Therefore, we recommend investing the time to conduct a needs and assets assessment before implementing a program. What other PFF programs exist on campus? Who runs and attends them? On what do they focus? What institutional resources, collaborations, and opportunities are available to achieve PFF goals? What are the barriers to participation and support by students and faculty? Empowered with this information, teaching centers can position themselves to collaborate with stakeholders on campus to create PFF programs that complement rather than compete with extant department- and college-level programs, in terms of both content and timing.

### Explore Opportunities for Collaborations

Early in the development of PFF programs, we recommend that teaching centers actively explore collaborations with academic and administrative units and solicit feedback from stakeholders on campus. For instance, CRLT partners with the Graduate School on each of its PFF programs. In addition to increasing the visibility of our programs and giving us useful advice, this partnership has been integral to garnering institutional and financial support for program development, implementation, and continuation. To create PFF programs that are inclusive and broadly appealing, yet tailored to meet specific professional development needs, CRLT also works closely with administrators responsible for overseeing graduate education and postdoctoral training in different schools and colleges. For instance, when designing the UM Graduate Teacher Certificate Program, we formed an advisory committee comprising associate deans and graduate students from four schools and colleges on campus. This committee provided feedback that was critical to overcoming barriers to program implementation, especially when developing flexible and inclusive program requirements that would not exclude graduate students from departments with limited teaching opportunities. Such committees also help teaching centers navigate the political and bureaucratic complexities of the university and establish *buy-in* from different academic units that PFF programs serve. This committee not only contributed to the initial success of the program, but it also continues to meet each year to discuss evaluation data and petitions from students and faculty regarding revisions to program requirements.

During program development, we also solicit feedback from the leaders of campus groups representing participants, such as the Rackham Graduate School Student Government, Students of Color of Rackham, Graduate Employees Organization (the union representing TAs on campus), and Postdoc Association. These meetings provide important feedback on program development and implementation while fostering grassroots enthusiasm for participation by the target audience. Actively soliciting stakeholder feedback also helps teaching centers create programs that fill conspicuous gaps in graduate student and postdoctoral training.

### Pilot and Evaluate New Programs on a Small Scale

Program evaluation is critical for PFF initiatives. Regardless of the model selected, we recommend that teaching centers start by piloting and evaluating a program that is limited in scope. In our PFF programs characterized by multiple sessions with the same cohort of participants, we frequently incorporate a midprogram participant evaluation. This approach not only models best practices in teaching, but it also allows program coordinators to gather and act on feedback about what is going well and what could be improved during the program. All programs conclude with a written evaluation. Periodically, we also survey alumni of our PFF programs after they have had subsequent teaching experiences or become faculty members, to reassess which program elements were most valuable to them and what was lacking. We use quantitative and qualitative evaluation data to revise and implement programs on a larger scale and to publicize programs, establish CRLT's reputation for excellence, and lobby for institutional support for continuing or expanding programs.

## Conclusion: Implications for Promoting a Culture of Teaching Excellence

PFF teaching initiatives can affect campus culture significantly, increasing the focus and value placed on professional development on teaching. To conclude this chapter, we explore how such cultural shifts can percolate through the university via the impact on graduate students, postdocs, faculty, and administrators. We also discuss the implications that may result for teaching centers regarding increased demands for their services.

In addition to preparing participants for the academic job search, evaluation data suggest that PFF programs may influence institutional culture in several ways. First, participants consistently report positive changes in their attitudes toward teaching, often expressed in terms of increases in confidence in their teaching skills or changes in their teaching practices that reflect research-based practice. Second, since 2008, the majority of the 162 participants completing the UM Graduate Teacher Certificate and Postdoctoral Short-Course expressed an increased desire to "seek out additional professional development opportunities regarding teaching in the future" (e.g., mean response of 4.0 out of 5.0, where 1 = *strongly disagree* and 5 = *strongly agree*), indicating that their behavior and values are likely to influence cultural norms at their future institutions, resulting in the increased importance of teaching.

PFF participants may also influence the culture in their current departments by actively promoting the value of PFF for teaching through conversations with colleagues. Although CRLT aggressively advertises its programs across campus, the most effective publicity may be by word of mouth. For example, in 2008, we recruited our first PFF Seminar participant from musicology. In 2009, we had four applicants from that comparatively small graduate program, each of whom applied based on the recommendations of the PFF alum. Similar increases in applications based on peer recommendations have been documented for other departments, ranging from philosophy to nursing and microbiology. Faculty members also inquire about and recommend our programs to their students and postdocs after hearing about them from PFF alumni. We are routinely invited to discuss our PFF opportunities for gatherings of graduate students in a variety of departments. In one department, we participate in the annual graduate student recruitment weekend, during which our PFF programs are highlighted as a resource and asset to help attract prospective students. For the Postdoctoral Short-Course, we require a letter of support from each applicant's supervising faculty member. These letters tend to describe effusively how this PFF opportunity will complement the postdoc's research training and mentorship. Although these examples are largely anecdotal, over time, they suggest a general increase across campus in the perceived value of PFF for teaching.

We have observed a concomitant increase in the demand for our teaching center's PFF for teaching services by graduate students and postdocs. Since implementation of the UM Graduate Teacher Certificate, attendance at workshops in the CRLT Seminar Series for graduate students and postdocs has increased on average by 42%, from 31 to 44 attendees per session. During the 2009–2010 academic year, 22% of participants from 29 workshops, ten people per session on average, attended to satisfy certificate requirements. The number of requests for consultations on classroom teaching and teaching philosophy statements has also increased by an average of 15 and 25 consultations per term, respectively. Program evaluation data confirm that these increases result from graduate students who are fulfilling certificate requirements. Each year, the PFF Seminar and Conference also generate 30–40 requests for consultations on teaching philosophy statements and classroom teaching from graduate students and postdocs, some of whom subsequently enroll in the UM Graduate Teacher Certificate, Intercampus Mentorship Program, and additional CRLT workshops on teaching.

PFF programs also involve faculty in several ways. Programs that include faculty panels, roundtable discussions, or guest presentations allow teaching centers to feature faculty who are leaders and innovators in teaching. For instance, several of CRLT's programs contain sessions on instructional technology and feature guest presentations and interactive demonstrations by faculty using student response systems ("clickers"), screencasting, and online discussion forums in a variety of teaching contexts to engage students actively and assess student learning. To help them receive credit and recognition for their teaching, we send letters of thanks to faculty participants and to their department chairs and deans. The letters describe the faculty participants' contributions to the program, include any laudatory program evaluation data, and highlight how their teaching methods serve as models for future faculty. We also feature participating faculty on the websites for PFF programs. Additionally, CRLT's Intercampus Mentorship Program and UM Graduate Teacher Certificate create and promote opportunities for faculty to mentor graduate students and postdocs explicitly on teaching. Given that graduate and postdoctoral mentorship at our institution have usually focused primarily on research skills, these activities represent a significant shift in mentorship culture and practice.

Because CRLT's PFF programs are developed, marketed, and funded in collaboration with the Graduate School, they also demonstrate the administration's commitment to teaching. PFF for teaching programs may also help administrators and faculty respond to external demands regarding graduate student and postdoctoral training. Recently, federal grant requirements (e.g., National Science Foundation) have changed, mandating mentorship plans for postdocs funded through research grant awards. PFF programs provide an institutional opportunity to serve this new demand by conspicuously leveraging the expertise of teaching centers.

The specific requirements of PFF programs may instigate institutional change at the departmental level. The UM Graduate Teacher Certificate requirements include participation in at least eight hours of orientation to college-level teaching and learning. Departmentally based teaching orientations must include both classroom climate and practice teaching sessions (e.g., see Pinder, 2007; Wright & Kaplan, 2007). If a department's TA training does not include these sessions, these requirements may stimulate a departmental review and discussion of TA training priorities and practices to ensure that its graduate students are eligible for the certificate. Furthermore, this stimulus may generate opportunities for a teaching center to consult with individual departments and colleges on designing sessions for departmental TA training.

In summary, this chapter has described how CRLT's approaches to PFF serve diverse stakeholders across UM's campus. Because one size may not fit all for the PFF needs of individual graduate students, postdocs, or departments, we have also made the case for offering an array of PFF programs, each of which should complement the strengths and limitations of the others. Implicit in our discussion of these programs is a set of values and assumptions about the role of good teaching in graduate student and postdoc development. We believe that preparing future faculty for teaching is central to a university's commitment to undergraduate and graduate education and postdoctoral training. By investing in and leveraging the PFF expertise of teaching centers, faculty and administrators can advance the culture of teaching excellence and make a positive difference on their own campuses and beyond.

# UNIVERSITY OF MICHIGAN GRADUATE TEACHER CERTIFICATE REQUIREMENTS

| Requirements | UM Graduate Teacher Certificate |
| --- | --- |
| A. Orientation to college teaching and student learning | 1. Documentation of at least eight hours of departmentally based GSI training, *which must include practice teaching and a classroom climate session* (sometimes offered as a one-credit 993 course) <br> *OR* <br> 2. Successful completion of the ELI 994 Course (*also satisfies Requirement B*) <br> *OR* <br> 3. Attendance at an entire CRLT Graduate Student Instructor (GSI) Teaching Orientation or Engineering GSI Teacher Training program |
| B. Learning about teaching | Successful completion of one of the following UM courses on college teaching[1]: <br> ENGR 580, ROMLING 528, BA 830&831, PIBS 505, ED 720, ED 790, ED 737, ED 834, HIST 812, PSYCH 958, MUSICOL 509, AAPTIS 837, ELI 994 (*ELI 994 also satisfies Requirement A*) <br> *OR* <br> Attendance at five CRLT, department, or disciplinary workshops on teaching methods, at least one of which must focus on multicultural, inclusive teaching practices OR instructional technology[2] <br> *OR* <br> Completion of one of the following Rackham-CRLT programs: May Preparing Future Faculty Seminar, Training for Multicultural Classroom Facilitation |
| C. Instructional practice | Two terms of teaching at UM[3], as certified by a course supervisor or GSI supervisor. This teaching must include direct contact with students in a classroom, studio, lab, or equivalent setting. *Positions involving only grading and/or office hours will not fulfill this requirement.* |

| | *AND*<br>One of the following consultations on teaching at UM: Midterm Student Feedback, classroom observation, classroom videotaping, or consultation on student ratings[4] |
|---|---|
| D. Mentorship on teaching | Participation as a mentee in a faculty mentorship on teaching, with a UM faculty member (2–3 meetings) or with a faculty mentor elsewhere (such as through the Rackham-CRLT Mentorship Program). The mentorship must include an endeavor above and beyond preparation to teach courses to which GSIs are appointed. Examples include, but are not limited to: (1) design, present, and receive feedback on a guest lecture; (2) prepare a syllabus, instructional materials, or assignments for a future course; or (3) conduct a research project on teaching and learning. |
| E. Reflection on instructional practice | Completion of a two-page statement of one's teaching philosophy[5] |

[1] "Successful completion" is defined as a B grade or better or a "Satisfactory (S)" grade in a pass/fail course. One-credit courses on teaching, such as 993 courses, do NOT satisfy Requirement B, but may satisfy Requirement A (see criteria above). As CRLT becomes aware of additional comprehensive UM courses on college teaching (usually three-credit, semester-long courses), they will become eligible to be added to the list for requirement B1). The UM Graduate Teacher Certificate Advisory Committee will review petitions each November and March. To submit a letter of petition, send an e-mail and the course syllabus to UMGraduateTeacherCertificate@umich.edu. Please see http://sitemaker.umich.edu/um.gtc for instructions on submitting course petitions. The Advisory Committee recommends that courses include appropriate modules on multicultural teaching and learning and instructional technology.

[2] Workshops focusing only on basic functionality of hardware or software rather than applications for teaching and learning do not satisfy the instructional technology requirement. Sessions at CRLT's October Preparing Future Faculty Conference do not satisfy requirement B2, because they do not explicitly focus on the development of teaching skills.

[3] Participation in the UM Graduate Teacher Certificate Program does NOT guarantee one a GSI appointment. Graduate students who cannot complete a second term of teaching as a GSI, for whatever reason, may petition the UM Graduate Teacher Certificate Advisory Committee (UMGraduateTeacherCertificate@umich.edu) to complete two of the three items under Requirement B in lieu of a second term of teaching.

[4] Consultations may be provided by a CRLT-trained consultant OR faculty member OR Graduate Student Mentor from the discipline of the GSI appointment.

[5] A CRLT-trained consultant will be assigned to evaluate teaching philosophy statements based on criteria specified by the program. If necessary, to satisfy the criteria, participants may resubmit revisions of their teaching philosophy.

# PART TWO

## SPECIAL EMPHASES AT CRLT

# 7

# THE ROLE OF A TEACHING CENTER IN CURRICULAR REFORM AND ASSESSMENT

*Constance E. Cook, Deborah S. Meizlish, and Mary C. Wright*

S ome teaching centers have assessment offices on their campuses and collaborate regularly with them. At the University of Michigan, no office is devoted solely to assessment of student learning outcomes, but CRLT has a long history of work on both curricular reform and assessment. We emphasize this work because it can lead to significant long-term improvements for student learning. Moreover, the involvement of the teaching center provides an opportunity to raise issues of pedagogy and pedagogical content knowledge in the context of the disciplinary and intellectual concerns of the faculty. As this chapter is being written, CRLT is contributing to ten university-wide projects run out of the provost's office. Additionally, deans from fourteen UM schools and colleges are using CRLT staff expertise for assessment projects, as are numerous department chairs. While the exact number and nature of CRLT curricular reform and assessment projects vary from year to year, there is a growing demand for our center's services. Word has spread at UM about the value of engaging CRLT in these endeavors. This chapter concerns the strategies CRLT uses to get involved in curricular reform and assessment, the ways we try to make those processes succeed, the range of services we provide, and the value to the academic units in having CRLT support.

## How a Teaching Center Can Help

One reason for highlighting CRLT's work on curricular reform and assessment is that the literature in these two areas largely overlooks the contributions of teaching centers. With occasional exceptions (e.g., Diamond, 1989, 2005; Gaff, 1983; Hutchings, 2010), the curriculum and assessment literature rarely mentions the value of partnering with teaching centers (see Gardiner, 1992, for an overview of the curricular reform literature). For example, Lattuca and Stark (2009) make only passing reference to the potential value of working with "instructional development centers" (p. 291). In the process, they repeat (but do not update) data collected over 20 years ago (Stark et al., 1990) showing that faculty avoid working with such specialists on curriculum issues. Likewise, Banta, Lund, Black, and Oblander's (1996) important collection of assessment case studies makes no specific reference to teaching centers as a valuable resource for assessment endeavors. Finally, Bok's (2006) influential book, *Our Underachieving Colleges*, mentions the role of teaching centers in improving postsecondary education only when discussing the dissemination of active learning practices.

In contrast, the literature on teaching centers increasingly emphasizes the importance of partnering with faculty and administrators on curriculum and assessment (Frantz et al., 2005; Sorcinelli et al., 2006). For example, Sorcinelli and her colleagues argue that involvement in assessment issues is crucial for faculty developers. Likewise, Diamond (2005) specifically highlights teaching centers as ideal institutional change agents. Yet, the faculty development literature also indicates that there is room for improvement. First, as Sorcinelli documents, there is a mismatch between the high importance center directors place on curriculum and assessment initiatives and the relatively limited number of services teaching centers offer in these areas. Second, where centers do offer services, they are more concentrated at the classroom level than at the unit or institutional level (Frantz et al., 2005). As Wehlburg (2008) notes, "Many institutions still have little interaction between those who collect and report assessment data and those who focus on improving teaching and learning" (p. 10). This is particularly surprising given that, as mentioned in chapter 3, the professional organization for faculty developers (the Professional and Organizational Development Network in Higher Education [POD]) specifically articulates a threefold mission, including faculty development, instructional development, and organizational development, all of which are integral to curricular reform and assessment (Diamond, 1989, 1998).

Research on faculty and administrator support for institutional effectiveness activities suggests why teaching centers are well positioned to facilitate these endeavors. Banta (1997) names a number of sources of resistance to engagement in institutional effectiveness activities, such as lack of faculty support and insufficient use of results. Indeed, research on assessment and curricular improvement suggests that for these activities to be well supported, administrators must believe that they stem from an internally driven need (as opposed to external pressures), that they can have personal involvement over their design and implementation, and that the activities have the potential for institutional change (Welsh & Metcalf, 2003b). Similar research on faculty suggests that an emphasis on the applications of assessment data—or "real results arising from instruction and efforts to improve" (Welsh & Metcalf, 2003a, p. 41)—is also critically important to achieve buy-in. Teaching centers can play important roles in fostering all of these dynamics. Staff at teaching centers typically have much experience working with academic administrators and faculty on critical assessment-related tasks, such as defining local instructional needs, helping faculty work collaboratively, facilitating conversations and events that will prompt curricular enhancement, and providing resources to support follow-up and implementation of changes.

What follows are several examples of CRLT projects in support of deans and department chairs who requested our help. The stories begin with the dean or chair telling us about a problem in his or her unit—something he or she would like CRLT's help in changing. Often, it is an ill-defined problem or set of questions. Usually these problems involve some aspect of the curriculum, but they are not always framed as curricular reform or assessment when they are brought to us initially.[1] Each set of stories highlights how CRLT was able to engage in an assessment or curricular reform effort through the best practice themes described by Welsh & Metcalf (2003a, 2003b): starting from the position of institutional improvement, emphasizing outcomes through data collection, facilitating the involvement of faculty and administrators in the design and implementation of the project, and using assessment for institutional change.

## Generating Faculty Involvement and Administrative Input

We have found that academic administrators often begin conversations with CRLT on curricular reform and assessment very cautiously. These are very sensitive topics in the academy (Banta, 2007; Fendrich, 2007; Hersh, 2007). Faculty naturally have a sense of ownership of the courses they teach, and they may think changes in the curriculum are unnecessary or question the need to assess student learning beyond their own efforts to grade student work. In addition, curricular reform and assessment projects can add substantially to faculty workload. As for the deans and chairs, their own reputations as successful administrators depend in part on handling curricular issues effectively, so they are not sure they should be putting their reputation in our hands. If CRLT does not do a good job, it could reflect badly on the dean or chair for involving us in the first place.

In response to this caution, we try to reassure administrators from the start by mentioning some of the projects we have done for their peers, and showing them that we are experienced and have a record of accomplishments in these and other areas. As the project proceeds, we involve them every step of the way, and we often also advise them on ways to generate the faculty input needed to make the process a success.

Involvement of faculty is critical to the success of reform projects (Welsh & Metcalf, 2003b). Yet, it sometimes seems that the hardest part of curricular reform is getting faculty together to make decisions. Often, our involvement in a project begins when an administrator contacts us about planning and implementing a meeting or retreat for faculty. It is not surprising that they come to us for this assistance. We have built a solid reputation on campus for hosting large events (like our TA and new faculty orientations or our Provost's Seminars on Teaching) devoted to teaching and pedagogy. We have developed or adapted several models useful for discussions of the curriculum.

For example, the dean of one of UM's largest colleges was considering launching a curriculum review. This dean was well aware of the difficulty of doing a full-scale review of the curriculum, with every issue on the table. He knew that both Harvard and MIT had recently engaged in reviews of their general education requirements and that, despite multiple task forces' devoting years to the review, neither institution had really accomplished curricular reform. He also knew that the perils of curricular reform go beyond the time, effort, and expense involved. It can lead to unpleasantness and factionalism among faculty, disrupt the sense of community, and become a full-time occupation for a dean who initiates the process (Schneider, 1999), making it hard to accomplish any other objectives.

To determine faculty views of the curriculum (and whether a full-scale review was necessary), the dean asked CRLT to organize three events that would provide faculty with a choice of opportunities to discuss the curriculum. The dean's invitation read as follows:

> Is it time for us to engage in sustained discussion of the curriculum, including the general education and distribution requirements? . . . Our curriculum may be fine as is, but I think we should discuss this more often than once every fifteen years.

About 60 faculty attended each of the three events, which occurred over a two-month period. The invitees were teaching award winners, executive committee members, department and program chairs, and a few key staff members. Instead of focusing on the intricacies of the curriculum, the dean wanted faculty to think carefully about their vision for the future, and have that vision guide the need for (and extent of) curricular change or revision. To achieve this, we worked with the dean to design a set of activities to surface these visions. He suggested that after a brief overview of the current curriculum we ask participants to craft a headline about the college curriculum they would choose to see in ten years in a publication such as *The Chronicle of Higher Education*—in other words, what did they want to have happen, and what would make it noteworthy? They would do this first as individuals, and then as a table group.

Having collected each table's favorite headlines, CRLT staff posted them on the walls around the room, and attendees were asked to vote for their top three choices, using colored dots. After the vote, each headline that received a large number of votes was assigned to a table for additional discussion. Participants chose the table where they wanted to sit based on the headline that table would be discussing. There were as many headlines discussed as there were tables. All tables considered the following issues in regard to the headline assigned to them: How does the current curriculum promote or impede implementation of that headline, and what additional steps would be necessary for the headline to be realized? CRLT staff took notes at each table, and at the end of the table discussions, the dean led a large-group debrief (see Figure 7.1 for an outline of the event).

What the dean learned from these discussions was that the faculty had no interest in a full-scale review of the curriculum. On the whole, they thought it was working. But they did say they had three major priorities for the curriculum of the future—more study abroad, more civic engagement, more active learning—as well as a desire for more assessment of student learning. To explore the details of each of their three top priorities, the dean

## FIGURE 7.1
### Agenda for Large-College Visioning Discussion

- Review of key curricular features and recent curricular developments
- Table Discussion: "Headline of the Future" exercise
- Vote
- Table Discussion: How to achieve headlines
- Debrief

then asked CRLT to organize half-day events at which one of the three priorities would be discussed in detail. Faculty and staff relevant to the topic were invited to attend these events, and there were table discussions similar in process to the three original discussions. The events allowed fuller exploration of the challenges involved in implementing each of the priorities. It became clear during the discussions that some of the challenges could be addressed through relatively simple bureaucratic changes, and the dean set about harvesting those low-hanging fruit (Weick, 1984). He then informed the faculty that he had acted on their recommendations. Other challenges were more complicated and would involve task forces and more detailed, long-term planning.

Our successful handling of these events helped lay the groundwork for our involvement in several additional projects. First, to further discussions of assessment, the dean asked us to expose key faculty to an array of assessment options. The dean hoped this would lower barriers to assessment by showcasing relevant activities under way at the college and department levels (e.g., student exit surveys, concept inventories, self-assessments) and providing opportunities for faculty to consider how to leverage existing practices (like capstone courses) for assessment purposes.

Second, with the faculty having identified assessment of student learning as a priority, the dean wanted to emphasize his own commitment to assessment by examining several of the college-level distribution requirements. In particular, he wanted to know whether the general education distribution requirements were teaching the skills and knowledge the faculty had agreed were important when the requirements were first adopted. He again asked for CRLT's help. (We discuss the specifics of this project later in this chapter.)

Over the years, CRLT has organized and facilitated a great number of faculty retreats like the ones described here. We make these processes successful by carefully designing events and then summarizing data and supporting follow-up activities. In doing so, we lessen the burden on deans and chairs and streamline faculty involvement so key issues can be addressed efficiently and effectively. We organize events that focus on positives and generate solutions to issues rather than simply air concerns.

## Support of the Collection and Analysis of Outcomes Measures

An institutional emphasis on outcomes, or results that illustrate if, how, and what students are learning, is critical to faculty support of institutional reform initiatives (Welsh & Metcalf, 2003a). We have found that curricular reform often founders because faculty views about the current curriculum are based only on anecdotal information and hypothetical conjectures. In the absence of data showing otherwise, it is easy for colleagues opposed to change to contend that the current curriculum is adequate, or for those who are eager for change to insist that change is essential. The absence of commonly shared evaluation data also makes it difficult to come to consensus about the direction the changes should take. Instructional consultants can help by providing evaluation and assessment data for the current curriculum so faculty decision making is empirically based.

In the following examples, faculty and administrators realized it was important to collect data about the current curriculum before rushing to judgment about making improvements. In each case, the data collection process (surveys, focus groups, and interviews) brought stakeholder voices into the decision-making process. The data convinced skeptical faculty that change was really necessary, and it also offered information for priority setting by highlighting the biggest issues and pointing to directions for change. The involvement in data gathering by a "neutral" CRLT consultant lent credibility to the process and helped convince faculty of the veracity of the evidence.

### Assessing General Education Requirements

Having identified assessment as a priority through the curriculum discussion we previously described, the dean asked CRLT to identify a viable strategy for assessing the college's quantitative reasoning (QR) requirement. We began by looking for models at peer institutions and found a rigorous methodology the University of Wisconsin used to assess its own QR requirement (Halaby, 2005). The survey was well validated, and the quantitative findings would be appealing to the audience of instructors teaching QR (e.g., math and statistics faculty). After a pilot test in the spring and summer, a large-scale survey was done of two groups of students: those who had never taken a QR course, and those who had. Results were analyzed to examine differences between the two groups of QR takers, differences for various groups of students taking QR courses (e.g., underrepresented minorities and others, men, and women), and what instructional strategies students found useful to help them learn analytical reasoning. The results were presented to departments that offered QR courses to show them their (generally quite positive) findings and in the interest of learning more about pedagogical best practices that might be disseminated more broadly. For more details about the process and findings, see http://www.crlt.umich.edu/assessment/lsaqrassessment.php.

## Conducting a Curriculum Review

A new dean with an ambitious agenda contacted us about supporting his efforts to conduct a major curriculum review. He was committed to a data-driven process and sought our assistance in designing and managing data collection on a variety of fronts. Over the course of several months, and with the advice and input of a small steering committee of faculty and senior staff, the instructional consultant helped the school design survey instruments for faculty, students, and alumni. These surveys were designed to elicit the importance each constituency placed on a set of proposed learning goals for the curriculum. The goals themselves had been generated through several rounds of faculty discussions. In addition to evaluating the importance of each objective, students and recent alumni were asked to evaluate the effectiveness of the current curriculum in reaching these learning objectives (see Table 7.1). These data helped the dean focus on several key areas for further discussion. Moreover, the dean asked his curricular review working groups to use this common pool of data to justify the recommendations put forward for faculty consideration.

## Addressing Multicultural Teaching and Learning

Student concerns can also drive curricular revisions. In one of our schools, persistent dissatisfaction among students of color prompted the dean to approach CRLT for assistance. CRLT consultants worked with a small faculty steering group to plan student focus groups to better understand student dissatisfaction. As Cook (2001) reported, the focus groups identified several concerns, including insufficient multicultural content in the curriculum, faculty who did not know how to handle sensitive topics in class, and a limited

## TABLE 7.1
### Sample Student Curricular Survey

The goals of this survey are:
- To provide us feedback on your experiences with the curriculum.
- To help us prioritize a list of potential learning objectives for the curriculum. (We are asking faculty and alumni to react to the same list. These rankings will help us evaluate our current roster of courses.)
- To tell us whether you've obtained any of these potential learning objectives—and from where in your educational experience.

| *Question Stems* | *Response Options* |
| --- | --- |
| How important should X be to the curriculum? | Very important, important, less important, not important |
| Please indicate to what degree you've obtained X in the current curriculum. | Yes, somewhat, not at all |
| Please indicate where in the curriculum you obtained each learning objective. | Required courses, elective courses, internships, practicum courses, not obtained |

sense of community in the school. As a result of these findings, CRLT was invited to design and facilitate a faculty retreat focused on multicultural teaching. The fruits of this process were documented later by an accreditation team, which rated the school as outstanding in its inclusion of multicultural materials in the curriculum and in its attention to issues of diversity.

### Evaluating the Contributions of a New Technology

Universities across the country face decisions about how best to allocate scarce resources to support instructional technology. At UM, a faculty member created a new instructional technology, LectureTools (http://www.lecturetools.org),[2] which allows students to use their laptops as a response system, similar to clickers, so an instructor can ask questions and then post student responses in real time. The software also lets students take notes and make drawings directly on lecture slides as well as anonymously ask TAs a question through a chat window during class. Students can rate their own understanding of each slide, giving the professor valuable feedback, and they can watch a video podcast of the lecture after it is over.

Knowing of CRLT's successful record of assessing other instructional technology innovations (see chapter 9), the university's instructional technology leader requested CRLT's assistance in determining the value of this software package for student learning. CRLT staff crafted a quasiexperimental design, recruiting faculty from a range of disciplines to use LectureTools and identifying a set of comparable courses to serve as a control. CRLT surveyed students in both sets of courses asking about the tools that helped them learn, the technical difficulty of using those tools, and the degree of distraction caused by laptop use in class. The findings indicated that students found value in LectureTools regardless of the discipline in which it was used. As a result, the provost's office invested more heavily in the software, making it more widely available and providing better user support (University of Michigan, 2010b).

### Assessing the Impact of a New Curricular Initiative

The UM president launched an initiative to encourage the development of interdisciplinary degree programs and team-taught courses for first- and second-year students by funding several programs and courses to serve as campus models (http://www.provost.umich.edu/programs/MLTT/). Because of CRLT's work on previous interdisciplinary initiatives, our instructional consultants were commissioned to work with each faculty team to create an assessment strategy for their individual courses while also designing a strategy to evaluate the overall impact of the initiative. Consultants helped several courses develop rubrics against which to measure student work, and we also designed a survey of all participating students to find out how they assessed their integrative learning. The resulting CRLT reports were given to individual instructors confidentially, especially the information about student reactions to course pedagogy, but the aggregate survey results went to the president to confirm the value of this initiative.

## Using Grants to Support Institutional Improvement Motivations

For faculty and administrators who "recognize the importance of institutional effectiveness initiatives for institutional improvement and self-knowledge" (Welsh & Metcalf, 2003b, p. 463), it is important that a teaching center offer support to foster instructional enhancement. CRLT, like some other teaching centers at research universities (Wright, 2000), has long supported curricular reform initiatives through direct grants.

Annually, CRLT funds nearly 100 UM faculty to engage in instructional improvement projects. Many of them concern curricular reform and assessment. For example, CRLT recently funded:

- a professional school's development of an e-portfolio system for student assessment;
- the writing center's evaluation of a college-wide, upper-level writing requirement;
- a team of STEM faculty to incorporate into their introductory courses an assessment of how students use course resources and the relationship between that use and student performance in the course; and
- an engineering faculty member to assess the use of screencasts in her own courses and the viability of that pedagogical innovation in a set of diverse courses across the College of Engineering.

In addition to these longstanding efforts, we recently created a new scholarship of teaching and learning (SoTL) grant program aimed at individual faculty. We are particularly proud of the structure of the SoTL grant program, which we call Investigating Student Learning, because it employs a multipronged strategy to support SoTL. The grant can fund individual faculty or faculty/graduate student/postdoc teams. We encourage the latter out of a belief that projects benefit from the support and collaboration that graduate students or a postdoctoral researcher can provide. Projects funded by the grant operate under a blanket agreement CRLT negotiated with our Institutional Review Board, obviating the need for individual faculty to handle the complexities of IRB approval. Grant activities begin with a daylong symposium where faculty meet with fellow grantees and CRLT consultants who help them refine and plan their projects. Over the course of the academic year, instructional consultants are available to help faculty work through any issues that might arise in their projects. Finally, at the end of the award period, all projects are highlighted in a poster fair at a major campus-wide event, providing faculty with recognition and visibility for their work (for more details, see http://www.crlt.umich.edu/grants/islgrant. php). We also give faculty information about disciplinary journals and meetings where they might disseminate their findings further.

## Connecting Assessment with Institutional Change

"Closing the loop," or implementing changes suggested by assessment efforts, is a critical step in cultivating faculty and administrative support for institutional effectiveness initiatives (Welsh & Metcalf, 2003a, 2003b). Even where there is faculty buy-in and data have been collected and reported, it is challenging for academic staff to use the information gained effectively for curricular change (Wehlburg, 2008). Once faculty have the evaluation data in hand, curricular design and enhancement may not occur because of time constraints or simply a lack of knowledge about what to do next. Instructional consultants can address these concerns by providing consultations and workshops that help faculty revise their courses and pedagogical practice. Ideally, these services, offered in conjunction with a particular initiative under way in the department or unit, can help faculty make direct connections to that initiative, increasing buy-in.

For example, as part of an extensive curricular review and assessment project, one of our professional schools identified professional writing instruction as a key strength of its curriculum. While the school was eager to maintain this strength, its existing structure for doing so had become untenable because it relied on a small group of faculty to provide this instruction. Having identified the problem, the school was uncertain how to address it. The CRLT consultant worked with the dean to identify a structural option (an advanced writing requirement) that would share the burden across a much broader swath of faculty. Should this proposal be adopted, the school will support it with a workshop to give the faculty a chance to create new approaches to responding to and grading student writing and increased resources to a school writing center that supports both faculty and students.

Other academic programs have come to us because their curricular review processes uncovered problems with the consistency and effectiveness of faculty feedback on student performance. In these cases, we have created workshops—such as one-on-one teaching skills in the clinic or using rubrics to provide formative feedback on student performance—to help faculty address these issues. This ability to support the pedagogical change initiatives brought about through curricular reform and assessment projects can be a teaching center's major contribution.

## Lessons From These Stories: Opportunities and Challenges for Teaching Centers

As Diamond (2005) noted, teaching centers are ideally suited to be institutional change agents and thus particularly well positioned to work on curricular reform and assessment. Given the numerous barriers to assessment and curricular reform, teaching centers have an important role in helping to construct institutional improvement processes (Banta, 1997; Welsh & Metcalf, 2003a, 2003b). First, they can encourage faculty buy-in and design processes that allow administrators to have personal involvement in curricular reform. Second, they can assist with the design and collection of data about student learning outcomes and processes, which can inform instructional discussions. Third, teaching centers are ideally positioned to offer consultations and workshops for faculty and administrators who come to the center with an internally driven question or need for enhancing their programs. Finally, many faculty developers have the background and experience to help implement changes suggested by assessment findings, through consultations, department discussions, and workshops. As other centers consider ways to support curricular review and assessment, the list of CRLT services detailed in the appendix to this chapter may be of help.

To say that teaching centers should be involved in curricular reform and assessment does not mean that it is easy to make this happen. There is a catch-22 about the involvement of teaching centers (and their instructional consultants) in curricular reform and assessment. As we noted at the outset of this chapter, to be able to help with these activities, academic administrators must be willing to trust the teaching center to make a positive contribution. As a result, a teaching center must communicate the value it can add to the process. However, as was noted in chapter 3, teaching centers do best when we let academic administrators take credit for their own initiatives, rather than trumpeting our own role in the process. Deans or chairs may prefer not to publicize the role the teaching center has played in helping them achieve those successes. If consultants claim credit for curricular and other improvements, faculty buy-in to those changes may be limited, and this may cause faculty to be reluctant to use our services in the future. Yet a teaching center must garner some external visibility in these efforts to capture enough university resources to do the work requested and to stimulate enough faculty interest to have a ready market for its services.

CRLT has taken numerous steps to navigate this catch-22. We have made sure to communicate our activities clearly to the provost and other administrators in the provost's office (of which we are a part). As a result, the provost has helped spread the word that the teaching center can assist administrators who want to engage in these activities. We have also learned to publicize our contributions quietly, noting them in one-sentence handouts or in bullets in our annual reports. The CRLT annual report lists what we do each year for every unit on campus, by name, so a dean or chair can see the long list of services for other units and contrast it with the short or nonexistent list of services for his or her unit (http://www.crlt.umich.edu/assessment/assessmentprojects.php). As we noted in chapter 3, we arrange meetings with senior leadership (particularly new leaders) on a regular basis, and the information in the annual report can be deployed strategically to highlight the work we are (and could be) doing. The goal is to indicate ways we can partner with academic leaders to accomplish their goals. Finally, we have a deliberate culture that seeks to leverage our connections to faculty and administrators in one arena to forge connections in others.

At CRLT this was particularly relevant during the university's 2010 accreditation effort where we played a major role in making visible the numerous assessment initiatives taking place on our large, decentralized campus. By leveraging our consultants' pedagogical and process expertise and our cross-campus connections, our center has solidly established itself as the locus of campus assessment work.

As this chapter makes clear, colleges and universities should be engaging their teaching centers in the curricular reform process and assessment of student learning outcomes. Moreover, to be relevant in the current climate, teaching center directors need to find ways to prioritize this work and make it visible. The range of expertise available in well-staffed teaching centers is ideally suited for this work. Teaching center consultants have expertise in pedagogical best practices, evaluation methods, and the design and facilitation of faculty gatherings necessary to consider curricular reform and assessment. Moreover, instructional grants administered by teaching centers can be used to leverage curricular reform and assessment initiatives further. Together, these resources can help support activities and overcome obstacles at all stages of the curricular review and assessment process.

CRLT provides the following services to support the assessment of student learning:

*Consulting*
- Discussion of the scholarship of teaching and learning
- Discussion of assessment plans for educational grants
- Consultation with chairs and deans on assessment of curriculum

*Facilitating Workshops and Retreats*
- Discussion of goals and competencies for concentrators
- Interpretation of data available in the department
- Development of questions for further data collection
- Discussion of curricular cohesion/gaps

*Assisting With Data Collection*
- Design and interpretation of student and alumni surveys
- Focus groups with students, faculty, staff (e.g., to collect baseline data, information on the impact of curricular changes, information on climate for learning)
- Collection and analysis of student work
- Discussion of revising student ratings to provide data for assessment purposes

*Providing Grants*
- Gilbert Whitaker Fund: Support for departmental, school, or college assessment projects
- Investigating Student Learning: Funding for scholarship for teaching and learning projects at the course level

*Offering Resources*
- Posting of examples of discipline-specific approaches to assessment
- Posting of web links and articles on assessment

*Supporting Dissemination of Results*

- Publicizing UM student data (e.g., CIRP and NSSE data and the UM Senior Survey results) and making it available to UM instructors for their own research and assessment projects
- Organizing poster fairs, seminars, and workshops where faculty discuss their assessment work, learn about assessment strategies, and discuss common challenges
- Providing advice about assessment conferences and journals for publication of assessment findings

## Endnotes

1. For example, CRLT is currently involved in multiple projects for professional schools with two-year master's programs. All face similar pressures: interdisciplinary programs with many competitors nationally and on campus, increasing enrollments characterized by student heterogeneity, and relatively small numbers of faculty (many with joint appointments in other schools). In each case these pressures have prompted efforts to review and assess the curriculum.

2. LectureTools was created by Perry Samson, UM professor of atmospheric, oceanic, and space sciences.

# 8

# STRENGTHENING DIVERSITY THROUGH FACULTY DEVELOPMENT

*Crisca Bierwert*

> The University of Michigan seeks to provide an academic environment where intercultural skills are developed and enacted among diverse campus constituencies, with community partners, and within classroom and research practices. . . . In this way education becomes a tool through which the *fact* of diversity is transformed to the exciting and productive *actions* of diversity, creating a climate and environment so stimulating and attractive that the experience of difference becomes a source of excellence and an instrument of achievement. (University of Michigan, 2007, p. 1)

This passage sets a context for reflecting on how teaching centers can strengthen diversity. Although the roles and responsibilities of a teaching center certainly do not cover the entire breadth of diversity initiatives and exchanges on any college campus, a teaching center can offer a great deal. Our knowledge and insight add to the intellectual richness of the academy; our practice enhances interactions from classrooms to boardrooms and communities.

Within the university, we contribute most to two main wings of diversity work. One wing enhances diversity by increasing the social backgrounds represented in campus communities, acknowledging the great value that people bring through their differences from others. This diversity is continuously expanding, adding to our knowledge, collaborations, and methods for approaching what is unfamiliar. The other wing of diversity work strives for social justice, including equity in access to and success in higher education, within the university itself and in communities outside of the university where we make a commitment to the empowerment of others.

This chapter outlines the strategies, policies, and programs the University of Michigan Center for Research on Learning and Teaching (CRLT) uses to strengthen both wings, by embedding multiculturalism into all programs, promoting student and faculty success and retention, supporting those who teach multicultural content, and forging alliances with others on campus. The conclusion of the chapter also offers a way of thinking about our contributions to diversity more broadly, a framework useful for strengthening all diversity efforts, whether directed at equity of access, social justice, or internationalization in higher education. As a whole, the chapter brings attention to the importance of faculty developers in promoting diversity efforts on campus, adding to the strong foundation laid in Ouellett (2005) and Kaplan and Miller (2007).

## Reaching the Broadest Audiences: Embedding Multiculturalism in More General Programs[1]

CRLT reaches the broadest audiences of faculty and TAs with messages about diversity by embedding multiculturalism into our core faculty development work. We design our programs with multicultural teaching goals as a priority, making explicit that the best teaching practices are those that are inclusive of all students and explaining why. In addition, our publications of all kinds, from websites to annual reports and brochures, include descriptions of multicultural goals and programs as an integral part of our work. We also identify multicultural learning outcomes as a priority in our grants programs to encourage applicants to focus on student diversity and to support innovations of faculty teaching specifically multicultural content. Embedding multiculturalism not only conveys our priorities, it also brings information on the value of diversity into the thinking of all faculty, even those who were not aware that these issues are relevant to their work. Furthermore, since these materials reach administrators as well as faculty and TAs, we contribute language that supports the university's broader goals of diversity indirectly while supporting teaching and learning directly.

We engage faculty and TAs in discussions of inclusive teaching from their first participation in CRLT programs, usually the teaching orientations we provide for faculty new to UM and for TAs new to teaching. Our plenary

sessions include information on student diversity and evidence for the efficacy of inclusive teaching, active learning, and the use of small groups. We
provide data from national and University of Michigan student surveys that
include a profile of our undergraduates' academic backgrounds, interests,
and aspirations, and show the distribution of their socioeconomic, racial,
and ethnic backgrounds. Participants discuss how these profiles compare to
those of universities or colleges where they have taught or been students.
Plenary sessions also include interactive theatre performances of "The First
Class," a sketch that raises issues of diversity (both visible and invisible) and
depicts the hopes, questions, and anxieties of both faculty and students in a
medium that is humorous yet thought provoking. (See chapter 11 for more
information on the theatre program.)

The plenary sessions lay the ground for breakout sessions, including at
least one that focuses explicitly on multicultural teaching. Other breakouts
also address multicultural dynamics and provide more specific strategies for
engaging the diversity of students. For example, a session at faculty orientation on using technology demonstrates how clickers can be used to elicit
student input anonymously, a strategy that works for faculty who want their
students to see the distribution of their viewpoints on sensitive topics and
for faculty who want to know the distribution of correct answers in a pre-
and postinstructional polling of students. For our TA orientations, we provide breakouts on "Getting Started" to all attendees, modeling small-group
work and talking about the value of engaging student diversity for student
learning. In "Leading Discussions" for TAs in the social science or humanities, our workshop leaders go into more depth on student engagement that
draws on their diversity, using case studies to trigger discussion of handling
multicultural classroom dynamics. Participants in these orientations leave
with experience in a broad repertoire of teaching skills—and the central
message of inclusion.

Outside of the orientations, we provide workshops for instructors
throughout the year on using pedagogical strategies and teaching in specific
contexts. In the same way that multicultural teaching goals underlie our
orientation programs, they guide these workshops: they model the principles
we espouse, they are evidence-based, and they engage participants in
exchange and reflection on ways to apply what they have learned to their
own teaching contexts. One challenge we face in workshops and in one-on-
one consultations is how to address existing achievement gaps (Lee, 2002).
It is important to know how to dispel rather than reinforce preconceptions
that may filter into classrooms and create a dampening atmosphere for

underrepresented students. (See Steele and Aronson, 1995, and Aronson, Fried, and Good, 2002, for example, on the phenomenon of stereotype threat and how to counter it.)

We respond to concerns that inclusive teaching means "dumbing down" courses by emphasizing research on the science of learning. For example, we point out that active, facilitated exchange among students produces significant gains in learning (Gurin, Dey, Hurtado, & Gurin, 2002), or that lecturing at a pace that allows students time to take notes and using interactive lecturing promote generative recall (deWinstanley & Bjork, 2002; DeZure, Kaplan, & Deerman, 2001). In addition, faculty are motivated to provide more scaffolding for course work when we call their attention to the differences between the learning processes of novices and those of experts (Brandsford, Brown, & Cocking, 2000; Brookfield, 1996), and to the value of identifying the implicit skills they draw on in their own scholarly work (Pace, 2004). By building this research into workshops and referring to it in consultations, we are able to replace a deficit model of achievement gaps with a model for success (cf. Bensimon, 2005).

## Student Success and Retention

As a university-wide unit, the closest we come to affecting student success directly is through assessment and consultations that specifically support the goals of academic units. For example, at the request of the dean of the liberal arts college, and in collaboration with department chairs, we conducted an assessment study to determine the factors that influence retention of women and underrepresented minority students as majors in science fields. Working with the departments, we developed a survey of students in the gateway courses to find out whether their intention to major in science changed during the term and, if so, why. We analyzed the results, considering indicators of academic background, success in the course, and whether the student was from a social group underrepresented in the field. We then worked with the gateway course instructors to enhance those aspects of the courses that could help students have a better learning experience and help the departments retain students in the sciences. (See chapter 10 for a full description of this project.)

At the individual course level, we often encourage faculty to analyze whether a teaching innovation has affected specific subgroups of students, as well as students overall. This is especially important for fields where women, minority, or international students comprise a small percentage of the students in a course, as their success or struggles can be invisible when looking at results in the aggregate. For example, we collaborated with a materials science and engineering (MSE) professor who received a grant from CRLT to create podcasts. She wanted to supplement selected lectures in a large gateway course and determine the impact of the podcasts on student performance. We worked with her over several terms as both she and her students learned to best use this resource. When we analyzed the use of podcasts, we looked at several indicators of student difference (overall performance in the course, GPA, major, gender, and race) and found significantly higher use rates for students with both high and low overall performance, and for students with majors whose content was least comparable to that in the MSE course. Analysis of particularly difficult test questions also revealed improved comprehension on the topics for which students had access to podcasts (Pinder-Grover, Millunchick, & Bierwert, 2008). As a result of this research, the faculty member learned that an innovative pedagogy was a significant resource for subsets of students who otherwise might struggle with the course. Equally important, she saw a marked improvement in the performance of the class as a whole.

## Faculty Success and Retention

CRLT supports underrepresented faculty primarily through our core workshops and individual consultations, which we offer to all faculty members. The connections that faculty from underrepresented groups make with CRLT consultants can provide long-term benefits. Initially we provide our professional expertise on teaching; course design; and, depending on the roles of the faculty members, departmental leadership and curricular reform.

When potentially marginalized faculty members come to see us about teaching and learning, we are a confidential resource outside the departmental hierarchy. We are not mentors, but we are supportive, and we represent institutional support for them. Not all minority faculty experience as obstacles the obvious features of minority status (being the only one from a particular group in the department, feeling marginalized, working in areas not yet well established in one's field). Some feel celebrated, their social distinctiveness equaled by recognition of their intellectual distinction. However, most report that constraints, impositions, or climate issues related to their minority social background have challenged them, even though they were successful in their careers (Cox, 2008; Stanley, 2006; Turner & Myers, 2000).

Finding a connection with a supportive ally or mentor at the institution is something named, in almost every story, as being critical to success.

Confidential consultations also help faculty members discuss difficult multicultural interactions. We can encourage new faculty members to forge alliances with colleagues, and we help them address issues of teaching as well, including those that involve their personal identities. When a faculty member of any rank experiences a challenge in the classroom that is explicitly racist or sexist—or that he or she experiences as such an assault—a CRLT consultation provides a confidential environment for talking through both the incident and strategies to respond. Less often, we consult on discomfiting interactions with colleagues, sometimes with a vulnerable faculty member and sometimes with a department chair who wants guidance on handling an issue.

We also offer a number of workshops targeted to issues of difference. One that regularly attracts a large audience is Gender and Authority in the Classroom. This workshop provides excellent resources and draws on a CRLT study showing that students are more demanding of women faculty than of men, and that women must overcome obstacles of student expectation to establish their authority in their classes (Kardia & Wright, 2004). The workshop includes valuable strategies for constructing a teaching persona that is compatible with both an individual's teaching style and the expectations of students.

For one minority constituency, international faculty, we host an annual event that helps them to network. We send an e-mail invitation to all teaching faculty to a reception and dinner for "international faculty," in recognition of the value that they bring to UM and in acknowledgment of the differences faculty experience when they have been educated abroad and come to teach in the United States. The provost and senior vice provost welcome this group, along with the directors of the International Center and the English Language Institute. Formal remarks are brief so that most of the evening is social. Rather than targeting the invitation, we invite all faculty and ask those who consider themselves international to attend; about 100 people come each year. It has been a great success, particularly for faculty members who have found others from their home country whom they did not know were on campus.

On the institutional level, we provide consultations with department chairs and deans—as well as yearlong training for new chairs and associate deans (see also chapter 3)—that help these key academic administrators improve the climate for faculty, students, and staff. Our theatre program also collaborates with a campus-wide ADVANCE program, which focuses on the recruitment and retention of a diverse and excellent faculty (http://sitemak er.umich.edu/advance/home). ADVANCE has commissioned three sketches that focus on the ways gender informs faculty hiring, mentoring, and tenure decisions. These sketches are performed regularly for academic administrators as part of ADVANCE's efforts to overcome institutional practices and habits of thought that marginalize women and faculty from underrepresented minorities. For example, each year the dean invites all faculty serving on executive committees in the liberal arts college to a dinner at which the CRLT Players perform "The Fence," a sketch about the tenure decision process. The sketch depicts numerous problematic interactions, many related to gender dynamics. The faculty members discuss the sketch, strategize about ways to intervene, and actually attempt to implement their interventions. The dean ends by emphasizing the college's commitment to a fair process and encouraging faculty to pay careful attention to intellectual and procedural processes that can avoid bias.

## Supporting Multicultural Teaching

Support for faculty teaching specifically multicultural content ranges from individual consultations to workshops that model strategies of productive engagement, and longer programs where faculty can go into more depth on pedagogical issues. This support is valuable not only to the faculty, but to the university more broadly. The programs we provide for those who are experts in multiculturalism strengthen their voices and thus add to the intellectual richness and diversity of university life.

One strategy we use in all of these settings is to suggest that faculty create guidelines for class discussion and review them with their students, inviting refinement and additions from the students themselves (http://www.crlt.umich.edu/gsis/P4_1.php). We have also created more detailed guidelines for instructors to use in times of crisis. For example, on the afternoon of September 11, 2001, we gathered to think through what instructors would need in classes in the next few days, prepared more elaborated guidelines to assist instructors who chose to lead discussions of the national crisis, and considered how instructors could respond to spontaneous student comments (http://www.crlt.umich.edu/publinks/tragedydiscussion.php). Key to our recommendations was encouraging instructors to frame such discussions with clear purpose, to know their own capacity for dealing with the powerful emotions of the time, and to respond with openness to what students might express. In later years, we created similar guidelines for instructors in the wake of the Supreme Court decision upholding affirmative action, the Southeast Asian tsunami of December 2004, Hurricane Katrina, a student's use of hate language that was widely publicized and fanned controversy on campus, and cyberbullying. These last examples apply to fewer class settings, but they serve the important purpose of supporting minority communities on campus. (For a site that has links to all these guidelines, see http://www. crlt.umich.edu/publinks/discussionguidelines.php.)

Consultations with faculty teaching multicultural content may involve helping them to deal with difficult classroom dynamics that result from course readings or discussions. We help them to diagnose origins of tension and to better handle student resistance, "hot" moments, and conflict in the classroom. We also help them develop strategies for student engagement when the concern is student silence rather than overt tension. Our website also has useful summaries of strategies to consider and cultivate (http://www .crlt.umich.edu/tstrategies/tsmdt.php).

Workshops on multicultural teaching help instructors clarify their goals and teaching strategies. Workshop participants are diverse not only in social, intellectual, and theoretical backgrounds but also in their expectations for student learning. Cross-disciplinary exchange of information is powerful in most faculty development workshops, and in the case of courses focused on multicultural content, it can be both a strength of the workshop and a challenge. Courses taught by these faculty may share the goals of developing discussion and dialogue skills, reflecting on one's own views and those of others, critically examining and evaluating information, formulating questions, and developing arguments or strategies. However, these courses—and thus the intentions of instructors participating in workshops—range from providing core background knowledge to developing skills for activism. Thus, despite sharing a general social purposefulness, and cognitive and affective complexity, the course goals and pedagogies differ tremendously in the amount of personal information students are expected to share and reflect on, and in the kinds of analytical assignments they do.

Our workshops on teaching with museums and archives have been particularly successful at navigating this dilemma because they draw a diverse audience, engage in multicultural issues, and have a concrete focus, but they do not have a specific theoretical orientation. In these workshops, faculty panelists discuss their teaching strategies, rationales, and examples of student learning outcomes in the form of ten-minute presentations. We ask them to focus on specific class assignments, rather than course design, since we have found that such examples are most useful to others. Customized workshops to support faculty teaching courses with experiential and service-learning components offer similar benefits, focusing on a common commitment— student and community engagement—with a wide range of implementations. For these efforts we collaborate with academic units in which such courses are taught, and with campus-wide offices, such as UM's Ginsberg Center for Community Service (http://ginsberg.umich.edu/) and the Arts of Citizenship program (http://www.artsofcitizenship.umich.edu/). Our contributions range from facilitating roundtable discussions to providing frameworks for assessment, consulting on the design of rubrics that provide formative feedback on skill development for students, groups and teams, and instructors. Valuable resources produced on our campus include the anthology *Engaging the Whole of Service Learning, Diversity, and Learning Communities* (Galura, Pasque, Schoem, & Howard, 2004) and a compendium of commentary and frameworks, *Service-Learning Course Design Workbook* (Howard, 2001).

We provide longer-term seminars for faculty and TAs as well. For TAs, we co-teach a six-week series of three-hour seminars, entitled "Multicultural Facilitation in the Classroom." Our partners in this teaching venture are instructors in the Program on Intergroup Relations (IGR) (http://www.igr.umich.edu/) who regularly teach semester-long courses on dialogue to undergraduates. Our seminar covers many strategies for facilitation and allows us to work with participants so they have a better grasp of their own social perspectives and positions of power. This training program is explicitly framed around concepts of power, privilege, and oppression. We give all participants copies of *Teaching for Diversity and Social Justice* (Adams, Bell, & Griffin, 2007), which provides pedagogical guidelines and an excellent compendium of frameworks for social justice teaching. Two of the six sessions are for practice teaching, where TAs bring in course content they are teaching and frame a discussion using small groups. We facilitate critiques of these practice sessions that provide lots of examples of strategies and opportunities for much meta-commentary and reflection.

For faculty, we initiated a Colloquium on the Science of Learning focusing on multicultural issues, with the support of a grant from the Teagle Foundation. For this project, we brought together a cohort of faculty, half of whom came from STEM disciplines and were particularly committed to the success of students who are underrepresented in their fields, and half of whom taught multicultural content. For each session, we selected brief readings and invited a UM scholar to talk about the related research on student learning. For example, we introduced them to Professor Patricia King's research on cognitive development of undergraduates (ages 18–22). King's work clearly identifies the phenomena of binary thinking, extreme relativism, and quasi-reflective thinking as kinds of cognition students must work through before they are able to reason in more nuanced ways (King, 2000; King & Baxter Magolda, 2005). Through readings and discussions with Professor King, faculty members learned that student reactions they perceived as ideological resistance in fact may reflect cognitive difficulty with unfamiliar structures of thought. This colloquium had a powerful impact on faculty participants, all of whom were already dedicated teachers. Over the course of our discussions, they formed new ideas about their students' experience, became much more open to student-centered teaching, and developed new strategies based on collegial exchange and the readings they had done. (For the Colloquium readings, see http://www.teaglefoundation.org/learning/pdf/scienceoflearningAB.pdf.)

## Forging Alliances

To have the maximum impact on campus, we work closely with key academic administrators and the many UM offices committed to diversity. Our primary alliances are with the deans and department chairs. These alliances have resulted in requests for ongoing programs and customized services, such as assistance with curricular reform and assessments involving multicultural goals. We also provide customized workshops at the request of a dean or chair who wants faculty members to engage in discussion or professional development on multicultural issues. For example, we collaborated on planning one school's Diversity Summit, helping to identify areas of concern and shape the program so issues could be addressed productively.

Forging alliances with others on campus who address diversity work is equally important. We regularly share program planning with other units dedicated to multicultural work. For example, we collaborate with the English Language Institute to co-teach a course on pedagogy for TAs educated abroad (http://www.crlt.umich.edu/gsis/igsicomm.php). Together with the UM National Center for Institutional Diversity (http://ncid.umich.edu/), we are developing a program for faculty teaching environmental justice. And the CRLT Players often collaborate with other diversity-focused offices, such as Services for Students with Disabilities (http://www. umich.edu/~sswd/) and the Office of Institutional Equity (http://www.hr. umich.edu/oie/) (on sexual harassment issues).

Sometimes the collaboration involves consultation or committee work rather than program development. We do not have a formal relationship with the units on campus that coordinate peer tutoring, for example, but we do offer consultation on diversity training with the directors of those programs. We also meet frequently with the directors of the Office of Academic Multicultural Initiatives (http://www.oami.umich.edu/), Multi-Ethnic Student Affairs (http://mesa.umich.edu/index.php?loc=home), and the Spectrum Center for LGBT students (http://spectrumcenter.umich.edu/) to get feedback on issues they hear from students, and to make sure they have current information on the services we provide to instructors on diversity issues related to teaching and learning. Our committee work includes participation and leadership of groups like the University Diversity Council that are centrally concerned with multicultural issues; others—like the Vice Provosts and Associate Deans Group or the Academic Services Board—are much broader in scope, and we speak to multicultural issues as they arise in discussions, adding our expertise and gathering valuable information to inform our own programs.

Alliance building not connected to specific programs or to current initiatives may appear to be outside the box of faculty development and may seem unattractive to faculty developers, especially given the burden of our workloads. However, for a faculty developer committed to multicultural goals, forming alliances with other diversity leaders is valuable not simply as a form of networking and an opportunity to make the teaching center more visible, but because of the professional value to the person. Even if there is no tangible, programmatic outcome, sharing a space with others, and being recognized in the circles of intellectuals and administrators on campus who are motivated by social justice goals, strengthen the multicultural faculty developer. For the faculty developer of color, or for a faculty developer with another minority identity, such alliances may build community connections and professional strength.


## Conceptualizing our Diversity Work[2]

Having discussed some specific goals and strategies of multicultural faculty development work, I return to a broader discussion of our impact on campus diversity. Thinking about our impact on the campus, not "just" our impact on teaching and learning, aligns with the AAC&U "Making Excellence Inclusive" initiative. Key to this initiative is shifting diversity from a narrow framework to one that envisions an institution of higher education as one "that systematically leverages diversity for student learning *and institutional excellence* [emphasis added]" (Williams, Berger, & McClendon, 2005, p. v). Two powerful and related ideas underlie this scheme. First, diversity goals may be measurable, but they are always in process. Second, dynamics of institutional hierarchy can cut across social inequalities in transformative ways.

Figure 8.1 is a template for documenting the impact of faculty development work on the diversity of a campus, a strong first step in analyzing impact. This template helps locate—and make more visible—the many kinds of diversity work discussed earlier in this chapter. Moving across the template, we can see how programs and practices that contribute to more obvious diversity work—affecting student success and retention, enhancing retention of underrepresented faculty, and supporting multicultural teaching—also contribute to other diversity goals and effects.

The framework also helps chart how multicultural skills can affect exchanges throughout the campus—past the classroom into interactions of the campus hierarchies. All of our workshops are based on principles of inclusion, and most are exemplars of multicultural training. Through our consultations and programs, we enhance the skills that instructors carry into other interactions: with students, with colleagues, and with staff. Thus, through the work on teaching, we affect not only classroom climate and engagement but also the leadership that faculty provide to guide the course of the university in the future.

In addition, we ourselves are considered to be campus leaders in multicultural exchange. Working with others, we take our skills and perspectives into program planning and into the processes of university committees. We are often called on to facilitate sensitive discussions and take leadership of campus initiatives. Our contributions help the institution move forward as an organization that effectively mobilizes our diversity. When we participate in decision-making committees and planning groups, and at all levels, social diversity moves from being fraught with unfamiliarity and awkwardness, unpacks previously unspoken assumptions, and becomes exciting.

We have such impact because universities are systems of practice. Nuanced interactions shape operations through intellectual, bureaucratic, political, and symbolic dimensions (Williams et al., 2005). The ability of

# FIGURE 8.1

## Template for Analyzing the Impact of Multicultural Faculty Development Work

| | 1. STATEMENTS OF VALUE: MISSION, POLICIES, ETC. | | 2. SOCIAL DIVERSITY DEMOGRAPHICS SUCCESS AT ALL LEVELS, INCLUDING CLOSING ACHIEVEMENT GAPS | 3. CLIMATE: PATTERNS OF BEHAVIOR AND ATTITUDES AND INTELLECTUAL LIFE OF DIVERSITY | | 4. CLIMATE THROUGH THE UNIVERSITY HIERARCHIES | 5. EXTERNAL ENGAGEMENT |
|---|---|---|---|---|---|---|---|
| | *Using Language That Supports Diversity and Equity* | *Teaching Inclusive and Active Learning Strategies* | *Supporting Underrepresented Faculty* | *Enhancing Classroom Dynamics, Instructor-Student Rapport* | *Supporting Multicultural and Social Justice Teaching and Learning* | *Consolidating Institutional Support, Forging Alliances, Teaching Skills* | *Supporting Community and Service Learning and Research Faculty* |
| LIST YOUR PROGRAMS HERE: | | | | | | | |
| | | | | | | | |
| | | | | | | | |
| | | | | | | | |
| | | | | | | | |
| | | | | | | | |

students, faculty, and staff to negotiate social diversity and to advocate for multicultural exchange thus affects how the university works. Without these abilities diffused throughout the institution, no mandate or desire for successful diversity is likely to succeed.

Some teaching centers prioritize multicultural programming as CRLT does (e.g., the Center for Teaching at the University of Massachusetts at Amherst), and others offer targeted resources on inclusion (e.g., the centers at Vanderbilt, University of Washington, and IUPUI). Multicultural work is ripe for teaching centers to play a leadership role. As faculty developers with multicultural expertise, we shape diversity because of what we do and because of how we do our work: through demonstrating effective, inclusive instruction and through modeling interactions that are attentive to diverse academic and social backgrounds. Our core knowledge of the teaching and learning literature, best pedagogical practices, and strategies for curricular and course design is enriched by the interaction skills we bring to our work. Our accomplishments come from negotiating differences that are both familiar and unfamiliar: listening keenly to others, facilitating productive dialogue, and negotiating a tremendous variety of social and intellectual differences. Our contributions to campus diversity are concrete, and they are also diffuse, helping to shape the breadth and openness of intellectual life to make the experience of diversity animated and rich and to prepare for diversities to come.

## Endnotes

1. See Cook and Sorcinelli (2005) for more on the strategy of embedding multiculturalism in faculty development.

2. This section builds on ideas developed in a workshop on multicultural organizational development (MCOD), organized for the AAC&U and POD, in January 2009, by Linda Marchesani, Leslie Ortquist-Ahrens, Matt Ouellett, Christine Stanley, Frank Tuitt, and Phyllis Worthy-Dawkins (see Ouellett & Ortquist-Ahrens, 2009). One of the best-known MCOD frameworks has been developed by Bailey Jackson and Rita Hardiman (Jackson, 2005).

# 9

# ENGAGING FACULTY IN EFFECTIVE USE OF INSTRUCTIONAL TECHNOLOGY

*Erping Zhu, Matthew Kaplan, and Charles Dershimer*

Teaching and learning with technology has been among the top ten IT issues in higher education for the past five years (Agee, Yang, & the 2009 EDUCAUSE Current Issues Committee, 2009; Allison, DeBlois, & the 2008 EDUCAUSE Current Issues Committee, 2008; Camp, DeBlois, & the 2007 EDUCAUSE Current Issues Committee, 2007; Dewey, DeBlois, & the 2006 EDUCAUSE Current Issues Committee, 2006; Ingerman, Yang, & the 2010 EDUCAUSE Current Issues Committee, 2010). As technology tools become increasingly available to students on college campuses, faculty report that the integration of instructional technology is one of their top challenges (Sorcinelli et al., 2006, p. 189). Teaching centers and/or technology departments are often charged with providing IT services and supporting faculty as they use technology. On many college and university campuses, faculty learn technical skills in hands-on workshops presented by an instructional technology unit. While technology specialists perform a valuable service in helping faculty develop their technical skills, these specialists often lack experience in university teaching and expertise in pedagogical research. This is a niche that teaching centers can fill, helping faculty think carefully about effective uses of technology, as well as disseminating best practices for using IT in the classroom.

Faculty attitudes toward teaching innovations involving technology vary widely. Rogers's (2003) innovation model divides faculty into four groups.

*Innovators* are those who are driven by their own passion for technology, take risks, and learn the technology on their own. *Early adopters* typically constitute the second wave to use a given tool, because they tend to wait until they understand the technology, what it offers, and what its drawbacks are. *Late adopters* are usually more interested in how a technology can help achieve specific instructional or curriculum goals. Finally, *laggards* perceive no need for a new technology because their teaching is already successful, or they are currently overwhelmed by teaching or other responsibilities (Kuhlenschmidt, 2010; Rogers, 2003). Due to different beliefs and technology skill levels, faculty adoption of technology usually goes through several stages, from nonreadiness to survival, mastery, and innovation (Holland, 2001). An innovator may use technology as a lever for fundamental changes in classroom structure and teaching behavior, an early adopter may use it as a teaching tool changing those aspects of teaching most closely related to the new technology, and a late adopter may use a tool as a supporting function that does not significantly affect teaching (Celsi & Wolfinbarger, 2002; Massy & Zemsky, 1995).

In this chapter, we explain how CRLT engages faculty in effective use of technology at all levels and for all purposes, and to influence classroom IT practices across the campus through an approach that focuses on technology promotion, support, and evaluation (see Figure 9.1). This approach attracts faculty with varied views about technology, provides multiple entry points for engaging them, and enables them to use technology at their own comfort level. We elaborate on each entry point, use specific examples to illustrate the details, and make connections among the different services and practices that make up the framework.

## Promoting Effective Use of Instructional Technology

The majority of faculty and TAs are now using some sort of instructional technology in teaching (Usability, Support, and Evaluation Lab, University of Michigan, 2008, 2009), but they use the interactive features of a course management system (e.g., chat, discussion, and wiki) much less frequently (Lonn & Teasley, 2009). Faculty and TAs also tend not to use, nor do they plan to use, Web 2.0 technologies in teaching, although they do use them for noninstructional purposes (Hartshorne & Ajjan, 2009). What hindered faculty and TAs from a more extensive use of technology was a lack of awareness about the "instructional value" of each technology

### FIGURE 9.1
**Framework for Effective Engagement**

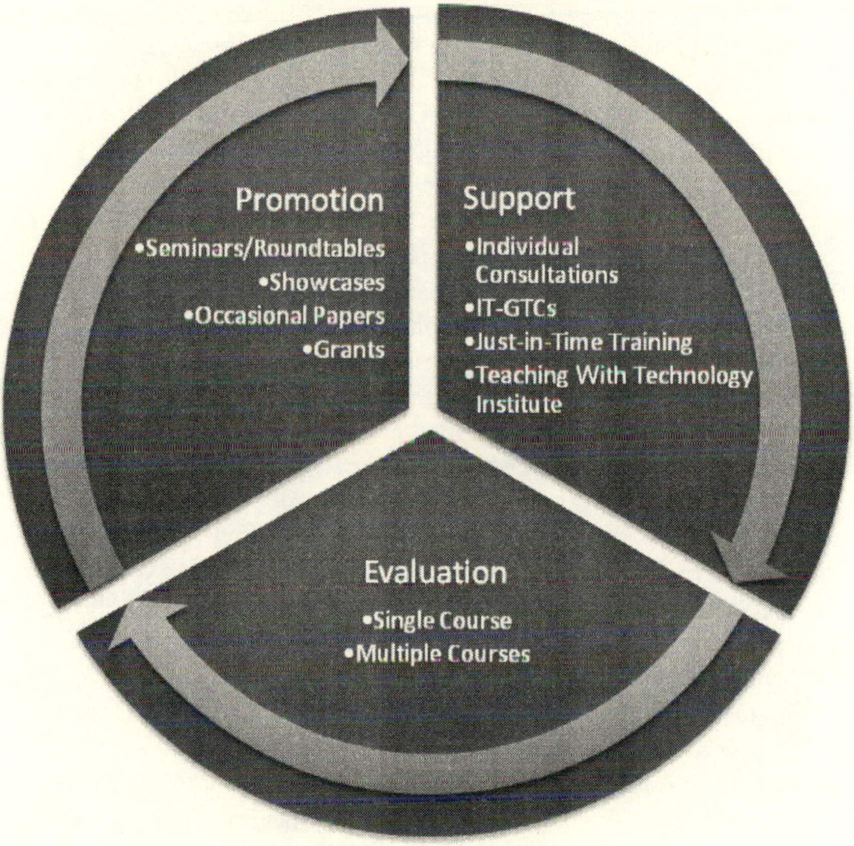

tool and how to integrate it into teaching to benefit students and improve learning (Center for Research on Learning and Teaching, University of Michigan, 2009). To help lower this barrier and ensure that faculty learn about technology tools and their value, we employ a number of promotion strategies (see Figure 9.1).

## *Seminars and Roundtables*

Instructional technology roundtables and pedagogical seminars are effective methods for promoting technology use in classrooms and are employed widely at teaching centers across the country. At CRLT these events are planned in advance for a given semester; are organized around an instructional theme, such as "online writing" or "enhancing feedback"; and require little preparation by CRLT staff (apart from scheduling, advertising, and room setup). Facilitated by CRLT consultants, these programs feature faculty members who demonstrate the classroom use of a new or emerging technology. At a roundtable discussion on blogs and wikis, for example, the faculty presenter gave a tour of his blog site and demonstrated how he integrated the blog into teaching and research (Cole, 2006). A seminar or roundtable session usually does not provide hands-on learning time; faculty can attend workshops on the basics of using blogs or wikis offered by a central technology support unit or seek assistance from college or department IT support staff in setting up a blog or wiki.

Thanks to careful selection of presenters, IT roundtables and seminars not only expose faculty to new and emerging tools, but, more important, they also introduce pedagogically sound practices for using technology tools. For instance, a seminar, titled "Big Class, Small Feel: Uncommon Teaching Using Commonplace Technologies," presented to faculty the idea of leveraging tools that students already own, such as cell phones and laptops, for in-class engagement. The faculty member demonstrated how, with the right software, these common tools can provide multiple avenues for each student to participate actively during the lecture, thus increasing class interactivity (Fishman, 2009). For several months after the presentation, CRLT received requests for more information about the instructional practices made possible by these tools. This pedagogy-focused IT seminar helped faculty think about significant shifts to new ways of interacting and communicating with and among students. The discussions enabled the faculty who attended these events to see the value of changing teaching behaviors and to reflect on their teaching practices and their roles as instructors.

## *Showcasing of Faculty Using Technology*

Faculty enjoy learning from their colleagues when CRLT gives them the opportunity to do so. Peer support actually has significant indirect effects on the actual integration of technology into teaching (Nicolle & Lou, 2008). We facilitate this kind of technology promotion by highlighting on the CRLT website examples of innovative ways faculty use technology (http://www.crlt.umich.edu/inst/techexamples.php). These examples are organized into sections around technology tools or curricular contexts, such as "Using technology tools and teaching strategies to promote active learning," and

"Using online tools to promote interaction and engagement with course content." We can refer to them in consultations; at new faculty orientations; and at many other events, such as the annual campus-wide technology conference, where faculty have the opportunity to learn about innovative technology uses in their own and other disciplines. We also published selected examples in a CRLT newsletter and distributed copies to all faculty in the university's 19 schools and colleges.

## CRLT Occasional Papers

Useful and relevant findings from instructional technology research and evaluation often draw faculty attention and encourage them to think more about technology and how to integrate it into teaching. However, many faculty members cannot afford the time needed to read journal articles on educational research and evaluation studies. We summarize recent research on current technology trends and instructional uses, suggest good practices with new technology, and publish the results as *Occasional Papers* to guide faculty practice. For example, *Teaching With Clickers* (Zhu, 2007) summarizes CRLT studies of student perceptions and provides recommendations for using clickers effectively in classrooms. *Lecture Capture: A Guide for Effective Use* (Zhu & Bergom, 2010) offers suggestions for making good use of lecture capture and podcasting to support student learning. All faculty receive copies of new *Occasional Papers*, and they can find all of them on our website (http://www.crlt.umich.edu/publinks/occasional.php).

## Grants

CRLT administers a variety of teaching grants for integrating instructional technology into teaching (http://www.crlt.umich.edu/grants/ttigrant.php). Grants enable innovators to explore new pedagogies and creative uses of technology and to redesign a course (or a series of courses) using these tools. For example, CRLT funded a small group of faculty who were exploring the use of handheld devices to promote active learning in large lecture classes. This early funding laid the foundation for the future adoption of clickers across campus. Another grant enabled a pair of faculty members to design a web-based learning module on exploratory bioinformatics research that allowed them to use active-learning methods to expose undergraduates to bioinformatics early in the curriculum.

Grants also provide opportunities for late adopters to catch up on technology integration. For example, some faculty who teach large undergraduate courses and want to incorporate multimedia elements do not have the time or expertise to digitize materials. Funds from CRLT's Multimedia Teaching Grant can be used to hire a student to help digitize and organize these resources. CRLT also offers small grants with rolling deadlines to help faculty get started with technology or plant the seeds for larger, external grants. For example, a non-tech-savvy faculty member used these funds to bring a number of guest speakers to a class virtually. A faculty member in engineering used monies to purchase equipment and software to seed an innovation for using laptops in the classroom. Several iterations later, this faculty member applied successfully for a much larger grant from the National Science Foundation. Teaching grants allow us to promote effective use of technology by enabling faculty to test and pilot innovative ideas, implement course redesign projects, and take small risks that may lead to more substantial results in the future.

## Providing Pedagogical and Technological Support

From our own consultations, as well as published research (Lin, Singer, & Ha, 2010; Moser, 2007; Nicolle & Lou, 2008), we know that faculty need pedagogical support when integrating new technology tools into classroom teaching. A teaching center is uniquely positioned to combine pedagogical and technical expertise, and CRLT uses a variety of methods to do this, ranging from short-term consultations to much more time-intensive faculty institutes.

### *Individual Consultation*

Instructional consultations attract faculty at all levels of proficiency because they allow for individualized learning, an important aspect of technology adoption at each stage and for each kind of user (Howland & Wedman, 2004). Innovators may enjoy sharing their use of cutting-edge technology with a consultant without feeling that they are intimidating or pressuring their colleagues (Kuhlenschmidt, 2010). They may be looking for experts to share their enthusiasm and provide resources to help push their innovations to the next level.

On the other hand, having waited for technology to become more stable before using it themselves, late adopters may initiate an individual consultation to discuss how to use a particular tool in teaching (Hagner & Schneebeck, 2001). One-on-one conversations with a consultant allow them to ask questions and discuss concerns. It is important for a consultant not only to showcase the classroom value of a new tool for addressing any identified instructional problems, but also to be honest about the up-front time investment that will be needed. Late adopters are usually comforted by actual (not potential) benefits of using technology to support their teaching and student learning.

With either group, consultations allow us to use the technical discussion as a platform for examining pedagogical practices and assumptions. For example, CRLT consulted with a faculty member who wanted to incorporate multimedia and animations into PowerPoint presentations to make slides more interesting. The CRLT consultant was able to help the faculty member explain what he meant by "interesting," encouraging him to rethink his initial goals for using media in the presentation. Together they discussed what learning activities could be created incorporating new media and how these activities might support student learning. The faculty member initiated the consultation to learn about adding video clips or animations to his slide presentations, but he left more knowledgeable about the pedagogical importance of active learning and student engagement.

### Instructional Technology Graduate Teaching Consultants (IT-GTCs)

IT-GTCs are a subset of CRLT's Graduate Peer Teaching Consultants (see chapter 5), whom we recruit and train to support fellow TAs, primarily around the applicaton of instructional technology. All the IT-GTCs have experience as TAs teaching independent courses or working with professors in a large class. They present IT seminars to teach returning and new TAs how to use technology in their recitations or lab sections. For example, IT-GTCs have led sessions on collaborative features in the university's course management system, showing TAs how to gather student input for a classroom discussion before it starts as well as how to keep a discussion going after face-to-face time ends.

IT-GTCs also help faculty implement large-scale technology projects in their courses. For example, in a large biology course, the professor decided to experiment with online quizzes and tests. One of our IT-GTCs helped design a bank of test items, piloted online quizzes with groups of students, refined the grading structure, and adjusted lecture content and sequence according to students' quiz performance. Another IT-GTC helped a faculty member start using the university's course management tool (CTools) for the first time. Because they are familiar with current technology trends and tools and know from their own experience as TAs what students are prepared to do, IT-GTCs work well with faculty innovators. They also work well with faculty who require more assistance. Since the IT-GTCs are still students themselves, it can feel less intimidating and embarrassing for faculty to talk to them about how to start using technology.

## Just-in-Time Training

Faculty need hands-on learning opportunities as well as guidance for integrating technology into their teaching. Workshops often provide a venue for such training. However, in a recent UM study, faculty reported spending an average of 58.6 hours per week on teaching, student advising, grant writing, and scholarly publications (Wright, 2010). Juggling so many duties makes it difficult for faculty to attend fixed-schedule workshops. "Just-in-time" coaching offers opportunities for busy faculty to learn specific skills when they are needed rather than having to wait for scheduled programs that might focus on more generic training.

For example, an instructor created a course management website before the start of a semester. However, a few weeks into the semester, she decided to add multiple-choice questions to help students review course material. The instructor requested an individual coaching session. A CRLT consultant went to her office, along with a staff member from the course management team. In two hours, the faculty member learned techniques for creating questions and designing online quizzes and was able to discuss with CRLT staff pedagogical considerations related to online testing as well as strategies for designing questions and giving online tests. A few days after the consult, the instructor had online tests ready for students to self-check their understanding.

## Intensive Training

Individual consultations and just-in-time coaching work well for most faculty, but one-on-one sessions do demand a lot of time from the CRLT staff. For a teaching center with a smaller staff, this approach may be less viable. In addition, fixed seminars may or may not fit faculty schedules. One solution to this dilemma is to designate a specific time each year for intensive technology training. CRLT, in collaboration with a range of other campus units, including the library and departmental IT units, plans just such an annual technology conference, called "Enriching Scholarship" (http://www.umich.edu/~teachtec/). This weeklong program is organized around three broad themes: teaching, research, and publishing. It is presented to faculty between semesters (usually in May), when they are generally not teaching and have time to explore new approaches before the summer begins. Each year, faculty can participate in over 100 hands-on sessions. Topics reflect current technology trends and pedagogical implications, such as image resources for the social sciences and humanities, using Adobe Connect to conduct synchronous graduate seminars online, and incorporating Picasa, Google video, and YouTube media.

This concentrated training program focuses on exposure to innovative ideas, development of hands-on technology skills, and discussion with peers and experts about how to incorporate new technologies into teaching. Faculty may attend one or several sessions related to different themes or tools, and there are opportunities to network and socialize with other faculty and staff who share similar interests or experiences.

## Teaching With Technology Institute

We have been successful in matching our training schedules and support services to faculty learning preferences and the needs created by faculty workloads. However, sometimes a faculty member wants to integrate a new tool into a new course or modify a course in light of a specific technology. In these cases, a single-session seminar is not suited to supporting course change. Faculty may not be clear about which teaching practices to change or modify to advance particular teaching and learning goals in a course using new technologies, nor do they always know the best tool for achieving these goals. Individual consultation and coaching are not an adequate solution. CRLT staff cannot devote the amount of time necessary to support individual faculty members with the consulting, training, and development needs associated with implementing a new project and still meet our goals of being accessible to the entire campus community.

To support this special need, CRLT created the Teaching with Technology Institute (TTI) (http://www.crlt.umich.edu/grants/ttigrant.php), which helps faculty make connections among pedagogy, technology, and disciplinary learning while exploring new instructional technology tools during course redesign (Figure 9.2). TTI provides a shared timeline and space for interested faculty and consultants from different campus technology units to co-create technology-based learning activities. The following discussion describes how this program leverages a successful collaborative structure to provide time-intensive faculty support.

## FIGURE 9.2
### Teaching with Technology Institute Overview

| | |
|---|---|
| **Proposal Selection** | • Form selection committee<br>• Select projects<br>• Designate consulting team |
| **Pre-Consultation** | • Clarify project goals<br>• Select appropriate tools<br>• Identify skills to be learned |
| **Hands-On Workshops** | • Practice using common tools<br>• Learn about new tools<br>• Develop familiarity with technology of choice |
| **Institute** | • Make presentations and receive feedback<br>• Consult on pedagogy and technology<br>• Create cohort of faculty and consultants |
| **Fall Implementation** | • Continue discussing pedagogical and technological issues<br>• Draft plans for project evaluation |
| **Wrap-Up** | • Present projects<br>• Exchange lessons learned<br>• Share student feedback and evaluation data |

Faculty interested in TTI submit an application describing their course-related technology projects. Based on criteria such as "inclusion of sound pedagogy in the plan for using technology in teaching" and "potential impact on student learning," a CRLT-led, cross-campus selection committee chooses up to ten faculty members for the institute. The committee comprises IT staff from different campus departments. Faculty whose proposals are selected receive a stipend of $2,500 for attending the institute and completing their project. Once faculty have been selected, project consultation teams are formed based on the skill sets and interests of the consultants, with teams generally consisting of an IT person and a CRLT consultant.

The institute is preceded by an initial consultation to help the faculty member clarify project goals and desired student-learning outcomes, explore a range of technology tools, and identify those most relevant to the project. In these early consultations, faculty may change their minds about the technology they want to use, with simple lower-tech tools often winning out over a more complicated initial choice. This switch in what is considered the most useful solution for faculty projects can occur because the early consultations always focus on student learning. This reverses the typical order of technology training that often puts technology ahead of pedagogy (Zhu, 2007).

Once an appropriate tool (or tools) has been selected for a project, consultants suggest individualized training sessions or available workshops at which faculty can acquire basic technology skills (if necessary). This strategy allows faculty to focus on mastering the particular features of a software application so they can design teaching modules or learning activities without being hampered by their lack of basic skills. These early consultations and training sessions are precursors to the kickoff meeting for the institute, a daylong event that brings CRLT staff, IT consultants, and faculty together for introductions, cohort building, and faculty presentations of initial versions of their projects.

After the kickoff meeting, the faculty, with support from institute staff, develop their projects throughout the late spring and early summer. Most faculty participants use the institute to complete a framework for designing learning materials, templates for teaching modules, or the actual technology-based teaching modules they will use in the course. Late in the summer, but before the start of the redesigned course, faculty participants work with CRLT consultants to draft plans for evaluating the impact of the project on student learning. The summer work ends with a day-and-a-half institute during which faculty present a revised version of their projects, discuss their plans for course implementation, and provide feedback on one another's projects.

During the fall semester, faculty participants deploy their projects, using materials created during the institute. Toward the end of the semester, everyone meets for the last time to share experiences, lessons learned, and feedback received from students. Faculty often develop plans to pursue additional funding for project evaluation or revisions to their projects. CRLT alone could not provide the time and individualized support each faculty member receives. By collaborating with and leveraging the skills of different departmental IT units, CRLT is able to offer a high-quality program that provides faculty with customized pedagogical and technical support for incorporating technology into their courses. In addition, meetings are kept to a minimum so faculty can spend their time focusing on implementing and evaluating their ideas.

## Evaluating Technologies Used in Teaching

Formal evaluation of technologies is a complex task, usually involving a team that includes developers, designers, trainers, and faculty users. Any technology tool can be evaluated on a number of dimensions, such as its features, cost, ease of use, security, and instructional value. What a teaching center brings to an evaluation team is the perspective of instructional value, or how well a technology supports teaching and student learning. We ask such questions as: "Under what conditions does technology have the most benefits for students?" and "What teaching strategies best support a particular technology tool?" (Ringstaff & Kelley, 2002). This helps steer the focus away from "Should we use technology?" to the more useful question, "How is technology best used, and what are the outcomes of different types of use?" In this section, we explain how CRLT evaluates the use of technology and its impact on teaching and student learning in different instructional settings: a single course and multiple similar courses within a college or school.

### *Evaluating Technology Use in a Single Course*

Many faculty on campus use technology in teaching, but few have time to evaluate its impact on teaching and learning because it is either too late to collect data or it takes too much time. CRLT encourages faculty to evaluate technology used in individual courses by planting the seed early and providing support as needed. For example, a faculty member in political science was interested in creating a series of case studies that students could access online. He wanted to post questions about the cases that would require students to research issues on their own, outside of class. He also wanted students to send their questions and comments about the cases to him so he could integrate their responses into his lectures. CRLT consultants worked closely with this faculty member to determine the most appropriate tool for this task, the potential impact on student learning as discussed in the literature, and the implications this innovation would have for both his teaching and student learning.

The idea of evaluation appealed to the faculty member, who initiated a series of consultations on evaluating his use of online cases and eventually applied for CRLT's Investigating Student Learning Grant to support the project (http://www.crlt.umich.edu/grants/islgrant.php). With grant funding, he worked with CRLT consultants to develop research designs and methods for data collection. When he used the cases in teaching, he collected students' responses to his questions, examined their essays and discussions, gathered quiz and test scores, and finally interviewed students. At the end of the course, CRLT helped with the data analysis. The evaluation of this particular project revealed both the real and perceived value of online cases with accompanying questions for student learning and helped the faculty member refine his practice as he continues using online cases in further iterations of the course. The faculty member shared his evaluation findings with colleagues more broadly and recommended good practices for using cases in teaching in the poster fair of a campus-wide technology conference.

## Evaluating Technology Use Across Multiple Courses in a College

Evaluation of a technology use across multiple courses in a college can be very powerful, helping to shape teaching practices with the technology and eventually promoting campus-wide adoption of a new learning technology. The following case explains how CRLT planned an evaluation to examine and promote the use of a technology—clickers—that was new to campus. CRLT identified best practices for using clickers in the classroom by collecting data on student perceptions and learning outcomes and sharing them with a broader audience on campus.

Clickers are wireless, handheld devices that provide real-time aggregations of students' responses to faculty questions during lectures. Faculty can pose a question to any size audience, and students can respond in multiple choice or short answer, depending on what form of input the clicker technology allows. In the early 2000s, clicker technology was gaining increasing attention from faculty and students across campus, and more requests were coming in for consultations about this technology. There were also doubts about the value of this technology and concerns about the extra cost to students. CRLT decided to evaluate clickers in a number of courses in one college to document how they were being used in classrooms and to identify which practices were particularly effective for enhancing teaching and student learning, as well as the practices to be avoided.

For three semesters, over 3,000 students and about 20 faculty members who used clickers completed online surveys that focused on examining students' perceptions of clicker technology and its impact on students' attention, engagement, and learning. Each semester, CRLT analyzed the data and identified practices that supported student learning and those that raised concerns or complaints from students. CRLT shared the findings from individual courses with the instructors teaching those courses and distributed the aggregate survey results to participating faculty members, other faculty interested in using this technology, and the broader campus community.

With the evaluation data, CRLT was able to identify and summarize effective practices worthy of wider dissemination, such as using clickers to assess students' prior knowledge and identify misconceptions before introducing a new subject, or using them to check students' understanding of new material. Faculty were very receptive to the practices identified and quickly put them to use in the classroom, because they were supported by research on college teaching (Chickering & Gamson, 1987). Over the three semesters, students changed from viewing clicker technology as "somewhat negative" in the initial adoption stage, to seeing it as "a helpful tool for learning" (Center for Research on Learning and Teaching, University of Michigan 2007). Clicker technology is now used across campus to promote active-learning strategies in large lectures. Whereas evaluating technology in a single course is fairly simple, doing so across multiple courses requires much greater coordination and collaboration and can have a correspondingly greater impact on teaching campus-wide.

## Taking a Collaborative Approach

A description of our practices would not be complete without a discussion of how we collaboratively leverage resources across campus to engage a range of faculty, from the technology novice to the expert, in using technology to support teaching and improve student learning.

Large universities usually run technology skills training out of one or more centrally supported training offices that provide high-quality technical support. However, the experience and range of expertise in a central support unit may be different from that in a college or departmental support unit.

This creates a situation where a faculty member may be introduced to technology skills but find it difficult to use them fully on an ongoing basis. Inconsistent technology support often impedes the successful use of technology in teaching and may prevent faculty from completing technology projects (Berge, 1998; University of Michigan, 2001, 2005). The same tools that worked smoothly in a central training room need to run hassle free in a lecture hall or at a departmental computer lab if they are to win over faculty and students. Unexpected technology glitches and loss of class time are common worst-case fears for faculty when they teach in unfamiliar instructional settings (Berge, 1998).

Collaboration helps us solve inconsistent support problems. It is particularly necessary on our campus because of UM's decentralized support structure, combined with the wide range of expertise needed to support faculty technology projects. It is impossible for a college or a department support unit to have staff with expertise over the entire range of faculty development, instructional design, software training, and classroom/facility support. On our campus, central and departmental technology units have staff who specialize in network infrastructure and hardware, or software applications and training. Department support staff know about classroom equipment and support, and CRLT has expertise in faculty development, course design, and the pedagogy of technology uses.

CRLT has developed strong working relationships with both central and departmental tech offices, which we can leverage to support both large-scale programs, such as our TTI, and short-term individual consultations. In addition, we map the available support to ensure that faculty have the information they need to work with common technologies. For example, we developed a matrix of the various lecture capture systems and support offices on campus so instructors would know what resources were available in their colleges or departments.

## Conclusion

The framework and the collaborative approach we use to engage faculty in effective use of technology allow us to reach faculty at every stage of technology use. They enable us to be flexible and creative, involving faculty in integrating technology into teaching at all three points of the framework: promotion, support, and evaluation. As we focus on one area of the framework, we do not lose sight of the others. When promoting a technology use, we prepare for its support. While supporting a faculty member in using a new technology, we prepare to promote its use in a broader context. When evaluating a technology tool, we once again plan for its support services and promote effective practices for using the technology across disciplines. We are confident that this framework and our collaborative approach are flexible and scalable so they can be adapted to supporting faculty who are teaching with technology at other institutions.

# ACTION RESEARCH FOR INSTRUCTIONAL IMPROVEMENT

*Chad Hershock, Constance E. Cook,*
*Mary C. Wright, and Christopher O'Neal*

During the past decade, CRLT has intensified its focus on research as a lever for strategically supporting and improving teaching on campus. A good example is the research project CRLT initiated in 2003 to investigate the factors influencing undergraduate retention and attrition in the sciences, with particular attention given to the role of TAs, who teach the majority of sections in introductory courses. Using this type of research to instigate data-driven institutional change was a new venture that was extremely time-consuming for multiple CRLT staff members over several years. However, CRLT's investment in this approach to faculty development was a strategic move targeted to (1) improve teaching in the introductory science courses in multiple departments; (2) demonstrate the teaching center's value more clearly to the dean and several department chairs in the liberal arts college; and (3) provide data to CRLT consultants that inform our work with TAs across campus.

What follows is a previously published article (Cook, Wright, & O'Neal, 2007), reprinted with permission of John Wiley & Sons, Inc., that describes the first three years of this initiative and illustrates how CRLT employs this type of action research to improve teaching on campus. Additionally, there is an epilogue summarizing the impacts of conducting action research on our teaching center's endeavors to improve the culture of teaching at UM over the last seven years.

# ACTION RESEARCH FOR INSTRUCTIONAL IMPROVEMENT

## Using Data to Enhance Student Learning at Your Own Institution[1]

*Constance E. Cook, Mary Wright, Christopher O'Neal*

### ABSTRACT

*Action research is a powerful tool that can be used by teaching centers to improve teaching and learning. This article describes an action research project conducted at the Center for Research on Learning and Teaching (CRLT) at the University of Michigan. The project concerns retention and attrition in science gateway courses, with particular attention given to the role of the Teaching Assistant. The article concludes with a discussion of six principles for teaching center staff who wish to conduct their own action research projects.*

The role of most teaching centers at universities across the country is to improve teaching and student learning, by creating a culture of pedagogical excellence, responding to instructors' needs, and advancing teaching and learning through new initiatives (Sorcinelli, Austin, Eddy, & Beach, 2006). In this article, we document one useful approach to enhance student learning through a methodology called "action research."

[1] Reprinted with permission from John Wiley & Sons from: Cook, C. E., Wright, M., & O'Neal, C. (2007). Action research for instructional improvement: Using data to enhance student learning at your institution. In D. R. Robertson & L. B. Nilson (Eds.), *To Improve the Academy: Resources for Faculty, Instructional, and Organizational Development, vol. 25* (pp. 123–138). Bolton, MA: Anker.

Coined by psychologist Kurt Lewin (1948/1997), action research (or action inquiry) generally refers to any research that is used as the basis and motivation for reform. Sorcinelli et al., in their discussion of the "evolution" of faculty development, describe a move from the 1950s and '60s Age of the Scholar (emphasizing support for faculty research) to today's Age of the Learner (supporting effective pedagogy and scholarship of teaching and learning) and tomorrow's Age of the Network, in which faculty and developer roles expand and collaboration becomes key to success. An action research approach is ideally situated for contemporary faculty development activities, as it emphasizes collaboration and supports student learning through data-driven investigation.

The Center for Research on Learning and Teaching (CRLT) at the University of Michigan illustrates the path of one teaching center to an action research approach. CRLT was established in 1962, and as its name implies, research was its primary focus for its first decades. In the 1980s, CRLT's emphasis moved to a mix of research and service to faculty, and by the 1990s, its focus was mostly on programmatic faculty development in response to the provost's mandate that teaching improvement was important and faculty development was the way to achieve it. This emphasis implies that there was no research at all, which was not the case; evaluation research was a regular part of the service CRLT provided. What the center rarely did, however, was initiate major research projects that went beyond investigation of a single course or curriculum.

In this new age, CRLT has broadened its own focus to embrace more of its research roots. We augment our faculty development programs with periodic research projects, and the research improves our programming. Our research usually is done at the request of academic leaders, especially deans, and it informs and improves the services we provide for them, as well as instructors' practice, curricula and institutional cultures. This type of research is a form of inquiry termed "action research," and it is a powerful tool by which teaching centers can improve instruction.

Lewin (1948/1997) described action research as a process, or a "spiral of steps each of which is composed of a cycle of planning, action, and fact-finding about the result of the action" (p. 146). Organizational action research is not new to higher education; using evaluation research to inform institutional change in higher education has been around since the master planning movement of the 1960s (Halstead, 1974; St. John, McKinney, & Tuttle, 2006). Since that time, action research has been used as a democratization method by which various constituencies can be brought into the change process (Armstrong & Moore, 2004; Benson & Harkavy, 1996; Park, 1999), an experiential tool to engage learners (Geltner, 1993; Krogh, 2001; Zuelke & Nichols, 1995), and a process to conduct classroom research (Cross & Steadman, 1996; Schön, 1983, 1987). There are many variants of action research, such as participatory action research, cooperative inquiry, empowerment research, community-based research, and feminist research (Reason, 1999; Small, 1995; Strand, Marullo, Cutforth, Stoecker, & Donohue, 2003).

There are several reasons why teaching centers are ideally suited to do action research. First, their institutional perspective is advantageous for this type of inquiry. While the organizational structure of teaching centers varies widely, most are central units with a broad mandate for change and the capacity to have an institution-wide perspective, not one rooted in a single school or college (Sorcinelli et al., 2006; Wright & O'Neill, 1995). This perspective can inform directors about the issues of concern to academic administration. Furthermore, the institutional position of a teaching center means that the staff know what data are available and are likely to be able to get permission to access it. Additionally, teaching centers, particularly larger ones, often are involved in evaluation projects, which means that data are near at hand and evaluation of action plans is efficacious (Wright & O'Neill, 1995).

Second, teaching center professional staff typically have the academic and professional backgrounds needed to conduct effective action research. Many have PhDs (Gillespie, 2001), and the action researcher's role as "catalyst" or "resource" (rather than "expert") parallels many consultants' approaches to their professional practice (Brinko, 1997; Stringer, 1999).

Finally, teaching centers are service organizations and their mission is to implement good ideas for improving teaching and learning on campus. When they analyze data and conclude that improvement is necessary and action needs to be taken, they already are positioned to use the data to implement an action plan, then evaluate its results. They can begin work on improving programs and services right away and are connected to campus faculty who are likely to agree to be early adopters of teaching innovations.

The most common type of teaching center–based action research is the solicitation of student opinions about a course through Small Group Instructional Diagnosis (SGID) or evaluation and the use of that feedback to improve the course (Nyquist & Wulff, 1988; Seldin, 1997). However, action research that extends beyond the individual classroom appears to be rare. Key exceptions include action research on graduate students' career goals in order to plan professional development programs (Bellows & Weissinger, 2005), use of student feedback to assess and revise departmental curricula (Black, 1998), initiatives to enhance students' writing and study skills (Zuber-Skerrit, 1992), and other projects that fall under the heading of assessment of student learning or the scholarship of teaching and learning. Additionally, the Center for Instructional Development and Research at the University of Washington has collected data on departments, such as grade distributions, class size, student ratings, and TA training, and used that data to help departments identify needs and effect improvements (J. Nyquist, personal communication, October 1996).

In spite of the many advantages that teaching centers have in conducting action research, these centers also face special challenges. Because they are service units, it is hard for professional staff to find time to do research that involves gathering data. Also, teaching center budgets are dependent on the decisions of academic administrators so it is important to be collaborative and helpful, not adversarial and critical. Furthermore, teaching center programs and services are rarely mandatory. Faculty use them because of their perceived value, so it is vital for a center to maintain a positive image on campus as a place that supports faculty and supports the academic units. To engage in behavior that alienates it from its faculty constituency would be self-defeating. These issues echo questions raised in action research that address politically-charged problems and engagement of multiple constituencies (Polanyi & Cockburn, 2003). Other questions raised in the action research literature that are relevant to teaching center staff who conduct such inquiries include:

- How do researchers manage tensions between their multiple roles as change agent, researcher, consultant, ally, and evaluator (Chesler, 1990; Elden, 1981)?
- How do researchers manage tensions between themselves and organization members about the interpretation of research, needed interventions, and how or whether to communicate results (Bishop, 1994; Greenwood & Levin, 1998; Israel, Schurman, & Hugentobler, 1992)?

Despite the challenges described above, teaching centers have much to gain from engaging in action research. In the following sections, to describe what we have learned about how to effectively conduct action research in a teaching center, we first present one case study to illustrate the process. We begin by situating CRLT's action research project within the national problem of retention in the sciences. We then describe the steps we took to engage in the action research project on the local level, that is, our work with three large science departments at the University of Michigan. Action research typically involves three key steps: planning, acting on findings, and reflection (Lewin, 1948/1997; Zuber-Skerrit, 1992), and we note our process in each of these stages. Finally, based on our experiences and the challenges noted above in the action research literature, we recommend six principles for conducting effective action research in a teaching center. Table 10.1 integrates the action research stages, our recommendations for teaching centers that wish to conduct action research stages, and what CRLT did in its study of undergraduate attrition in the sciences.

## The National Problem

Nationally, retention in science has become a matter of real importance, as educational institutions try to slow the sizable flow of undergraduates out of scientific fields (Campbell, Jolly, Hoey, & Perlman, 2002; National Science Foundation, 2003; Strenta, Elliot, Adair, Matier, & Scott, 1994). For two decades, the National Science Foundation (NSF) has been especially active in addressing attrition through a series of grants, workshops, publications, conferences and other interventions designed to improve science retention at U.S. universities. In 2004, the Government Accountability Office reported that NSF and twelve other federal agencies spent $2.8 billion on programs intended to increase the number of students pursuing studies in science, technology, engineering, and mathematics (Selingo, 2005). Attrition in the sciences is especially problematic in the undergraduate years because approximately 40% of the students who come to college intending to major in the sciences ultimately decide to major in something else (Astin & Astin, 1993; Seymour & Hewitt, 1997; Strenta et al., 1994). Many of those who leave the sciences are capable students with the aptitude to do well in science (Montgomery & Groat, 1998; Seymour & Hewitt, 1997; Tobias, 1990), and the attrition problem is particularly acute for women and people of color (Astin & Astin, 1993; Holstrom, Gaddy, Van Horne, & Zimmerman, 1997; Seymour, 2001; Xie & Shauman, 2003).

Not much literature exists on the role of Teaching Assistants (TAs) in attrition or retention, and the literature that does exist reports that the TA is not an important factor (Seymour & Hewitt, 1997). Nonetheless, most

## TABLE 10.1
### CRLT Action Research Stages, Principles, and Steps

| Action Research Stage | Principles to Guide Action Research in a Teaching Center | What CRLT Did in the Study of Student Attrition in the Sciences |
|---|---|---|
| **Planning** | 1. Focus on research that is central to a teaching center's mission. | 1. Undertook a study central to CRLT's mission of promoting a university culture that values teaching and supports learning environments in which diverse students can excel |
| | 2. Shape the action research project so it answers questions of national importance while also being relevant and specific to local problems. | 2. Designed a study that responded to local needs (Task Force report and departments' goals) as well as the national problem of retention in the sciences |
| | 3. Obtain the buy-in of both the administrators motivating the study and the faculty and units that are the subject of study. | 3. Met with dean and departments to gain support for study |
| **Acting** | 4. Communicate the results of the study in a way that generates support for improvements without alienating the individual units or people who will have to implement those improvements. | 4. Presented results of study to departments and engaged in collaborative strategizing |
| | 5. Enhance credibility for the project by modifying the teaching center's own programs and practice when research findings indicate a need. | 5. Made improvements to CRLT's TA training programs |
| **Reflecting** | 6. Stay involved in the change process after research is complete to facilitate, guide, and evaluate reforms. | 6. Developed action research principles, worked with departments to enact changes, and planned for future evaluation of reforms |

undergraduate science, technology, engineering, and math (STEM) majors are educated at research universities that employ large numbers of TAs in science courses (National Science Board, 2004). Students in the sciences often depend more on TAs to help them to learn basic concepts than do students in disciplines outside the sciences, especially because students find it more difficult to learn from science faculty and also because science faculty delegate more teaching responsibility to TAs (Seymour & Hewitt, 1997; Seymour, Melton, Wiese, & Pedersen-Gallegos, 2005).

## CRLT Research Project

The CRLT action research project grew out of the experience of the 2002 *University of Michigan Task Force on Testing and Training Prospective Graduate Student Instructors* (Cook et al., 2002). The Task Force was composed of a group of academic leaders from the major undergraduate schools at the University of Michigan: the College of Literature, Science, and the Arts; and the College of Engineering. It was convened to consider how to improve the training of TAs, particularly those who were teaching in the sciences. Lacking relevant data, the task force suggested that CRLT begin an action research project to gather relevant data for future decision-making.

### *Planning the Action Research Project*

Attrition in the sciences is especially likely in the first two years of college (Seymour & Hewitt, 1997), so CRLT's research focused on the part of the leaky pipeline known as the "gateway course." The gateway course is the initial college course in the sciences taken by a first- or second-year student who has studied science in high school and expects to major in science in college. After the Institutional Review Board (IRB) approved the study, CRLT surveyed more than 3,600 undergraduate students in the gateway courses for prospective science majors. The survey was distributed immediately following the completion of the survey course, and questions concerned students' intention to major in the sciences both before and after they enrolled in the course, as well as reasons for this decision and their views on their TAs. The high response rate (73%) is likely attributable to a small set of prizes offered to students taking the survey. To supplement survey data, we gathered information from the registrar on student grades in these classes and any additional courses they took in the sciences in two subsequent semesters. We also collected data on the science TAs: demographic characteristics, number of terms as University of Michigan graduate students and as TAs, undergraduate English language background, and end-of-term student ratings. Additionally, we examined the TA training programs in each of the departments.

## Acting on Research Findings

This project generated three main findings that were especially relevant to the Task Force's initial questions:

1. Most TAs in Michigan's science departments performed very well. Only a very small percentage of TAs could be classified as "problematic."
2. Lab climate was one of the most important factors influencing students' plans to stay in or leave the sciences. Other factors that played a role in their decisions were their course grades, their math grades, and what they learned about careers.
3. Retention of students in Michigan science programs was high, but still worrisome when considered in the long term, especially for female students.

This research project eventually led to reforms in the training of science TAs at the University of Michigan. The research findings were presented to chairs in the three departments surveyed, and CRLT staff collaboratively strategized with them on implications for their TA training programs and curricula. As a result of these discussions, two departments are revising their introductory courses significantly, two departments are implementing new evaluation and support systems for TAs (one department already had an effective system in place), and all three departments developed greater awareness of the impact of TAs on student performance and retention. We have recently initiated a follow-up study in one of the departments to assess the impact of their TA training and course reforms.

## Reflecting

CRLT was a constant partner in this change and continues to be active in helping departments institute and evaluate these reforms. However, like much action research, this project was politically charged and required careful navigation by the center in order to emerge from the research project with allies in the departments instead of enemies. In the following section, we discuss six principles that we feel were key to our project's success.

*Principle 1: Focus on research that is central to a teaching center's mission.* Teaching centers are busy, often overcommitted, places. Because of their unique position on campus as an interface between students, faculty, departments, and administrators, they are also susceptible to mission creep. For a center to commit resources and staff to an action research project, that initiative must support a center's core mission. For CRLT, our central purpose is to "promote a university culture that values and rewards teaching, respects and supports individual differences among learners, and encourages the creation of learning environments in which diverse students can learn and excel."

This action research project on the TA's role in attrition and retention in the sciences was an excellent fit with this mission. While the research was enormously time-consuming for CRLT, we saw it as a project that could have a great impact on teaching and learning, especially through better TA training, and it even would support the center's multicultural mission by positively impacting science enrollments of underrepresented groups.

*Principle 2: Shape the action research project so it answers questions of national importance while also being relevant and specific to local problems.* This principle may seem counter-intuitive to centers struggling to improve teaching and learning on their own campuses. However, there are a number of reasons to focus on national issues. First, the more teaching centers are connected to reform at the national level, the more they will be seen as legitimate players in shaping higher education. When tasked with investigating TA training in the sciences at the university, CRLT decided to focus on science student retention as one key measure of TA effectiveness. This decision has added prestige and exposure for the center through presentations of the research at national forums. That exposure has led to more willingness to engage with the center on these issues at the campus level. Second, faculty are immersed in their own departmental cultures and attuned to issues that are highlighted by their disciplines at the national level (Gouldner, 1957). By choosing to focus on student retention in the sciences, as one measure of TA effectiveness, CRLT was focusing on an issue of real concern in the sciences. Department administrators, previously unexcited about a project on TA training, became very engaged with issues of student retention.

*Principle 3: Obtain the buy-in of both the administrators motivating the study and the faculty and units that are the subject of study.* Because the 2002 Task Force highlighted the dearth of data to inform its report, the need for a research project on the role of TAs was clear. That catalyst was very helpful in paving the way for the CRLT research project. Furthermore, we were fortunate to have a new dean in Michigan's liberal arts college who was eager to improve teaching and learning and who was willing to put his authority behind actions designed to accomplish those objectives. He is not a scientist and wanted to know more about the science instruction provided by his college, so he saw this research project as a way to inform himself. It is important to note that without his interest and support, the research could not have gone forward.

However, for this research project to succeed, the support of the dean and each of the chairs and associate chairs from the involved departments was necessary. We decided to meet individually with each department's administrators to stress that the survey data analysis on their departments was going to each of them directly (rather than going to the dean first) so they could decide independently what improvements and interventions might be helpful. Not surprisingly, some individual instructors and departments were not eager to have us collect data on their students and TAs. A fourth department opted out of the study altogether. We should note that due to the success of this initial research project the dean is now working with the chair of this department to do a similar study of its TAs.

Once general buy-in to the project was achieved, CRLT worked with key faculty in the departments to determine the relevant gateway courses for study and agree on the research design. We worked with the departments until we gained their trust and finally agreed on specific courses and specific protocols for the research. This step was crucial not only for performing the research, but it also helped prime the departments to act on the research findings.

*Principle 4: Communicate the results of the study in a way that generates support for improvements without alienating the individual units or people who will have to implement those improvements.* While the dean had supported the study, and the department chairs and faculty helped to create the questionnaire, only CRLT was involved in data analysis and decisions about how to report the results. We began by giving aggregate results to the dean and associate deans. In these reports we did not release specifics about the strengths and weaknesses of the departments. Next, we met individually with representatives from each department and presented both aggregate results and their specific departmental results. Strengths were emphasized and weaknesses candidly discussed, along with our suggestions for improvement. This respect for the authority of the department chairs helped to create a safe space for the chairs to initiate their own changes to TA training. Toward the end of the action research project, the dean asked about the departmental data and wanted information about the receptivity of the departments to curricular reform and TA training improvements. In our communications to the dean we emphasized the responsiveness of the departments and the substantial investment in training and curricular reform being undertaken there (one department allocated over $250,000 to the reforms suggested by our study).

*Principle 5: Enhance credibility for the project by modifying the teaching center's own programs and practice when research findings indicate a need.* Although many of the implications of our research fell within the purview of the science departments, CRLT also made a commitment to examining its own TA training programs. Our survey data showed that a special concern for undergraduates was communication with the TA, and student communication problems were named for both English-educated and non-English-educated TAs. First, we presented aggregate results to the university's English Language Institute, which, together with CRLT, helps coordinate the training for new TAs educated abroad in a non-English medium. Many of the international TAs communicated very well, thanks to a variety of factors: careful screening of graduate students during the admissions process, workshops and courses offered by the English Language Institute and CRLT, and more rigorous testing of TAs' English classroom competency before they were assigned to the classroom. However, at the meeting, we were able to strategize about how to enhance the training even further, such as by creating stronger early feedback and support systems for TAs after they enter the classroom.

Second, we focused on CRLT's training program for all TAs. Prior to the initiation of the study, recommendations of the 2002 *Task Force on Testing and Training Prospective Graduate Student Instructors* included two improvements to enhance the communication skills of all TAs, domestic and international. The first improvement was an individual practice teaching session (sometimes called micro-teaching) for every TA who attended the CRLT's central orientation. For two hours, all the TAs were divided into groups of six, each group with a trained instructional consultant. Each TA presented to the group a five-minute lesson in her own field and then received feedback on her teaching from the consultant and other TAs. Prior to the study, this portion of CRLT's TA orientation was optional, but findings of our research study confirmed the necessity of making this experience mandatory for all attendees. Given the hundreds of TAs who attend the University of Michigan TA orientations, this was a labor-intensive initiative, but the TAs reported it was the best part of the orientation and made them more confident as they began teaching classes. We were then able to recommend this practice to departments that hold their own TA training programs.

The second improvement to orientation was the addition of a one-hour interactive session on communication strategies. It describes and models ways to organize classes, use visual aids, and create interactivity among students. It also presents information about Michigan undergraduates in terms of academic background, social background, variations in learning styles, and patterns of intellectual development, to give TAs a good sense of the extent of diversity they will find in the classroom. Many TA developers know that because orientation programs have limited time, decisions about what to include in these programs can be difficult. However, because of the study's findings on TA-undergraduate communication, we confirmed that this was a highly valuable part of the orientation that should be maintained.

Indeed, a follow-up formal evaluation of these elements in CRLT's TA evaluation confirmed that practice teaching and the session on communication strategies were valuable additions. Respondents reported that the sessions had a favorable impact on their sense of preparation for teaching at the university and their abilities to give effective presentations, teach a diverse group of students, create a positive classroom climate, use active learning methods, plan a lesson, and give feedback to students about what they are learning.

*Principle 6: Stay involved in the change process after research is complete to facilitate, guide, and evaluate reforms.* While all the science departments had well-established TA training programs separate from CRLT's own, it was clear from the student survey responses that there was considerable variation between departments in the effectiveness of their students' learning experiences. Students had rated some departments' TAs highly and qualitative comments did not suggest that there be substantial changes in training. For other departments, the message was less favorable. Students especially criticized some TAs for poor communication skills and unclear or problematic grading systems. CRLT offered to provide the new practice teaching and communications modules for TAs to future departmental training programs, but it was important to find interventions that would improve instruction during the upcoming fall term.

To supplement their own training, two of the departments decided to initiate an early evaluation of TAs, asking students to fill out instructor ratings early in the semester so that problematic instructors could be identified quickly and the departments, along with CRLT staff, could offer support to those TAs and help them improve their teaching over the course of the semester. One department went so far as to arrange a follow-up training session for all TAs during one of the days of fall break so that all new instructors, not just those identified as problematic, could receive additional training. Another department arranged to have graduate student mentors, or advanced TAs hired to assist with TA development in the departments, consult with TAs who were struggling.

Based on the data from the survey of students, two departments determined that the problems with gateway courses went deeper than TA instruction and could be attributed to the nature of the courses themselves. One of those departments immediately embarked on a costly and time-consuming curricular reform effort that involved multiple instructors and all of its gateway courses. Another department has just begun the effort to revise and improve its course offerings.

As noted by Lewin (1948/1997) a complete action research cycle involves not only action, but also "fact-finding about the result of the action" (p. 146). For the interventions in all three departments, CRLT provided assistance, for example, overseeing some of the early evaluation, offering instruction at the follow-up training sessions, and providing benchmark data for the course revisions. A good action research project involves evaluation of the changes, and that, too, will be a CRLT responsibility.

## Conclusion

At CRLT, we learned a great deal from our action research. We learned that our own TA orientation could be improved, and we had the data to guide that improvement process. We learned that the dean and his department chairs are eager to improve instruction and welcome data that offer advice about how to do so. We also learned that our offers of assistance with the interventions were as important as the data. The departments lack the capacity to initiate all these changes on their own without assistance. So we provided some of the staffing for the reform efforts. Perhaps the biggest lesson for us at CRLT was the power of data. We operate in a university that prides itself on research excellence, and we found that our carefully-designed research project, producing high quality data, was an effective way to get the attention of faculty and administrators and accomplish teaching improvement objectives.

## Epilogue

CRLT's continued engagement in action research has advanced our mission of improving teaching on campus in several noteworthy ways. First, these action research projects were CRLT's entrée into several departments with which we had limited or no previous working relationships, and they strengthened existing relationships in other departments. Such access to departments provided CRLT with valuable information on their curricula, teaching practices, and TA training. As a result, we were able to position ourselves strategically to offer and provide customized, needs-based services for each department over a period of several years, including consulting on reforms to the training and early evaluation of TAs and providing customized workshops on pedagogy and assessment to faculty and TAs.

Second, CRLT's approach to navigating the action research process resulted in sustained relationships and partnerships with key faculty and administrators. In one science department, after investing over $250,000 worth of reforms to introductory courses and TA training, the chair asked CRLT to gather longitudinal data to assess the impact of revisions to introductory courses on student retention. This evaluation revealed a statistically significant increase in retention and provided additional data to improve teaching and TA training. Furthermore, it demonstrated how CRLT's expertise and services could help the department focus resources and target the areas for reform most likely to produce results. As the leadership changed within departments, CRLT maintained its involvement by building on its history of assistance with curriculum assessment and reform. For example, under a new chair, one science department is now revising the lecture format and pedagogy for its introductory courses. Based on our relationships with senior faculty formed during the initial action research, CRLT was positioned effectively to consult on this next round of curriculum revisions and will also assist with the evaluation of the reforms.

Third, department chairs have communicated that it is relatively easy for faculty to collect assessment data on their courses. However, these data may sit in filing cabinets indefinitely because faculty have limited time to analyze the data or implement the next steps in the reform process. Teaching centers are uniquely positioned not only to provide these assessment services, but also to stimulate and guide a productive, timely process for moving forward with curriculum reforms.

Finally, the dissemination of the research results across campus (without identifying individual departments or instructors) provided pedagogical support to faculty across science and engineering disciplines who did not participate in the studies but are eager to increase student retention. For instance, CRLT publishes *Occasional Papers* on teaching and learning that are available online and distributed in hard copy to faculty across campus. Following the action research project, CRLT authored an *Occasional Paper* that distilled our research results and a review of the extant literature into simple, practical strategies that positively influence student retention in science and engineering and can be readily implemented by individual faculty in their classes "next week" (Kendall Brown, Hershock, Finelli, & O'Neal, 2009). Additionally, we designed a data-driven, interactive, faculty development workshop based on our action research data. This workshop can be customized for different disciplines by modifying the examples and activities that model, highlight, and practice teaching strategies shown to have a positive impact on student retention. We have also infused the teaching principles distilled from our action research into the curricula of our preparing future faculty programs for graduate students and postdoctoral scholars (see chapter 6). Consequently, our action research has created opportunities for CRLT to improve teaching through multiple, data-driven interactions with individual instructors and departments across campus.

# II

# ROLE-PLAY AND BEYOND

Strategies for Incorporating Theatre
Into Faculty Development

*Matthew Kaplan and Jeffrey Steiger*

The CRLT Players Theatre Program (http://www.crlt.umich.edu/the
atre/index.php) is dedicated to the application of theatre arts to faculty development. Some universities and colleges house troupes that
perform sketches on student issues (e.g., date rape, cheating and plagiarism,
alcohol abuse) for incoming student orientations or programs in classrooms
and dorms. The CRLT Theatre Program represents, to our knowledge, the
first fully institutionalized theatre program to perform for faculty and graduate students, with a focus on issues of teaching and learning and faculty work
life. Most of the sketches are fairly short (ten minutes) and usually include
character-audience interaction. After the performance, the actors stay in
character and talk with the audience members, who can learn more about
their motivations, thoughts, and attitudes. Sometimes sketches are replayed
based on those discussions, or audience members join the scene and attempt
to change the dynamics. Longer plays (20–30 minutes) include multimedia
elements, music, and dance. Extensive, facilitated discussions follow all of
the Players' performances so the audience can grapple with the issues and
their reactions to them and with the divergent viewpoints present in any
group of faculty or graduate students.

The Players are used extensively in the center's programming, with performances included in campus-wide orientations and seminars as well as
customized retreats and workshops for departments and schools. Partnerships and collaborations extend to other university units, such as ADVANCE

at the University of Michigan (http://sitemaker.umich.edu/advance/home), which has funded development and performance of three sketches on faculty work life (LaVaque-Manty, Steiger, & Stewart, 2007), and the College of Literature, Science, and the Arts, which commissioned a set of vignettes on sexual harassment for TA training.

Demand for performances has grown over the years, both at UM and nationally. In 2009–2010, the Players performed for 2,200 audience members over a span of more than 40 performances. The growth of the program, from a single sketch on the chilly climate for women in science classes to a list of more than 25 sketches on a wide range of topics, attests to the power of theatre as a faculty development tool that sparks substantive conversations among academics.

While we are well aware of the potential of theatre, we also realize that our current structure (three professional staff and a troupe of 25 part-time actors) will remain beyond the reach of most teaching centers, at least initially, and certainly in an era of fiscal constraint. This chapter focuses, instead, on ways to benefit from a particular theatrical approach—role-playing—that offers many of the benefits of theatre without the need to create a full troupe.

## What Makes Theatre Successful?

Before turning to role-plays in particular, it is important to consider the aspects of theatre that make it a successful tool for faculty development. A 2006 *Change* magazine article (Kaplan, Cook, & Steiger, 2006) outlined four features of theatre that we felt made it particularly well suited to professional development in an academic context:

- **Serious issues presented with humor.** Serious issues that are often difficult to discuss (such as sexual harassment or gender discrimination in the hiring or tenure process) are presented with humor, providing a release of tension and increasing audience members' willingness to engage with the issues. Humor ensures that participants do not feel "preached at" and decreases their resistance to difficult conversations.
- **Emotional engagement while maintaining distance.** Theatre taps into the power of emotions for promoting learning, as participants see and hear about the impact of difficult situations (such as a science TA who is contributing to the chilly climate for women students in

his class or a doctor telling a patient she has cancer). At the same time, audience members can maintain some distance, since this is not a depiction of their own classroom, clinic, or department, but a composite that allows for recognition without feelings of defensiveness.

- **Credibility combined with a suspension of disbelief.** Considerable research goes into the creation of sketches, from results of published literature to discussions, focus groups, and preview performances with feedback. As a result, we often hear that sketches are surprisingly realistic. At the same time, we can take advantage of the willingness of audience members to suspend disbelief. This allows us to condense multiple issues into a single, short interaction, which promotes a very rich discussion without destroying the sketch's credibility.
- **Meaning generated through presentation and active learning.** The sketches themselves function as dramatic research presentations, raising the issues but avoiding clear-cut solutions. The discussions and exercises that follow take advantage of the power of active learning and engagement and push participants to grapple with the issues and with the divergent opinions of their colleagues and to develop a rich understanding of the topic at hand.

Evaluations done on the impact of CRLT Players' performances indicate that the sketches have an immediate and a lasting impact on audience members. In surveys conducted six months after sketches on instructor responses to student disability, 80% of respondents reported that the sketch had affected their teaching (Kaplan et al., 2006). The ADVANCE Program at UM reports that that audience members gave high ratings (4.0 and higher on a five-point scale) to the usefulness of the issues presented in the sketches on faculty work life and the degree to which the performances and discussions increased understanding of the issues in sketches (LaVaque-Manty et al., 2007). And both studies collected open-ended responses that revealed the depth of impact theatre can have on audience members. For example, a TA who saw the chilly climate sketch wrote the following:

> I teach a lab course. Often I see women being the note-taker in the lab, rather than actively participating in the experiments. In those cases, I now intervene immediately to remind my students that they will all need individual lab skills. (Kaplan et al., 2006, p. 36)

A faculty member who saw the sketch on a faculty meeting about hiring said,

> I think that the skit raised a number of points about departmental dynamics. Certainly every member of departmental executive committees should see it. It simply helps people be aware of the pitfalls common to interpersonal communication. (LaVaque-Manty et al., 2007, p. 217)

Others have written about the impact of interactive theatre as well, for example, documenting the power of this approach for helping women engineering faculty navigate the gender dynamics of their departments (Chesler & Chesler, 2005).

How then can teaching centers take advantage of this type of theatre without creating their own troupes? We believe role-playing offers an effective yet accessible way for faculty developers to draw on the power of drama for programs and internal processes.

## Role-Playing in Faculty Development

The following section provides background on role-plays and examines a variety of ways they can be used.

### History

The use of role-play as a pedagogical tool has a rich history, spanning multiple disciplines, and deserving of careful attention beyond the scope of this chapter. Psychiatrist and psychosociologist Jacob Moreno is often credited with the creation and use of psychodrama—the specific application of drama, or role-play—as a therapeutic agent. Inspired by and based in the philosophies of Paulo Freire, theatre practitioner Augusto Boal wrote extensively about the uses of theatre exercises and interactive scenes, or "Forum Theatre," as a means to role-play social, personal, and political conflict to foster dialogue and conflict strategies and solutions (*Theatre of the Oppressed*, 1979; *Games for Actors and Non-Actors*, 1992; *The Rainbow of Desire*, 1995). Viola Spolin's work on improvisation is often credited as the basis for American comedy improvisation, in particular Second City (which later spawned *Saturday Night Live*), which is considered the iconoclastic home for comedy improvisation. Spolin's writing had a significant impact on the use of games and role-play in the theatre and classroom as well (*Improvisation for the Theater*, 1963). Spolin reached a broader audience of instructors with the publication of *Theater Games for the Classroom: A Teacher's Handbook* (1986), which was specifically intended to broaden the pedagogical uses of her techniques for the classroom.

Today, role-play is used in a variety of disciplines and educational settings, including medical education (Benbassat & Baumal, 2002; Heru, 2003; Jones, 2001; Mann et al., 1996), business (Anselmi, 2004; Liebowitz, 2003; Yazisi, 2004), history (Erb, 2003; Morris, 2003), antiracist teaching (McGregor, 1993), second language acquisition (Kodotchigova, 2001), and social work (Halperin, 2002). At CRLT, we regularly use role-play in a variety of venues, including our training of graduate students to become graduate student consultants.

## Role-Plays Using Actors: Trigger Vignettes

CRLT's artistic director works with faculty committees to craft trigger vignettes, short scenes that depict difficult or problematic dynamics and spark conversation about how faculty can respond. Possible vignette topics include departmental climate and communications, authority in the classroom, office hours, and interactions between faculty and students in the clinic. Impetus for vignette development may come from chairs or deans, faculty committees, or even university-level administrators. The following examples illustrate how vignettes are created and used.

Unlike the low-impact role-plays described previously, trigger vignettes involve advanced preparation and a greater level of scripting. They often use actors, who tend to be comfortable with improvisation and risk taking, which is very important for both planning and performance. Our troupe consists of professional actors and academics (graduate students, lecturers, and CRLT staff) who are comfortable on stage. Trained actors bring a performance skill set, whereas academics know the content and are familiar with the issues under discussion. The key to working with any performer is a leader/facilitator who understands both theatre and academic content (or a collaboration between two people who bring skills from each side of this equation).

The director and actors meet with the faculty group commissioning the vignette. This meeting lasts about 90 minutes and has two parts. The first part is very similar to a faculty focus group; it helps the director and actors learn more about the goals for the performance and the issues faculty hope to address, such as common trends, any history of these issues in the department, examples of problematic moments or dynamics related to the issues, and the range of believable circumstances or dynamics (compared with scenarios that might be considered too extreme). The second part involves scripting the scenarios. The actors are an important part of this process. Based on the preliminary focus group, the director will suggest to the faculty two or three situations that seem to represent a number of the issues raised. The actors then improvise short scenes based on each of these scenarios. The director stops after each and asks the faculty questions to refine the improvisations into vignettes: What rang true? What was missing? What was out of place? What technical language needs refining? The actors and director take notes, and the actors then replay the scenario, with the director checking in one last time with faculty. After the meeting, the director creates a more fleshed-out vignette using a specific outline format described in the following example. The actors and the director then meet for a 30-minute rehearsal just before the performance to run through and review the vignettes.

## Faculty-Staff Relations

CRLT collaborates with the provost's office on a professional development program for department chairs and associate deans, the Provost's Campus Leadership Program (http://www.provost.umich.edu/programs/faculty_development.html). In addition to roundtables for all chairs and associate deans, we conduct an orientation for those new to these positions, among the most demanding and time-consuming administrative jobs at the university (for more information on the program, see chapter 3 in this volume and Wright et al., 2010). Part of the difficulty faculty experience in making the transition to administration is the responsibility for supervision and smooth functioning of departmental support staff, including key administrators, secretaries, and others. While they certainly interact with these personnel as faculty members, they are not involved in the smooth functioning of the office team, the relationship between staff and other faculty, or the interactions among office staff prior to assuming their administrative roles. In addition, administrators at this level must learn to depend on staff to guard their time and help them set and stick to priorities in order not to be overwhelmed by minutiae, even if this means redefining established relationships and communication patterns with their colleagues.

As part of the program for new chairs and associate deans, CRLT used the 90-minute trigger vignette development process described previously to create two scenarios for the orientation program for new chairs and associate deans. In this case, the focus group included the supervisor of key administrators in all departments in our largest college, plus CRLT's director. The limited size of this discussion was appropriate since both participants were extremely well informed about the relevant groups: The administrative supervisor knew from her years of work with departmental administrative staff the struggles faculty faced as they made the transition to administrators; CRLT's director had interviewed experienced chairs and associate deans as part of a needs assessment that went into creating the orientation. This discussion led to the identification of two trigger vignettes: one in which a staff member who has clearly been a friend of the new chair for many years comes to discuss a conflict with another member of the administrative staff and asks the chair for support, and a second in which the key administrator arrives late, exhibits further examples of disorganization, and is dismissive of the chair's request for a more structured and well-defined working relationship.

As discussed previously, after this initial meeting, the director created the vignettes by sketching out an outline; this consisted of a series of *beats*, short moments that define the arc of the story. See Figure 11.1 for an example using the first vignette.

The outline is not a full-blown script. Instead, the actors are given key lines they must speak when performing the vignette. The spaces between the lines are filled by improvisation based on the actors' knowledge of the scene (from either their participation in the focus group or their work in rehearsal) and their understanding that the next beat needs to fit with their invented dialogue. By creating an overarching structure, the outline lets actors feel comfortable improvising. Moreover, potentially stilted dialogue becomes fresh in each new performance, drawing the audience in and helping its members identify with the scene, which is key to using the vignette as a springboard for a productive discussion of the issues.

The post-vignette discussion includes time for interaction with the characters (the actors do not step out of character until the very end of the workshop). This exchange draws faculty into the scene and deepens their understanding of the topic and the characters' motivations, something that is essential for determining how to respond effectively should they confront a similar situation. Typical interactions between characters and audience members include requests for more information, questions, and comments. In addition, CRLT's artistic director has developed two dramatic techniques that are particularly effective for raising issues that otherwise remain unspoken.

The first technique is called "time-out/time-in." At a given moment the facilitator reminds audience members that a character might not be able to

## FIGURE 11.1
### Example of a Trigger Vignette Outline

**Beat 1: The late arrival**

A. → (Key admin's entrance): "Hello, so sorry, my mother-in-law again . . ." (she tripped on stairs)

B. → (Key admin's story): "Stairs like Mount Everest to her . . ."

C. → (Chair politely trying to interrupt: "O.K.," "Well . . .")

**Beat 2: Time to start**

A. → (Chair's response): "I was waiting for you. . . ." "I really needed you here. . . ."

B. → (Key admin's defense): "I'm ready . . . so let's start. . . . I have my pad. . . ."

C. → (Chair's clarification): "Again, I don't know if we have the time . . ."

D: → (Key admin's defense): "Well, let's see what we can get done. . . . I'm ready. Let's go"

**Beat 3: False start**

A. → (Chair's agenda): "We have to talk about the Provost's Seminar, the curriculum. . . . We need to know X, Y, Z. . . ."

B. → (Chair's problem): "Since Cindy is now at home until noon, we are going to have to tend to . . ."

C. → (Chair's rethinking): "You know, I just can't do this right now. I have a meeting coming up. . . ."

D. → (Key admin departs quickly and with attitude)

**Beat 4: Let's talk**

A. → (Chair tries again): "Sit down . . . let's talk."

B. → (Chair puts issues on table): "You've been late, I need you here. . . ."

C. → (Key admin's defense, aggrieved): "My mother-in-law . . . the move-in, etc. . . ."

D. → (Chair's response): "It has been hard not having you here on time. . . ."

E. → (Key admin's request): "Cindy's situation [arriving at noon] would work for me, and ease things. . . ."

F. → (Chair's end line): "You're kidding, right . . . ?"

---

speak frankly due to the presence of the other character(s). The facilitator offers to let the audience speak to one of the characters privately. That character is in "time-in," while the other characters are in "time-out," unable to hear anything that is being discussed. This method adds another important layer to the discussion, as it implicitly raises issues of power dynamics and what we feel we can and cannot say.

We refer to the second technique as "switch." Toward the end of the presentation, the facilitator asks the audience to imagine the exact same scene—same dialogue, personalities, issues at play—but with different casting. The actors retake their original positions on stage and assume a signature physical gesture indicative of their character (which is worked out in rehearsal). When the director says, "Switch," the actors physically switch positions, inhabiting different characters from the ones they played, and using the signature physical gestures of the new characters. Audience members are then asked to consider what changed for them and what stayed the same when, for instance, a character who had been portrayed by a White woman is now being depicted by a male actor of color. We have found that audiences often gasp with surprise as they confront what had been invisible preconceptions about race, gender, and other aspects of identity. The ensuing exchange adds depth to the conversation and allows us to explore issues that are often quite difficult to raise directly without provoking shame, defensiveness, or silence. This is another example of the power of theatre to allow audience members to reach their own insights rather than feeling as if they are being lectured to or shamed into recognizing their blind spots.

These vignettes are co-facilitated by the CRLT Players director and the administrative supervisor. The co-facilitation is unusual for the CRLT Players, but it is a key ingredient in the success of these particular vignettes, and it is a strategy faculty developers can use to explore a very broad set of issues using vignettes. The staff member in this case has years of experience working with faculty chairs and can add her insights and cautions, and push faculty to see aspects of the problem they otherwise may not have noticed. As does any faculty developer, the CRLT Players director brings a background in facilitation, which enables him to keep the discussion on track, to prevent the conversation from becoming too didactic, and to record the good ideas that arise.

## Role-Plays Without Actors

Some of the ways in which we use role-plays involve minimal preparation and do not require trained actors. Two examples show how this process works in very different settings: our process for hiring instructional consultants and a training session for consultations.

### Hiring Instructional Consultants

As mentioned in chapter 1, we take hiring very seriously, because our reputation rests on the quality of the work we do. Our interview process involves multiple components, one of which is using role-plays to give us insight into the abilities, attitudes, and dispositions candidates would bring to one-on-one consultations. We have developed a set of role-plays around two major classroom-level concerns—a general pedagogical issue (e.g., lack of student participation) and a classroom diversity issue (e.g., inclusion/exclusion of students from different backgrounds)—plus one department-level issue (e.g., creating a new professional development program for TAs or faculty). Each of these scenarios reflects real-life consultations that we see often at CRLT.

Role-plays take place with all of our consulting staff present. We provide a brief setup for each scenario on the spot and then have various members of our staff play the instructor while the candidate plays the consultant. We emphasize in advance that we do not have a single, correct answer in mind. Instead, we are interested in gaining insight into how candidates would approach consultations (e.g., the questions they ask, the resources they bring to bear, their ability to make a client comfortable). We have also scripted a set of background characteristics for the instructor played by our consultants so that they play the role and answer questions consistently from one candidate to the next. The role-plays themselves are fairly brief, lasting approximately three to five minutes. Candidates are then asked to step back and reflect on how they think the consultation went, why they took the approach they did, and what they might do differently.

While individual consultations are only one aspect of the job, we find that these role-plays give us tremendous insight into how candidates think, and how they would interact with clients in general. Just as theatre asks an audience to compare the actions on stage to their own behaviors, these role-plays can open up a discussion about the relationship between candidates' theories about faculty development (e.g., a desire to foster dialogue rather than provide answers) and the approach they took to the role-plays. In addition, this piece of the interview shows us how they would react to difficult situations for which there are no clear-cut correct answers. Finally, while each of us speaks individually with the candidates, the role-plays offer a common experience, which we can then relate back to aspects of our one-on-one conversations.

We use a similar but more streamlined process for selecting the peer teaching consultants (PTCs) we employ to enable us to meet the demand for services for TAs (see chapter 5).

### Training for Consultations

Once we hire new staff (instructional consultants and graduate teaching consultants), we provide a set of training workshops to help them learn our approach to consultations. We include role-plays in two of these programs, one on observing classes and collecting midterm feedback and a second on consultations concerning student ratings of instruction.

The workshop on observing classes and MSFs (see chapter 4) includes an introduction to taking objective notes while observing a class, using those notes to consult with an instructor, and learning how to run the MSF process in a classroom. Role-plays are essential for helping new consultants get a feel for the language they will use, the types of questions and resistance they might face, and the type of preparation they need to do for a consultation. In this workshop, we show brief sections (five minutes) from videos of UM instructors. While they watch, participants practice taking objective notes (i.e., tracking what happens while avoiding making judgments). After seeing and discussing a sample role-play between the workshop facilitators, participants watch two additional videos and take turns playing the role of consultant and instructor with a partner. A debrief follows each role-play during which the participants reflect on effective strategies, challenges, and questions they have. In setting up these role-plays, we discuss Brinko's (1997) model for consultations, which ranges from providing answers to confronting clients. In choosing videos, we look for a range of instructor personalities and approaches (from very confident but didactic lecturers to struggling discussion leaders) so participants will need to think carefully about the type of approach to take given the needs of the client and students.

By acting out the consultations, participants have a chance to play with their approach in a low-stakes environment. In effect, they are getting to try on a consultant persona and receive feedback on how effective their approach is. They also get to see other approaches by watching their partners and the facilitators. Moreover, these interactions give them a sense of the emotional components of consulting—for both the consultant and the client—that are impossible to access using other methods.

In the workshop on consulting around student ratings, participants receive an overview of the research on student ratings as well as a guide to help them interpret the summary report results (both numerical data and open-ended comments). To jump-start the conversation, the workshop facilitators role-play a consultation in which the participants are told to think of themselves as co-consultants. At various points, the facilitator playing the consultant turns to the audience of participants and asks them for ideas on how to proceed. As they make suggestions, the consultant can probe for their rationale, and then try out their ideas in the role-play. A variety of approaches to the same issue can be used, and if it seems appropriate, the consultant may ask a participant to take over the role-play and try out the approach he or she is suggesting.

This type of role-play creates a common experience and makes the most of the tension between distancing and engagement outlined in our discussion of why theatre is effective. The participants are not fully on stage, so they do not feel put on the spot and can maintain a certain critical distance. On the other hand, they are brought into the fictive world of the role-play as co-consultants, so they can think carefully about their own reactions as the scene progresses.

## Consulting With Faculty on Using Role-Playing

In addition to incorporating role-plays into our own programs, we have worked with faculty on campus who wish to use drama in their classrooms or for professional conferences. Following are examples of this type of work:

- **Genetic counseling.** One of the challenges students face in this pro-gram is learning how to deliver difficult news. In particular, they will need to inform patients of medical test results indicating that the child they are expecting has serious health and ability issues. At the beginning of a clinical training course, the faculty member invited the CRLT Players to facilitate a discussion on students' assumptions, perspectives, and experiences regarding disability, and to teach role-playing skills that could be used over the course of the term. To accomplish the latter goal, the CRLT Players director engaged the class in a discussion of how role-plays are structured, helped them generate guidelines for respectful feedback, and set up scenarios for them to practice role-playing and giving feedback to colleagues.

- **Environmental justice.** As part of a presentation for the People of Color Environmental Summit, a faculty member worked with the CRLT Players on practical strategies for challenging the perspectives of community members and policy makers on the impact of environ-mental issues on marginalized communities. This collaboration led to the creation of trigger vignettes, such as a scene depicting an interac-tion between a mayor and a community member lobbying for atten-tion to environmental issues at a neglected school. After watching the scene, conference participants had an opportunity to replace the community member and try different strategies to lobby the mayor. This was followed by a full-group discussion of effective approaches. Based on the success of the presentation, the faculty member decided to include role-playing activities in his courses. He asked students to create their own scenes and present them to fellow classmates to generate a dialogue about the complexity of course topics.

- **School of social work.** The CRLT Players artistic director consulted with faculty in the school of social work as they developed a course module to train a cadre of students in role-playing skills. He talked to the instructors about the typical theatrical approaches for preparing actors (e.g., active-listening skills, emotional commitment to a scene, improvisation, not breaking out of character), the principles that govern effective scenes (described previously), and the importance of creating an open space for actors to examine their own assumptions and move beyond stereotypical portrayals. Students from this course are available to role-play scenarios that might be used in the context of other courses or school of social work events.

## Conclusion

During the past ten years we have learned that theatre has the power to open up difficult conversations among faculty, TAs, and academic administrators. Moreover, our experience indicates that more informal productions, such as role-plays, present different and unique strengths, and they can be as effective as more fully scripted, longer sketches. Role-plays and vignettes also have unique advantages. They are usually quite short, which enables us to integrate them into our programs, and they do not take long to create, which means we can be responsive to programming needs (both ours and those of the units with whom we work) without the long lead time required to create a full-blown sketch. While vignettes benefit from the participation of trained actors, we have had great success using role-play strategies in a number of situations with members of our staff or even administrators stepping into the roles. And we have found that students and faculty in UM's theatre department and at other local campuses are willing and eager to work with us in cases where we prefer to use actors. Teaching centers can gain valuable allies though such cross-campus collaborations, allowing them to take full advantage of the power of theatre to enrich their faculty development programs.

# CONCLUSION

## Responding to Challenges Faced by Teaching Centers at Research Universities

*Matthew Kaplan with contributions from:*
*Terry Aladjem, Lori Breslow, Susanna Calkins, Deborah DeZure,*
*Robyn Dunbar, Jean C. Florman, Marne Helgesen, Alan Kalish,*
*David Langley, Gregory Light, Angela Linse, Michele Marincovich,*
*Joan Middendorf, Allison Pingree, William C. Rando, Mary Deane*
*Sorcinelli, Kathy Takayama, Pratibha Varma-Nelson, Suzanne*
*Weinstein, and Mary-Ann Winkelmes*

### Introduction

Institutions of all types attend to their educational missions, but at a research university, the focus on good teaching feels countercultural. Teaching centers on research university campuses face unique challenges as they work to fulfill their mission of improving teaching and student learning.

We thought it would be useful in this final chapter to broaden our scope from CRLT and the University of Michigan to include our colleagues at peer institutions who operate in similar environments. As we mentioned in the introduction to this volume, CRLT is a member of two groups—the Committee on Institutional Cooperation (CIC) and Ivy (Plus) Teaching Center Directors—to whom we often turn when we face challenges in our research university environment. In addition, we have often sought advice from experienced practitioners who have a long history of involvement with faculty development (including service to POD). We asked these insightful and successful center directors to share with us the challenges they face and the strategies they have developed to overcome them through innovative programming and careful management of their resources. Their submissions fell into four broad categories: institutional-level challenges, engaging faculty and students and supporting engaged pedagogy, discipline-specific programming, and programming to address specific instructor career stages. We are grateful to them for responding and sharing the wisdom of their practice with us. We trust you will find their insights as useful as we do.

## Institutional-Level Challenges

As teaching centers become better established and academic administrators see their value, we are being asked to do more varied types of work. While we are often excited to be seen as more central and valued on campus, this development raises significant issues for us. How do teaching centers handle major initiatives that threaten to overwhelm their resources? How can we maintain our mission focus ("stay within our box," as we say at CRLT) while still serving the real needs of those who set the course for our institutions? The following examples provide insights and models for ways to address this challenge.

### ANCHORED OR ADRIFT: RESPONDING TO CENTER AND INSTITUTIONAL PRIORITIES

*Mary Deane Sorcinelli, associate provost for faculty development, Office of Faculty Development, University of Massachusetts Amherst (http://www.umass.edu/ofd) (The author thanks Allison Pingree, Center for Teaching, Vanderbilt University, for helpful conversations on this topic.)*

Institutional requests for faculty development programs that sponsor or support pedagogical innovations in general education, blended and online learning, first-year seminars, learning and teaching commons, and new classroom spaces have mushroomed over the last few years. Some centers have also been called upon to provide broader professional development assistance in areas such as mentoring, scholarly writing, chair leadership, and work/life balance. In general, supporting institutional needs and initiatives such as these is valuable. It allows a center to engage in a more expansive range of faculty work; to build new networks with departments, schools and colleges, and campus administration; and to collaborate with other support services.

It also adds to a center's portfolio of expertise and experience, and allows for projects that otherwise might be impossible to administer, finance, or navigate politically. But supporting priorities outside a center's core mission also can invite "mission drift."

How does a center respond to these requests in a way that reinforces rather than weakens its core mission and guiding principles? Over the years, our center has developed the following series of questions that serves as a "check and balance" when we need to calibrate institutional requests with our core mission:

- Does the initiative fit within our center's mission and values? For example, is it faculty-driven versus top-down, developmental versus evaluative, voluntary versus mandated?
- What will be the role of our center (e.g., staff tasks, level of sponsorship, time commitment)? Will we be expected to contribute as a full partner in the design, delivery, and assessment of the program; donate funds; or only handle administrative logistics?
- Will the program represent our center well? Lending our name to a poorly organized event, an event with a speaker we haven't vetted, or a program that is mandatory or regulatory in nature (e.g., faculty misconduct, sexual harassment) rather than elective and self-developing, could negatively affect how we are perceived.
- What resources will we need—staff and budget—and will there be a good return on our investment of time, toil, and funds?
- How broad will the audience be? Joining an initiative focused on a small number of faculty (e.g., a teaching fellowship or learning community) might need to be balanced with a campus-wide workshop that draws 100 participants.
- How can our center partner with other units (e.g., research affairs, library) or academic leaders (e.g., department chairs, deans, provost) to further mutual agendas for enhancing faculty careers?

Anchoring programs to your center's core mission allows you to steer a course that makes strong connections among faculty needs, institutional priorities, and the expertise of your center.

### FINDING A WAY FOR THE TEACHING CENTER TO SUPPORT INSTITUTIONAL CHANGE WHILE BEING PERCEIVED AS HELPFUL BY FACULTY MEMBERS

*Alan Kalish, director, University Center for the Advancement of Teaching, The Ohio State University (http://ucat.osu.edu)*

At a very large university like Ohio State, institutional initiatives can be perceived by some members of our faculty as administrative whims or fads. However, when an initiative seeks to advance the quality of teaching and learning, this falls directly within the mission of our center, and we look for ways to support our faculty in making these changes succeed for our students.

Our center handled one such challenge by playing an important supporting role when the university went from a quarter system to a semester system. The mandate to change academic calendars came from our state Board of Regents and drove similar changes across Ohio. Our staff members were consistently and extensively involved in the semesters project, serving ex officio on all major, university-level committees.

In our conversations with faculty, center staff stated clearly that we weren't driving the change, but we could assist both academic units and individuals. Whether they were excited to envision their curriculum anew, or resistant to the daunting task of redesigning their programs, many felt unsure about how to make such major changes to courses and curricula.

To address this need, our staff members collaborated to create course and curriculum design institutes, which have been very successful providing the tools, time, and collegial support to dig in and design or redesign a course or a curriculum. See http://ucat.osu.edu/semesters.html for details.

## DISCERNING APPROPRIATE INVOLVEMENT OF OUR CENTER IN RELATION TO NUMEROUS ONGOING EDUCATIONAL INITIATIVES AT THE INSTITUTIONAL LEVEL

*David Langley, director, Center for Teaching and Learning, University of Minnesota (http://www1.umn.edu/ohr/teachlearn)*

Large institutions have many educational priorities, and the list should be familiar: (1) internationalizing the curriculum, (2) assessing liberal education, (3) incorporating learning outcomes into undergraduate courses, (4) improving teaching and learning in technology-enhanced active learning spaces, and (5) infusing writing-enriched curriculum into undergraduate majors.

One successful approach for helping us decide whether to engage is to signal our intentions for involvement through a goal statement—"leading, advancing, and supporting campus initiatives that influence the educational mission of the university." Right up front, we indicate both a willingness and the responsibility to be a player on large-scale educational initiatives that affect the campus.

Second, our decision to be involved requires weighing (1) higher administration's energy and emphasis surrounding the initiative, (2) the degree to which our involvement would "move the needle" in a substantial way to complete the initiative, and (3) staff availability and skill to provide a quality contribution. In addition, honest discussion with one's supervisor (in our case, a vice president) does wonders to keep one's priorities in check!

Our strategic risk management process—weighing the risk of involvement against the impact of the initiative—continues to bear fruit as our breadth of involvement has increased in recent years. We are fortunate to have staff who do not merely serve as members of a task force but are often catalysts in moving a project forward.

### Addressing Important Professional Development Needs That Go Beyond the Scope and Mission of Our Center

*Allison Pingree, director, Center for Teaching, Vanderbilt University (http://cft.vanderbilt.edu)*

Our center handled this challenge by building a collaborative of stakeholders to address issues across units. Traditionally, Vanderbilt has taken a decentralized approach to graduate education, channeling most of its resources through individual schools and departments, rather than the Graduate School. While this approach has depended on departments and individual advisors to provide career preparation and professional development for graduate students, the students themselves have reported that the quality and quantity of such offerings often has been insufficient.

In response to those concerns and to the success of Preparing Future Faculty programs across the country, we launched a Future Faculty Preparation Program (F2P2) in 2000; during the following five years, more than 300 graduate students participated. Nonetheless, over time it became clear that continuing to address these needs would exceed our center's mission, expertise, and budget. We thus adapted F2P2 into a Teaching Certificate program that focuses on the scholarship of teaching and learning: http://cft.vanderbilt.edu/programs/teaching-certificate-program/.

Not wanting the broader needs to go unmet as a result of our own streamlining, however, we left the frameworks and resources from F2P2 as a self-directed web guide: http://cft.vanderbilt.edu/teaching-guides/audiences/future-faculty/. In addition, I met with two colleagues (assistant provost in the Graduate School and an associate dean for graduate education) to discuss ways we might address the needs that were beyond the scope of our center's Teaching Certificate program; the result was creation of the Graduate Development Network.

Now in its fifth year, this consortium consists of representatives from more than a dozen units—administrators, faculty, and students who play a role in supporting graduate students (http://www.vanderbilt.edu/grad school/gdn/index.html). At monthly meetings, we have shared resources, updated each other on programs and initiatives, even applied for and received internal funds for career development events and resources. In short, we are building collectively a support structure for professional development that none of us could or should address on our own.

## RESPONDING TO AN INSTITUTIONAL MANDATE TO CREATE ROBUST, DEPARTMENT-LEVEL TEACHING ASSISTANT AND GRADUATE ASSISTANT DEVELOPMENT IN TEACHING

*Robyn Dunbar, senior associate director, and Michele Marincovich, director, Center for Teaching and Learning, Stanford University (http://ctl.stanford.edu)*

Our center created a number of resources to support an unfunded Faculty Senate mandate that departments establish discipline-specific TA training programs (in addition to general training provided by the center). We catalyze department efforts with annual TA training grants and reach out to faculty newly in charge of department programs to help orient them to their roles. Capitalizing on a longstanding department liaisons program (http://ctl.stanford/edu/teachingta/ctl-liaisons-and-consultants.html), we engage cross-departmental conversation and share effective practices in quarterly meetings and at an annual Faculty-TA Conference on TA Training. The online document "What's Working in TA Training" (www.stanford.edu/dtp/CTL/TA/whats_working.pdf) provides an infrastructure of effective practice, showcases specific departmental examples, and—in an expansion of our graduate teaching consultants corps (http://ctl.stanford/edu/teachingta/ctl-liaisons-and-consultants.html)—the center's MinT (Mentors in Teaching—http://www.stanford.edu/dept/CTL/mint/index.html) program now trains and supports approximately 50 department-based TA mentors across campus. The net impact of the university decision requiring departments to train their own TAs has been even stronger integration of the center into the campus infrastructure of teaching support. The spin-offs have been significant, including further integration of the center into broader departmental conversations about teaching, learning, and curriculum development.

## Pent-Up Campus Demand

*Marne Helgesen, director, Center for Instructional Excellence, Purdue University (http://www.cie.purdue.edu/)*

When I began as director of a newly created teaching center, I encountered an acute campus case of "pent-up demand." Campus leaders had been strategizing for a center and director for more than eight years, and they felt the center needed to respond to this demand quickly, thereby building campus respect. In responding to this challenge, I learned the following lessons:

- It is essential to forge partnerships and make commitments involving key people strategically and quickly.
- It is important to schedule meetings with every campus dean, as well as central administration campus leaders, to identify needs, problems, and potential programs to be created (or eliminated), and to create links across the disciplines.
- Bringing tried-and-true programs from other institutions saves time (no sense in reinventing the wheel). The generosity of colleagues at other teaching centers can be important here, too.
- Centers should adhere to the philosophy that you can get a great deal accomplished if you don't mind who gets the credit.
- In its first years, a new center can operate effectively on a restricted budget, based on the tenet that success and respect can come from the creation of substantive, relevant programs that do not require extra funds.

## Engaging Faculty and Students and Supporting Engaged Pedagogy

In many ways, we could say that teaching centers are in the business of engagement. We try to engage the faculty in our services and, more broadly, in substantive and transformative conversations to help them think critically about how they can promote student learning more effectively. This often includes looking for strategies to help faculty engage their students in the learning process by moving away from a dependence on traditional pedagogies. It also includes support for those faculty who are dedicated to having their students engage the community outside of the academy. The authors of the following pieces offer practical advice for helping us promote engagement at various levels.

## Engaging Faculty in Serious Discourse About Pedagogy

*Terry Aladjem, executive director, Derek Bok Center, Harvard University*
*(http://bokcenter.harvard.edu)*

As an old teaching center at a very old university, our services are much appreciated, our faculty know and respect us, and many of them are excellent teachers. However, they are not engaging in a serious discourse about pedagogy with us or with one another.

To address this challenge, we believe we need to create (1) a series of compelling points of reference; (2) a vocabulary; and, ultimately, (3) a curriculum of common interest to faculty that charts future directions, with which they might begin such a conversation. To that end we have undertaken three initiatives:

1. We (and others) have brought in speakers of the highest caliber who challenge our faculty to make changes based on research they have undertaken, and who have served as points of reference in a developing conversation. Ken Bain and Carl Wieman (brought to Harvard for a Dudley Herschbach lecture on science teaching) both had powerful effects, and Sherry Turkle is slated to speak about the teaching and learning of the future.
2. Our senior staff created a pedagogy seminar (for ourselves and others) in which we have all been reading reports on cutting-edge research in cognitive science, assessment, and commentary on higher education, from which we have begun to generate a well-founded vocabulary to address faculty concerns.
3. With a grant from the Teagle Foundation, we are launching a seminar called "Designing the Course of the Future" for graduate students. The readings and themes from this course reflect a curriculum the center will offer to graduate students through departmental teaching colloquia and a certificate program, but, ultimately, to faculty as well, through graduate seminars they are creating to design courses, and in a seminar of their own as interest "trickles up."

## Reaching Faculty

*Angela Linse, executive director, and Suzanne Weinstein, director of instructional consulting, research, and assessment, Schreyer Institute for Teaching Excellence, The Pennsylvania State University (http://www.schreyerinstitute.psu.edu)*

Reaching faculty is one of the ongoing challenges Penn State's teaching center faces. Although this issue is not unique, the size and geographic dispersion of our faculty significantly complicates the process. The Schreyer Institute serves over 8,000 faculty of all ranks at 24 campuses throughout Pennsylvania who teach traditional, hybrid, or online courses to 90,000 highly diverse students.

The instructional consultants at the Schreyer Institute have implemented a variety of methods to increase faculty awareness and use of our services. Previously, we offered workshops, events, and funding on topics we selected. In recent years, our focus has shifted more to outreach and assessment of faculty and academic unit needs and interests. Among our most successful efforts are:

- **Unit liaisons**. Each of our 158 single- and multilocation academic units has its own instructional consultant, which provides a personal touch in this very large system. Unit Liaisons learn about the faculty and the curriculum, communicate regularly with unit heads, and visit faculty meetings. These activities have resulted in increases in individual consultations, tailored workshops, website traffic, and participation in our university-wide teaching and learning events.
- **Faculty communities hub**. We co-designed and now manage an electronic space to facilitate communication and collaboration among geographically dispersed faculty. The hub has evolved to include discipline-based, interdisciplinary, curricular, research, co-curricular, and administrative communities.
- **Grants**. Three types of grants advance teaching, learning, and assessment. Our competitive grants fund individual, community, and multicampus projects; Regional Colloquy grants support multicampus teaching and assessment events; and special projects grants support broad-impact projects aligned with strategic priorities.

## ENGAGING FACULTY WHO PRIORITIZE RESEARCH OVER TEACHING

*Susanna Calkins, associate director, and Gregory Light, director, Searle Center for Teaching Excellence, Northwestern University (http://www.northwestern .edu/searle/)*

This challenge involves reaching faculty who (1) do not think of themselves as teachers; (2) rarely, if ever, engage with the center about teaching; and (3) often have a very poor understanding of teaching as the facilitation of deeper learning (i.e., they view teaching merely as the transmission of facts). Many of our programs and services address these three related issues. For example, in addition to offering an array of faculty development workshops, as well as a substantial yearlong faculty development program (the Searle Fellows program), we collaborate with faculty on educational research grants, with our interactions ranging from individual consultations to complete project evaluations. To further this effort, we created grant-writing and mentoring workshops to help faculty write the educational and mentoring components of their grants (e.g., NSF CAREER awards, NIH training grants for doctoral students). We also designed a set of undergraduate research workshops to provide undergraduates with a better understanding of what it means to do science research at a deep level. For more detailed descriptions of these programs, see Calkins and Drane (2010) and Streitwieser, Light, and Pazos (2010).

## Student Engagement: The Switch From a Teaching to a Learning Perspective

*Joan Middendorf, associate director, Center for Innovative Teaching and Learning, Indiana University (http://citl.gwu.edu)*

Faculty often mimic their own teachers, thinking about all the things they know and everything it would be "good" for their students to know. Disciplinary skills necessary to operate in their field are tacit and thus they do not model some of the most basic and essential thinking skills for their students (Diaz, Middendorf, Pace, & Shopkow, 2008).

We have found that three critical actions help faculty to make the switch to a student learning–based perspective:

1. Creating a community by engaging with faculty from other disciplines and outside their own department. Another instructor's problems are easier to understand than one's own.

2. Turning teaching problems into questions (Bass, 1999). Faculty members identify a learning bottleneck from their own classes, which motivates them in the same way as selecting their own research questions does. They all follow the same process with their own problems, uncovering their tacit thinking, modeling it for students, and providing students practice and feedback. The decoding-the-disciplines model (Pace & Middendorf, 2004) grew out of trial and error with faculty.

3. Assessing to cement faculty understanding of the new perspective. Professors assess performance on their bottleneck operation with their own students. Besides providing feedback to the faculty about how their students learned, these assessment results measure our program efficacy, not just satisfaction.

To our surprise, faculty from these decoding-the-disciplines learning communities have gone on to undertake SoTL studies, publish their work, and receive millions of dollars in grants to continue their efforts.

## SUPPORTING FACULTY MEMBERS WHO DO PUBLICLY ENGAGED TEACHING AND SCHOLARSHIP

*Jean C. Florman, director, Center for Teaching, University of Iowa (www.centeach.uiowa.edu)*

Our approach to this challenge was to provide intensive on-the-ground training as well as opportunities for faculty members to build institutional frameworks that genuinely value community engagement. Several years ago, 30 faculty members who sought to develop service-learning courses participated in an intensive Center for Teaching Service Learning Institute, a five-day training in the pedagogy conducted by Bentley College Professor of English Edward Zlotkowski. Almost 50 courses resulted, in addition to new and enriching ties between the university and the community.

In 2009 two faculty participants created and conducted another Center for Teaching–sponsored faculty institute, From Engaged Teaching → Engaged Scholarship. Among other outcomes, faculty participants were inspired to write a book chapter about collaboration to build a Martin Luther King Jr. park memorial, participate in Temple University's Inside-Out Prison Exchange Program, and create a museum exhibit to showcase the publicly engaged work of university scholars and teachers.

An alumnus of these faculty development institutes created The Crossroads Institute, which jump-started work by a dozen faculty members to incorporate volatile topics and deliberative dialogue into their courses. Several participants in these Center for Teaching institutes have now become administrative leaders who actively support community engagement. In addition, institute faculty members are deeply involved in the Provost's Task Force on Publicly Engaged Arts, Scholarship, and Research.

## Discipline-Specific Programming

At CRLT we have long recognized that our impact can be most profound when we focus on programs and services tailored to needs and signature pedagogies of a specific discipline. However, we also know that, as a central office, we must serve the whole campus. The authors in this section provide models for ways to offer discipline-based programming within the context of a comprehensive teaching center.

### ATTRACTING SCIENCE FACULTY

*Kathy Takayama, director, Harriet W. Sheridan Center for Teaching & Learning, Brown University (http://www.brown.edu/Administration/Sheridan_Center)*

Active, regular participation in Teaching and Learning Center events by science faculty can be a formidable challenge in research universities. Yet at Brown, our *Science Fridays* (*SciFri*) group has been meeting regularly for two years and has evolved into an engaged, interactive community. Junior and senior faculty from the STEM disciplines gather every second Friday at lunchtime to share and explore ideas about teaching.

A key factor in the success of SciFri is building trust and community among faculty, all of whom are time-poor and overcommitted but care deeply about teaching. SciFri is a forum for faculty to share their interests, ideas, and innovations, along with their challenges and frustrations about teaching science. The discussions are co-facilitated by an enthusiastic, highly respected geosciences professor (who is a Sheridan Faculty Fellow) and a Sheridan Center staff member (who has a STEM background). Resources and activities relevant to topics of interest (e.g., learning styles, visual literacy, and scientific literacy) are incorporated into SciFri gatherings. Senior faculty often invite and introduce new junior faculty to SciFri, a powerful affirmation for junior faculty by their senior colleagues of the importance and excitement of teaching. Faculty *want* to come, because they enjoy the conversations and the company. Through the shared values of this community, faculty have found a useful and engaging forum for intellectual debate and professional development.

### BEING BOTH COMPREHENSIVE AND DISCIPLINE-SPECIFIC

*Pratibha Varma-Nelson, executive director, Center for Teaching and Learning, Indiana University–Purdue University Indianapolis (http://ctl.iupui.edu)*

A typical challenge at a research university is for a teaching center that serves the whole campus to find ways of being relevant to faculty in specific disciplines. Our center handled this challenge by taking a more discipline-based approach to our work. We did this by

- creating a Guest Lecture series that honors nationally recognized scholars who have made a contribution to their discipline as well as teaching and learning within their discipline. The 2010 lecture was given by 2001 Nobel Prize Laureate in Physics, Carl Wieman (http://ctl.iupui.edu/winterseries/2010/);
- finding ways to form deeper partnerships with faculty by collaborating with them to write education proposals to NSF;
- broadening the background of center personnel beyond education by hiring a director with a chemistry background and a STEM (science, technology, engineering, and mathematics) education specialist;
- offering a new grant opportunity, called the Curriculum Enhancement Grant, and assigning a center staff member to each project to bring about more lasting changes (http://ctl.iupui.edu/Programs/CEG.asp);
- customizing programming for a department by partnering with faculty from the department to co-present and develop workshop descriptions, examples, and strategies; and
- deliberately including representatives from a variety of disciplines on the Center for Teaching and Learning Advisory Board.

## BALANCING CENTRALIZED AND DISCIPLINE-SPECIFIC FACULTY DEVELOPMENT SERVICES

*Mary-Ann Winkelmes, campus coordinator for programs on learning and teaching, University of Illinois at Urbana-Champaign (http://www.teachingandlearn ing.illinois.edu/)*

Disciplinary expertise on teaching, learning, and even faculty development topics has grown dramatically in recent years. To incorporate this rich, evolving new knowledge, any centralized faculty development office must embrace and partner with discipline-based experts. Ultimately, this might mean transferring some people and resources from the center to the peripheries where valuable, discipline-specific pedagogical work is happening. But a centralized presence is still needed to help coordinate and connect the important work on the peripheries, to identify shared interests, foster collaboration, and avoid wasteful redundancies. Finding and maintaining an effective balance between centralized and discipline-based faculty development efforts is challenging. Some centers resist partnering with discipline-based experts, seeing them as a threat or as a competitor for limited resources. Such centers slowly grow less relevant to their faculty constituents who teach in the disciplines.

At Illinois, we address this challenge by supporting the work of 14 college-based, discipline-specific, faculty-run Teaching Academies (http://www.teachingandlearning.illinois.edu/directory.html), helping them connect their efforts around topics of shared interest. Starting in the 2009–2010 year, the Office of the Provost and Vice Chancellor for Academic Affairs appointed a Faculty Fellow (http://www.teachingandlearning.illinois.edu/facultyfellows.html) to each college Teaching Academy, after soliciting nominations from the college deans. The Fellows work within their colleges to support the teaching efforts of their faculty colleagues. A small, centralized office supports collaboration across college Teaching Academies to explore teaching and learning topics across disciplines (http://www.teachingandlearning.illinois.edu/audioarchive.html) and to offer faculty development resources that are codified, archived, and shared.

## Programming to Address Specific Career Stages

Just as the needs and pedagogies of faculty differ across the disciplines, so, too, do the needs of instructors at various points in their careers. Authors in this section address programming for specific groups served by teaching centers, focusing especially on faculty who have achieved tenure and are looking for direction for the next stage in their careers, and on how to support doctoral students about to enter the academy.

### UNDERSTANDING AND SUPPORTING MID-CAREER FACULTY

*Deborah DeZure, assistant provost for faculty and organizational development, Office of Faculty and Organizational Development, Michigan State University (http://fod.msu.edu)*

A suggestion by our Advisory Board led us to "map the terrain of the mid-career experience" by conducting a qualitative study about the experiences, challenges, and needs of mid-career faculty at Michigan State University as perceived by faculty and chairs. This turned out to be an important source of data, since there had been relatively little research on this career stage.

We learned that many newly tenured mid-career faculty were unclear about the road ahead. They did not know the expectations and criteria for promotion to full professor, nor did they know the array of productive career options available to them. In response, we developed a seminar entitled "Orientation to the Mid-Career Experience: From Associate Professor to Professor—Productive Decision-Making at Mid-Career." We also learned that mid-career faculty carry the lion's share of managerial and leadership responsibilities in departments without access to leadership development (offered solely to academic administrators). In response, we initiated a workshop series for faculty, entitled "Workshops for Faculty Leaders," to support the skills required in their informal leadership roles— for example, running effective meetings, and conflict management.

Beyond our campus, there has been great interest in our study of mid-career faculty, which won the POD 2007 Robert Menges Award for Outstanding Research in Faculty Development and appeared in *Change* (Baldwin, DeZure, Shaw, & Moretto, 2008). The orientation for mid-career faculty won the 2009 POD Innovation Award, and "Workshops for Faculty Leaders" was a finalist for a 2010 POD Innovation Award.

## PROVIDING OPPORTUNITIES FOR DOCTORAL STUDENTS TO TEACH IN WAYS THAT FOSTER LEARNING

*Lori Breslow, director, Teaching and Learning Laboratory, Massachusetts Institute of Technology (http://web.mit.edu/tll)*
The particular challenge we faced was to develop a program that was rigorous enough to provide doctoral students with a sound grounding in teaching and learning while taking into account the pressure they are under to complete their research. Our center handled this challenge by creating the Graduate Student Teaching Certificate Program.

The program consists of seven two-hour workshops, and topics include using research into learning to inform teaching, designing a course and creating a syllabus, constructing effective assignments and exams, using interactive pedagogies, planning and presenting a lecture, teaching in a multicultural classroom, and articulating a teaching philosophy statement. Each two-hour workshop requires students to do pre-reading and complete an assignment. For example, for the foundational workshop on learning, students read articles on constructivism, cognitive psychology, and retention and transfer. They are asked to create a worksheet in which they first summarize findings from that research, and then describe how they might implement or have implemented those findings in a practical way in the classroom. The reading and assignment take approximately two hours to complete, which was feasible for the students and would provide the rigor we were looking for. In addition, the students must participate in a microteaching workshop.

To make the program as flexible as possible, we allow students to start with any workshop during the year. (However, we strongly urge them to begin with the workshop on learning, which we offer at the beginning of the fall and spring semesters.) They have two years to complete the program, although we find that almost three-quarters finish within one academic year. This is the third year we have offered the program, and to date, 60 students have attained a certificate, and an additional 200 are in the pipeline.

### Creating Meaningful Teaching Opportunities for PhD Students

*William C. Rando, assistant dean and director, Graduate Teaching Center, Graduate School of Arts and Sciences, Yale University (http://www.yale.edu/ graduateschool/teaching/index.html)*

Our center handled this challenge by helping to develop and organize the Associates in Teaching (AT) Program. Working with the dean and associate deans of the Graduate School of Arts and Sciences, we created a new role for graduate teachers, the Associate in Teaching. In this role, a graduate student collaborates with a faculty partner to design and co-teach an undergraduate course.

The program has multiple benefits for graduate students, faculty members, and undergraduates. Graduate students get an unprecedented opportunity to design and deliver a new course or a much-updated version of an existing course. They also co-teach with an experienced member of the Yale faculty, which provides many opportunities for mentoring, modeling, and reflecting on teaching. Faculty members benefit from approaching existing courses in entirely new ways, and the co-teaching generates opportunities for feedback and reflection. Undergraduates revel in the rich interplay between the co-teachers and the dynamic environment that results from two minds leading the class. The center consults with each of the teams and sponsors conversations among them.

## Conclusion

The common thread running through these narratives is the creativity and adaptability needed to make a teaching center flourish at a research university. This might mean finding ways to be responsive to institutional priorities that seem to stretch our resources and expertise. Or we may need to find ways to tailor our programs to specific audiences whose needs are particularly acute at a given moment. Refusing to take on these challenges is not an option: many centers have spent years trying to move "from the basement office to the front office" (Chism, 1998) and have succeeded precisely because of their responsiveness to campus needs, their ability to seize the opportunities that present themselves. Moreover, educational development is a field defined by promoting and responding to change. It is that very challenge that drew many of us to this profession and keeps us so engaged with our work. Given the track record of teaching centers, as the examples in this volume demonstrate, demand for our expertise will certainly increase as our institutions seek to meet the challenges of the 21st century.

Abbott, R. D., Wulff, D. H., Nyquist, J. D., Ropp, V. A., & Hess, C. W. (1990). Satisfaction with processes of collecting student opinions of instruction: The student perspective. *Journal of Educational Psychology, 82*(2), 201–206.

Adams, M., Bell, L., & Griffin, P. (Eds.). (2007). *Teaching for diversity and social justice.* New York: Routledge.

Agee, A. S., Yang, C., & the 2009 EDUCAUSE Current Issues Committee. (2009, July/August). Top-ten IT issues, 2009. *EDUCAUSE Review, 44*(4), 44–59.

Albright, M. J. (1988). Cooperation among campus agencies involved in instructional improvement. In E. C. Wadsworth (Ed.), *A handbook for new practitioners* (pp. 3–8). Stillwater, OK: New Forums Press.

Allison, D. H., DeBlois, P. B., & the 2008 EDUCAUSE Current Issues Committee. (2008, May/June). Top-ten IT issues, 2008. *EDUCAUSE Review, 43*(3), 36–61.

Angelo, T. A. (1995). Reassessing (and defining) assessment. *AAHE Bulletin, 48*(3), 7–9.

Angelo, T. A., & Cross, K. P. (1993). *Classroom assessment techniques: A handbook for college teachers* (2nd ed.). San Francisco: Jossey-Bass.

Anselmi, K. (2004). Modular experiential learning for business-to-business marketing courses. *Journal of Education for Business, 79*(3), 169–175.

Armstrong, F., & Moore, M. (2004). Action research: Developing inclusive practice and transforming cultures. In F. Armstrong & M. Moore (Eds.), *Action research for inclusive education: Changing places, changing practice, changing minds* (pp. 1–16). London: RoutledgeFalmer.

Armstrong, P., Felten, P., Johnston, J., & Pingree, A. (2006). Practicing what we preach: Transforming the TA orientation. In S. Chadwick-Blossey & D. R. Robertson (Eds.), *To improve the academy: Resources for faculty, instructional, and organizational development, Vol. 24* (pp. 231–246). Bolton, MA: Anker.

Aronson, J., Fried, C., & Good, C. (2002). Reducing the effects of stereotype threat on African American college students by shaping theories of intelligence. *Journal of Experimental Social Psychology, 38*(2), 113–125. doi:10.1006/jesp.2001.1491

Association of American Colleges. (1985). *Integrity in the college curriculum: A report to the academic community.* Washington, DC: Author.

Association of American Colleges and Universities (AAC&U). (2010). *Preparing future faculty.* Retrieved from http://www.aacu.org/pff/index.cfm

Astin, A. W., & Astin, H. S. (1993). *Undergraduate science education: The impact of different college environments on the educational pipeline in the sciences.* Los Angeles: Higher Education Research Institute, University of California.

Austin, A. E. (2002). Preparing the next generation of faculty: Graduate school as socialization to the academic career. *The Journal of Higher Education*, *73*(1), 94–122.

Austin, A. E. (2010). Supporting faculty members across their careers. In K. J. Gillespie, D. L. Robertson, & Associates (Eds.), *A guide to faculty development* (2nd ed., pp. 363–378). San Francisco: Jossey-Bass.

Austin, A. E., Connolly, M. R., & Colbeck, C. L. (2008, Spring). Strategies for preparing integrated faculty: The Center for the Integration of Research, Teaching, and Learning. In K. O'Meara, C. L. Colbeck, & A. E. Austin (Eds.), *Educating integrated professionals: Theory and practice on preparation for the professoriate* (pp. 69–81). New Directions for Teaching and Learning, No. 113. San Francisco: Jossey-Bass. doi:10.1002/tl.309

Baldwin, R., DeZure, D., Shaw, A., & Moretto, K. (2008, September/October). Mapping the terrain of mid-career faculty at a research university: Implications for faculty and academic leaders. *Change: The Magazine of Higher Learning*, *40*(5), 46–55. Retrieved from http://www.changemag.org/Archives/Back%20Issues/September-October%202008/abstract-mapping-the-terrain.html. doi:10.3200/CHNG.40.5.46-55

Banta, T. W. (1997, Winter). Moving assessment forward: Enabling conditions and stumbling blocks. In P. J. Gray & T. W. Banta (Eds.), *The campus-level impact of assessment: Progress, problems and possibilities* (pp. 79–91). New Directions for Higher Education, No. 100. San Francisco: Jossey-Bass. doi:10.1002/he.10007

Banta, T. W. (2007). Can assessment for accountability complement assessment for improvement? *Peer Review*, *9*(2), 9–12.

Banta, T. W., Lund, J. P., Black, K. E., & Oblander, F. W. (1996). *Assessment in practice: Putting principles to work on college campuses*. San Francisco: Jossey-Bass.

Barkley, E. F., Cross, K. P., & Major, C. H. (2005). *Collaborative learning techniques: A handbook for college faculty*. San Francisco, CA: Jossey-Bass.

Baron, L. (2006). The advantages of a reciprocal relationship between faculty development and organizational development in higher education. In S. Chadwick-Blossey & D. R. Robertson (Eds.), *To improve the academy: Resources for faculty, instructional, and organizational development, Vol. 24* (pp. 29–43). Bolton, MA: Anker.

Bartlett, T. (2002, March 22). The unkindest cut. *The Chronicle of Higher Education*. Retrieved from http://chronicle.com/article/The-Unkindest-Cut/21885/

Bass, R. (1999). The scholarship of teaching and learning: What's the problem? *Inventio: Creative Thinking About Learning and Teaching*, *1*(1).

Bean, J. C. (2001). *Engaging ideas: The professor's guide to integrating writing, critical thinking, and active learning in the classroom*. San Francisco: Jossey-Bass.

Bellows, L., & Weissinger, E. (2005). Assessing the academic and professional development needs of graduate students. In S. Chadwick-Blossey & D. R. Robertson (Eds.), *To improve the academy: Resources for faculty, instructional, and organizational development, Vol. 23* (pp. 267–283). Bolton, MA: Anker.

Benbassat, J., & Baumal, R. (2002). A step-wise role playing approach for teaching patient counseling skills to medical students. *Patient Education and Counseling, 46*(2), 147–152.

Bennett, W. J. (1984). *To reclaim a legacy: A report on the humanities in higher education.* Washington, DC: National Endowment for the Humanities.

Bensimon, E. M. (2005, Fall). Closing the achievement gap in higher education: An organizational learning perspective. In A. Kezar (Ed.), *Organizational learning in higher education* (pp. 99–111). New Directions for Higher Education, No. 131. San Francisco: Jossey-Bass. doi:10.1002/he.190

Benson, L., & Harkavy, I. (1996). Communal participatory action research as a strategy for improving universities and the social sciences: Penn's work with the West Philadelphia Improvement Corps as a case study. *Educational Policy, 10*(2), 202–222.

Berg, J. M., Dutton, J. E., & Wrzesniewski, A. (2008). *What is job crafting and why does it matter? Theory-to-Practice Briefing.* Retrieved from http://www.bus.um ich.edu/Positive/POS-Teaching-and-Learning/TheorytoPractice.htm

Berge, Z. L. (1998). Barriers to online teaching in post-secondary institutions: Can policy changes fix it? *Online Journal of Distance Learning Administration, 1*(2). Retrieved from http://www.westga.edu/~distance/Berge12.html

Bishop, R. (1994). Initiating empowering research. *New Zealand Journal of Educational Studies, 29*(1), 175–188.

Black, B. (1998). Using the SGID method for a variety of purposes. In M. Kaplan & D. Lieberman (Eds.), *To improve the academy: Resources for faculty, instructional, and organizational development, Vol. 17* (pp. 245–262). Stillwater, OK: New Forums Press.

Blackburn, R. T., & Lawrence, J. H. (1995). *Faculty at work: Motivation, expectation, satisfaction.* Baltimore, MD: Johns Hopkins University Press.

Blumberg, P. (2010). Strategic committee involvement: A guide for faculty developers. In L. B. Nilson & J. E. Miller (Eds.), *To improve the academy: Resources for faculty, instructional, and organizational development, Vol. 28* (pp. 63–81). San Francisco: Jossey-Bass.

Boal, A. (1979). *Theatre of the oppressed.* New York: Urizen Books, 1979. Republished by Routledge Press in New York/London in 1982.

Boal, A. (1992). *Games for actors and non-actors.* New York: Routledge Press.

Boal, A. (1995). *The rainbow of desire.* New York: Routledge Press.

Boice, R. (1991a). New faculty as teachers. *The Journal of Higher Education, 62*(2), 150–173.

Boice, R. (1991b, Winter). Quick starters: New faculty who succeed. In M. Theall & J. Franklin (Eds.), *Effective practices for improving teaching* (pp. 111–121). New Directions for Teaching and Learning, No. 48. San Francisco: Jossey-Bass. doi:10.1002/tl.37219914810

Boice, R. (2000). *Advice for new faculty members: Nihil Nimus.* Needham Heights, MA: Allyn & Bacon.

Bok, D. (2006). *Our underachieving colleges: A candid look at how much students learn and why they should be learning more.* Princeton, NJ: Princeton University Press.

Border, L., & von Hoene, L. (2010). Graduate and professional student development programs. In K. J. Gillespie, D. L. Robertson, & Associates (Eds.), *A guide to faculty development* (2nd ed., pp. 327–345). San Francisco: Jossey-Bass.

Bothell, T. W., & Henderson, T. (2004). Evaluating the return on investment of faculty development. In C. Wehlburg & S. Chadwick-Blossey (Eds.), *To improve the academy: Resources for faculty, instructional, and organizational development, Vol. 22* (pp. 52–70). Bolton, MA: Anker.

Brandsford, J., Brown, A., & Cocking, R. (Eds.). (2000). *How people learn: Brain, mind, experience and school.* Washington, DC: National Academy Press.

Brinko, K. T. (1997). The interactions of teaching improvement. In K. T. Brinko & R. J. Menges (Eds.), *Practically speaking: A sourcebook for instructional consultants in higher education* (pp. 3–8). Stillwater, OK: New Forums Press.

Brinko, K. T., & Menges, R. J. (Eds.). (1997). *Practically speaking: A sourcebook for instructional consultants in higher education.* Stillwater, OK: New Forums Press.

Brookfield, S. (1996). Through the lens of learning: How experiencing difficult learning challenges and changes assumptions about teaching. In L. Richlin & D. DeZure (Eds.), *To improve the academy: Resources for faculty, instructional, and organizational development, Vol. 15* (pp. 3–15). Stillwater, OK: New Forums Press.

Calkins, S., & Drane, D. (2010). Engaging faculty in conversations about teaching through a research proposal workshop. In L. B. Nilson & J. E. Miller (Eds.), *To improve the academy: Resources for faculty, instructional, and organizational development, Vol. 28* (pp. 265–277). San Francisco: Jossey-Bass.

Callan, P. M., Jones, D., Ewell, P. T., & Breneman, D. W. (2008). *Measuring up 2008: The national report card on higher education.* San Jose, CA: The National Center for Public Policy and Higher Education.

Cameron, K. (2008). *Positive leadership: Strategies for extraordinary performance.* San Francisco: Berrett-Koehler.

Camp, J. S., DeBlois, P. B., & the 2007 EDUCAUSE Current Issues Committee (2007, May/June). Top-ten IT issues, 2007. *EDUCAUSE Review, 42*(3), 12–31.

Campbell, P. B., Jolly, E., Hoey, L., & Perlman, L. K. (2002). *Upping the numbers: Using research-based decision making to increase diversity in the quantitative disciplines.* Newton, MA: Educational Development Center.

Celsi, R. L., & Wolfinbarger, M. (2002). Discontinuous classroom innovation: Waves of change for marketing education. *Journal of Marketing Education, 24*(1), 64–72. doi:10.1177/0273475302241008

Center for Research on Learning and Teaching, University of Michigan. (2007). [Qwizdom Student Survey]. Unpublished data.

Center for Research on Learning and Teaching, University of Michigan. (2009). [IT Needs Assessment Survey]. Unpublished data.

Centra, J. A. (1976, November). *Faculty development practices in U.S. colleges and universities.* Princeton, NJ: Educational Testing Service.

Chesler, M. A. (1990). Action research in the voluntary sector: A case study of scholar-activist roles in health care settings. In S. A. Wheelan, E. A. Pepitone, & V. Abt (Eds.), *Advances in field theory* (pp. 265–280). Newbury Park, CA: Sage.

Chesler, N. C., & Chesler, M. A. (2005). Theater as a community-building strategy for women in engineering: Theory and practice. *Journal of Women and Minorities in Science and Engineering, 11*(1), 1–13.

Chickering, A., & Gamson, Z. (1987). Seven principles for good practice in undergraduate education. *AAHE Bulletin, 39*(8), 3–7.

Chism, N. V. N. (1998). The role of educational developers in institutional change: From the basement office to the front office. In M. Kaplan & D. Lieberman (Eds.), *To improve the academy: Resources for faculty, instructional, and organizational development, Vol. 17* (pp. 141–153). Stillwater, OK: New Forums Press.

Chism, N. V. N. (2005). Promoting a sound process for teaching awards programs: Appropriate work for faculty development centers. In S. Chadwick-Blossey & D. R. Robertson (Eds.), *To improve the academy: Resources for faculty, instructional, and organizational development, Vol. 23* (pp. 314–330). Bolton, MA: Anker.

Chism, N. V. N., & Szabó, B. (1996). Who uses faculty development services? In L. Richlin & D. DeZure (Eds.), *To improve the academy: Resources for faculty, instructional, and organizational development, Vol. 15* (pp. 115–128). Stillwater, OK: New Forums Press.

Chism, N. V. N., & Szabó, B. (1997). Teaching awards: The problem of assessing their impact. In D. DeZure & M. Kaplan (Eds.), *To improve the academy: Resources for faculty, instructional, and organizational development, Vol. 16* (pp. 181–200). Stillwater, OK: New Forums Press.

Cohen, M. D., March, J. G., & Olsen, J. P. (1972). A garbage can model of organizational choice. *Administrative Science Quarterly, 17*(1), 1–25.

Cohen, P. (1980). Effectiveness of student-rating feedback for improving college instruction: A meta-analysis of findings. *Research in Higher Education, 13*(4), 321–341.

Cole, J. (2006, January). *Blogs and wikis: What do they add to research and publishing?* Presentation given at the Center for Research on Learning and Teaching, University of Michigan.

Connolly, M. R., & Millar, S. B. (2006). Using workshops to improve instruction in STEM courses. *Metropolitan Universities Journal, 17*(4), 53–65.

Cook, C. E. (1980). *Nuclear power and legal advocacy: The environmentalists and the courts.* Lexington, MA: Lexington Books.

Cook, C. E. (1998). *Lobbying for higher education: How colleges and universities influence federal policy.* Nashville, TN: Vanderbilt University Press.

Cook, C. E. (2001). The role of a teaching center in curricular reform. In D. Lieberman & C. Wehlburg (Eds.), *To improve the academy: Resources for faculty, instructional, and organizational development, Vol. 19* (pp. 217–231). Bolton, MA: Anker.

Cook, C. E. (2004). Developing infrastructure. In B. Cambridge (Ed.), *Campus progress: Supporting the scholarship of teaching and learning* (pp. 11–19). Washington, DC: American Association for Higher Education.

Cook, C. E. (2008, May/June). Study abroad for Chinese university presidents: How China is reforming higher education. *Change: The Magazine of Higher Learning, 40*(3), 32–39. doi:10.3200/CHNG.40.3.32-39

Cook, C. E., Gerson, J., Godfrey, J., Kerner, N., Larsen-Freeman, D., Mullane, E., . . . Smaill, A. (2002). *Report of the task force on testing and training prospective graduate student instructors.* Ann Arbor, MI: University of Michigan.

Cook, C. E., Kaplan, M., Nidiffer, J., & Wright, M. (2001, November). Preparing future faculty—faster. *AAHE Bulletin, 34*(3), 3–7.

Cook, C. E., & Marincovich, M. (2010). Effective practices at research universities: The productive pairing of research and teaching. In K. J. Gillespie, D. L. Robertson, & Associates (Eds.), *A guide to faculty development* (2nd ed., pp. 277–292). San Francisco: Jossey-Bass.

Cook, C. E., & Sorcinelli, M. D. (2005). Building multiculturalism into teaching development programs. In M. Ouellett (Ed.), *Teaching inclusively: Resources for course, department and institutional change in higher education* (pp. 74–83). Stillwater, OK: New Forums Press.

Cook, C. E., Wright, M., & O'Neal, C. (2007). Action research for instructional improvement: Using data to enhance student learning at your institution. In D. R. Robertson & L. B. Nilson (Eds.), *To improve the academy: Resources for faculty, instructional, and organizational development, Vol. 25* (pp. 123–138). Bolton, MA: Anker.

Cox, A. (2008). *Women of color faculty at the University of Michigan: Recruitment, retention, and campus climate.* Ann Arbor, MI: University of Michigan Center for the Education of Women.

Cross, K. P., & Steadman, M. H. (1996). *Classroom research: Implementing the scholarship of teaching.* San Francisco: Jossey-Bass.

Dalkey, N. C., & Helmer, O. (1963). An experimental application of the Delphi method to the use of experts. *Management Science, 9*(3), 458–467.

D'Eon, M., Sadownik, L., Harrison, A., & Nation, J. (2008). Using self-assessments to detect workshop success: Do they work? *American Journal of Evaluation, 29*(1), 92–98. doi:10.1177/1098214007312630

Dewey, B. I., DeBlois, P. B., & the 2006 EDUCAUSE Current Issues Committee (2006, May/June). Top-ten IT issues, 2006. *EDUCAUSE Review, 41*(3), 58–79.

deWinstanley, P. A., & Bjork, R. A. (2002, Spring). Successful lecturing: Presenting information in ways that engage effective processing. In D. F. Halpern & M. D. Hakel (Eds.), *Applying the science of learning to university teaching and beyond* (pp. 19–31). New Directions for Teaching and Learning, No. 89. San Francisco: Jossey-Bass. doi:10.1002/tl.44

DeZure, D., Kaplan, M., & Deerman, A. (2001). *Research on student notetaking: Implications for faculty and graduate student instructors.* CRLT Occasional Paper

No. 16. Ann Arbor, MI: Center for Research on Learning and Teaching, University of Michigan.

Diamond, M. R. (2004). The usefulness of structured mid-term feedback as a catalyst for change in higher education classes. *Active Learning in Higher Education*, *5*(3), 217–231.

Diamond, R. M. (1989). *Designing and improving courses and curricula in higher education: A systematic approach*. San Francisco: Jossey-Bass.

Diamond, R. M. (1998). *Designing and assessing courses and curricula: A practical guide* (2nd. ed.). San Francisco: Jossey-Bass.

Diamond, R. M. (2005). The institutional change agency: The expanding role of academic support centers. In S. Chadwick-Blossey & D. R. Robertson (Eds.), *To improve the academy: Resources for faculty, instructional, and organizational development, Vol. 23* (pp. 24–37). Bolton, MA: Anker.

Diaz, A., Middendorf, J., Pace, D., & Shopkow, L. (2008). The History Learning Project: A department decodes its students. *Journal of American History*, *94*(4), 1211–1224.

Dotson, W. H., & Bernstein, D. J. (2010). A model for putting a teaching center in context: An informal comparison of teaching centers at larger state universities. In L. B. Nilson & J. E. Miller (Eds.), *To improve the academy: Resources for faculty, instructional, and organizational development, Vol. 28* (pp. 82–97). San Francisco: Jossey-Bass.

Dweck, C. S. (2002). Messages that motivate: How praise molds students' beliefs, motivation and performance (in surprising ways). In J. Aronson (Ed.), *Improving academic achievement: Impact of psychological factors on education* (pp. 37–60). New York: Academic Press.

Eble, K. E., & McKeachie, W. J. (1985). *Improving undergraduate education through faculty development*. San Francisco: Jossey-Bass.

Elden, M. (1981). Sharing the research work: Participative research and its role demands. In P. Reason & J. Rowan (Eds.), *Human inquiry: A sourcebook of new paradigm research* (pp. 261–266). Chichester, UK: John Wiley & Sons.

Erb, S. (2003). A taste of Chautauqua: Historical investigation and oral presentation. *Journal of Adolescent and Adult Literacy*, *47*(2), 168–175.

Fendrich, L. (2007, June 8). A pedagogical straitjacket. *The Chronicle of Higher Education*, p. B6.

Ferren, A., & Mussell, K. (1987). Strengthening faculty development programs through evaluation. In J. Kurfiss (Ed.), *To improve the academy: Resources for faculty, instructional, and organizational development, Vol. 6* (pp. 133–143). Stillwater, OK: New Forums Press.

Finelli, C. J., Ott, M., Gottfried, A. C., Hershock, C., O'Neal, C., & Kaplan, M. (2008). Utilizing instructional consultations to enhance the teaching performance of engineering faculty. *Journal of Engineering Education*, *97*(4), 397–411.

Finelli, C. J., Wright, M. C., & Pinder-Grover, T. (2010). Consulting the Delphi: A new idea for collecting student feedback through the Two Survey Method. *Journal of Faculty Development, 24*(2), 25–33.

Fishman, B. (2009, October 8). *Big class, small feel: Uncommon teaching using commonplace technologies.* Presentation for the Center for Research on Learning and Teaching.

Frantz, A. C., Beebe, S. A., Horvath, V. S., Canales, J., & Swee, D. E. (2005). The roles of teaching and learning centers. In S. Chadwick-Blossey & D. R. Robertson (Eds.), *To improve the academy: Resources for faculty, instructional, and organizational development, Vol. 23* (pp. 72–90). Bolton, MA: Anker.

Gaff, J. (1983). *General education today: A critical analysis of controversies, practices, and reforms.* San Francisco: Jossey-Bass.

Galura, J., Pasque, P., Schoem, D., & Howard, J. (2004). *Engaging the whole of service learning, diversity, and learning communities.* Ann Arbor, MI: Ginsberg Center for Community Service, University of Michigan.

Gardiner, L. F. (1992). *Designing a college curriculum: Overview, planning aids, and selected resources.* Professional Resource No. 4 (copyright by Gardiner).

Gardner, S. K. (2007). "I heard it through the grapevine": Doctoral student socialization in chemistry and history. *Higher Education, 54*(5), 723–740. doi:10.1007/s10734-006-9020-x

Geltner, B. B. (1993, October). *Collaborative action research: A critical component in the preparation of effective leaders and learners.* Paper presented at the annual meeting of the University Council for Educational Administration, Houston, TX.

Gillespie, K. (2001, October). *Marketplace reality and our dreams of the profession.* Paper presented at the annual meeting of the Professional and Organizational Development Network in Higher Education (POD), Atlanta, GA.

Gillespie, K. J. (2010). Organizational development. In K. J. Gillespie, D. L. Robertson, & Associates (Eds.), *A guide to faculty development* (2nd ed., pp. 379–396). San Francisco: Jossey-Bass.

Gillespie, K. J., Robertson, D. L., & Associates (Eds.). (2010). *A guide to faculty development* (2nd ed.). San Francisco: Jossey-Bass.

Glenn, D. (2009, August 18). Wary of budget knife, teaching centers seek to sharpen their role. *The Chronicle of Higher Education.* Retrieved from http://jobs.chronicle.com/article/Wary-of-Budget-Knife-Teaching/48049/

Glenn, D. (2010, February 5). College teaching needs to get better now, educators warn. *The Chronicle of Higher Education,* p. A12.

Gouldner, A. W. (1957). Cosmopolitans and locals: Toward an analysis of latent social roles. *Administrative Science Quarterly, 29*(3), 281–306.

Greenwood, D. J., & Levin, M. (1998). *Introduction to action research: Social research for social change.* Thousand Oaks, CA: Sage.

Groscurth, C., Hershock, C., & Zhu, E. (2009, October). *Assessing teaching assistants' instructional technology training needs: Research and practice.* Workshop presented at the annual meeting of the Professional and Organizational Development Network in Higher Education (POD), Houston, TX.

Gurin, P., Dey, E., Hurtado, S., & Gurin, G. (2002). Diversity and higher education: Theory and impact on educational outcomes. *Harvard Educational Review, 72*(3), 330–366.

Hacker, A., & Dreifus, C. (2010). *Higher education? How colleges are wasting our money and failing our kids—and what we can do about it.* New York: Times Books.

Hagner, P. R., & Schneebeck, C. A. (2001). Engaging the faculty. In C. A. Barone & P. R. Hagner (Eds.), *Technology-mediated teaching and learning* (pp. 1–12). San Francisco: Jossey-Bass.

Hake, R. R. (1998). Interactive-engagement versus traditional methods: A six-thousand-student survey of mechanics test data for introductory physics courses. *American Association of Physics Teachers, 66*(1), 64–74.

Halaby, C. N. (2005, October). *Two assessment studies of the general education quantitative reasoning "A" requirement at the University of Wisconsin–Madison.* Report to the General Education Assessment Council Subcommittee on the Effectiveness of the Quantitative Reasoning "A" Requirement. Madison, Wisconsin: University of Wisconsin–Madison. Retrieved from http://www.ls.wisc.edu/gened/Reports/commA_surveyreport.pdf

Halperin, D. (2002). The play's the thing: How social group work and theatre transformed a group into a community. *Social Work With Groups, 24*(2), 27–46. doi:10.1300/J009v24n02_03

Halstead, D. K. (1974). *Statewide planning in higher education.* Washington, DC: U.S. GPO.

Hartshorne, R., & Ajjan, H. (2009). Examining student decisions to adopt Web 2.0 technologies: Theory and empirical tests. *Journal of Computing in Higher Education, 21*(3), 183–198. doi:10.1007/s12528-009-9023-6

Hativa, N., & Marincovich, M. (Eds.). (1995, Winter). *Disciplinary differences in teaching and learning: Implications for practice.* New Directions for Teaching and Learning, No. 64. San Francisco: Jossey-Bass.

Hersh, R. H. (2007). Going naked. *Peer Review, 9*(2), 4–8.

Heru, A. M. (2003). Using role playing to increase residents' awareness of medical student mistreatment. *Academic Medicine, 78*(1), 35–38.

Hines, S. R. (2010). *An investigation of program assessment practices at established centralized TLCs: The findings report.* Unpublished manuscript, Saint Mary's University of Minnesota.

Holland, P. E. (2001). Professional development in technology: Catalyst for school reform. *Journal of Technology and Teacher Education, 9*(2), 245–268.

Holstrom, E. I., Gaddy, C. D., Van Horne, V. V., & Zimmerman, C. M. (1997). *Best and brightest: Education and career paths of top science and engineering students.* New York: Commission on Professionals in Science and Technology.

Horii, C. V. (2010). Transforming Teaching Cultures: Departmental Teaching Fellows as Agents of Change. In L. Nilson & J. Miller (Eds.), *To improve the academy: Resources for faculty, instructional, and organizational development, Vol. 28* (pp. 359–378). San Francisco: Jossey-Bass.

Howard, J. (2001, Summer). *Service-learning course design workbook* [Companion volume]. Michigan Journal of Community Service Learning. Ann Arbor, MI: Ginsberg Center for Community Service, University of Michigan.

Howland, J., & Wedman, J. A. (2004). Process model for faculty development: Individualizing technology learning. *Journal of Technology and Teacher Education, 12*(2), 239–262.

Hunt, N. (2003). Does mid-semester feedback make a difference? *The Journal of Scholarship of Teaching and Learning, 3*(2), 13–20.

Huntzinger, M., McPherron, P., & Rajagopal, M. (2011). The TA consultant program: Improving undergraduate instruction and graduate student professional development. In J. E. Miller & J. E. Groccia (Eds.), *To improve the academy: Resources for faculty, instructional, and organizational development, Vol. 29* (pp. 246–259). San Francisco: Jossey-Bass.

Hussey, T., & Smith, P. (2009). *The trouble with higher education: A critical examination of our universities.* New York: Routledge.

Hutchings, P. (2006). A tug toward the center: Pat Hutchings at POD on the scholarship of teaching and learning. *The National Teaching and Learning Forum, 16*(1), 5–7.

Hutchings, P. (2010). *Opening doors to faculty involvement in assessment.* Retrieved from http://www.learningoutcomeassessment.org/occasionalpaperfour.htm

Ingerman, B. L., Yang, C., & the 2010 EDUCAUSE Current Issues Committee. (2010, May/June). Top-ten IT issues, 2010. *EDUCAUSE Review, 45*(3), 46–60.

Israel, B. A., Schurman, S. J., & Hugentobler, M. K. (1992). Consulting action research: Relationships between organization members and researchers. *Journal of Applied Behavioral Science, 28*(1), 74–101.

Jackson, B. (2005). The theory and practice of multicultural organization development in education. In M. Ouellett (Ed.), *Teaching inclusively: Resources for course, department and institutional change in higher education* (pp. 3–20). Stillwater, OK: New Forums Press.

Jacobson, W., Wulff, D. H., Grooters, S., Edwards, P. M., & Freisem, K. (2009). Reported long-term value and effects of teaching center consultations. In L. B. Nilson & J. E. Miller (Eds.), *To improve the academy: Resources for faculty, instructional, and organizational development, Vol. 27* (pp. 223–246). San Francisco: Jossey-Bass.

Johnson, W. B., & Huwe, J. M. (2003). *Getting mentored in graduate school.* Washington, DC: American Psychological Association.

Jones, C. (2001). Sociodrama: A teaching method for expanding the understanding of clinical issues. *Journal of Palliative Medicine*, 4(3), 386–390.

Kalish, A., Armstrong, P., Border, L. L. B., Chandler, E. O., Horii, C. V., Maurer, V., . . . & von Hoene, L. (2009, October). *Structured professional development for graduate and professional students: A taxonomy.* Workshop presented at the annual meeting of the Professional and Organizational Development Network in Higher Education (POD), Houston, TX.

Kaplan, M., Cook, C. E., & Steiger, J. (2006, May/June). Using theatre to stage instructional and organizational transformation. *Change: The Magazine of Higher Learning*, 38(3), 32–39. doi:10.3200/CHNG.38.3.32-39

Kaplan, M., & Miller, A. T. (Eds.). (2007). *The scholarship of multicultural teaching and learning.* New Directions for Teaching and Learning, No. 111. San Francisco: Jossey-Bass.

Kardia, D. B., & Wright, M. C. (2004). *Instructor identity: The impact of gender and race on faculty experiences with teaching.* CRLT Occasional Paper, No. 19. Ann Arbor, MI: Center for Research on Learning and Teaching, University of Michigan.

Keller, G. (1983). *Academic strategy: The management revolution in American higher education.* Baltimore, MD: Johns Hopkins University Press.

Kendall Brown, M., Hershock, C., Finelli, C. J., & O'Neal, C. (2009). *Teaching for retention in science, engineering, and math disciplines: A guide for faculty.* CRLT Occasional Paper, No. 25. Ann Arbor, MI: Center for Research on Learning and Teaching, University of Michigan.

King, P. M. (2000, Summer). Learning to make reflective judgments. In M. B. Baxter Magolda (Ed.), *Teaching to promote intellectual and personal maturity: Incorporating students' worldviews and identities into the learning process* (pp. 15–26). New Directions for Teaching and Learning, No. 82. San Francisco: Jossey-Bass. doi:10.1002/tl.8202

King, P. M., & Baxter Magolda, M. B. (2005). A developmental model of intercultural maturity. *Journal of College Student Development*, 46(6), 571–592.

King, P. M., & Kitchener, K. S. (1994). *Developing reflective judgment: Understanding and promoting intellectual growth and critical thinking in adolescents and adults.* San Francisco: Jossey-Bass.

Kodotchigova, M. A. (2001). Role play in teaching culture: Six quick steps for classroom implementation. *The Internet TESL Journal*, 8(7), 1–7. Retrieved from http://itcslj.org/Techniques/Kodotchigova-RolePlay.html

Krogh, L. (2001, March). *Action research as action learning as action research as action learning . . . at multiple levels in adult education.* Paper presented at the Fourth Annual Australian Vocational Education and Training Research Association Conference, Adelaide, Australia.

Kucsera, J. V., & Svinicki, M. (2010). Rigorous evaluations of faculty development programs. *The Journal of Faculty Development*, 24(2), 5–13.

Kuhlenschmidt, S. (2010). Issues in technology and faculty development. In K. J. Gillespie, D. L. Robertson, & Associates (Eds.), *A guide to faculty development* (2nd ed., pp. 259–274). San Francisco: Jossey-Bass.

Kuhlenschmidt, S. (2011). Distribution and penetration of teaching-learning development units in higher education: Implications for strategic planning and research. In J. Miller & J. Groccia (Eds.), *To improve the academy: Resources for faculty, instructional, and organizational development, Vol. 29* (pp. 274–287). San Francisco: Jossey-Bass.

Kuhlenschmidt, S., Weaver, S., & Morgan, S. (2010). A conceptual framework for the center: Going beyond setting priorities. In L. B. Nilson & J. E. Miller (Eds.), *To improve the academy: Resources for faculty, instructional, and organizational development, Vol. 28* (pp. 25–36). San Francisco: Jossey-Bass.

Kulik, J. A. (2009, March). *On-line teaching evaluations at the University of Michigan: A preliminary appraisal.* Unpublished report. Office of Evaluations and Examinations, University of Michigan, Ann Arbor.

Langley, D. (2008, July). *Success metrics at the Center for Teaching and Learning at the University of Minnesota.* Memo presented at CIC Teaching Center Directors' Meeting, Chicago, IL.

Lattuca, L. R., & Stark, J. S. (2009). *Shaping the college curriculum: Academic plans in context.* San Francisco: Jossey-Bass.

LaVaque-Manty, D., Steiger, J., & Stewart, A. J. (2007). Interactive theater. In A. J. Stewart, J. E. Malley, & D. LaVaque-Manty (Eds.), *Transforming science and engineering: Advancing academic women* (pp. 204–222). Ann Arbor, MI: The University of Michigan Press.

Lee, J. (2002). Racial and ethnic achievement gap trends: Reversing the progress toward equity? *Educational Researcher, 31*(1), 3–12.

Levin-Rozales, M. (2003). Evaluation and research: Differences and similarities. *The Canadian Journal of Teaching Evaluation, 18*(2), 1–31.

Lewin, K. (1997). *Resolving social conflicts.* Washington, DC: American Psychological Association. (Original work published 1948)

Lewis, K. G. (2010, Summer). Pathways toward improving teaching and learning in higher education: International context and background. In J. McDonald & D. Stockley (Eds.), *Pathways to the profession of educational development* (pp. 13–24). New Directions for Teaching and Learning, No. 122. San Francisco: Jossey-Bass. doi:10.1002/tl.394

Lewis, K. G., & Povlacs, J. T. (Eds.). (2001). *Face to face: A sourcebook of instructional consultation techniques for faculty/instructional developers.* Stillwater, OK: New Forums Press.

Liebowitz, J. (2003). Teach people skills totally online? *College Teaching, 51*(3), 82–85.

Light, G., Calkins, S., Luna, M., & Drane, D. (2008). Assessing the impact of faculty development programs on faculty approaches to teaching. *International Journal of Teaching and Learning in Higher Education, 20*(2), 168–181.

Lin, C., Singer, R., & Ha, L. (2010). Why university members use and resist technology? A structure enactment perspective. *Journal of Computing in Higher Education*, 22(1), 38–59. doi:10.1007/s12528-010-9028-1

Lonn, S., & Teasley, S. D. (2009). Saving time or innovating practice: Investigating perceptions and uses of Learning Management Systems. *Computers & Education*, 53(3), 686–694.

Lovitts, B. (2008). The transition to independent research: Who makes it, who doesn't, and why. *The Journal of Higher Education*, 79(3), 296–325.

Mann, B. D., Sachdeva, A. K., Nieman, L. Z., Nielan, B. A., Rovito, M. A., & Damsker, J. I. (1996). Teaching medical students by role playing: A model for integrating psychosocial issues with disease management. *Journal of Cancer Education*, 11(2), 65–72.

Marincovich, M. (1997). Training new consultants at Stanford: The TA consultants program. In K. T. Brinko & R. J. Menges (Eds.), *Practically speaking: A sourcebook for instructional consultants in higher education* (pp. 305–326). Stillwater, OK: New Forums Press.

Marincovich, M., Clerici-Arias, M., Denman, M., & Wright Dunbar, R. (2007). Developing effective consulting skills. In C. Ross, J. Dunphy, & Associates (Eds.), *Strategies for teaching assistant and international teaching assistant development: Beyond micro teaching* (pp. 62–67). San Francisco: Jossey-Bass.

Marincovich, M., & Gordon, H. (1991). A program of peer consultation: The consultants' experience. In J. Nyquist, R. Abbott, D. Wulff, & J. Sprague (Eds.), *Preparing the professoriate of tomorrow: Selected readings in TA training* (pp. 176–183). Dubuque, IA: Kendall/Hunt Publishing.

Marincovich, M., Prostko, J., & Stout, F. (Eds.). (1998). *The professional development of graduate teaching assistants.* Bolton, MA: Anker.

Massy, W., & Zemsky, R. (1995, June). *Using information technology to enhance academic productivity.* Retrieved from http://net.educause.edu/ir/library/html/nli0004.html

McDonald, J. (2010, Summer). Charting pathways into the field of educational development. In J. McDonald & D. Stockley (Eds.), *Pathways to the profession of educational development* (pp. 37–45). New Directions for Teaching and Learning, No. 122. San Francisco: Jossey-Bass. doi:10.1002/tl.396

McGregor, J. (1993). Effectiveness of role playing and antiracist teaching in reducing student prejudice. *Journal of Educational Research*, 86(4), 215–226.

Median salaries of college administrators by job category and type of institution, 2004–5. (2005, March 4). *The Chronicle of Higher Education*. Retrieved from http://chronicle.com/article/Median-Salaries-of-College/9238

Meizlish, D., & Kaplan, M. (2008). Valuing and evaluating teaching in academic hiring: A multidisciplinary, cross-institutional study. *The Journal of Higher Education*, 79(5), 489–512.

Meizlish, D., & Kaplan, M. (2010, November). *Preparing new professors for a research university's teaching mission.* Poster presented at the annual meeting of the Professional and Organizational Development Network in Higher Education (POD), St. Louis, MO.

Meizlish, D. S., Pinder-Grover, T. A., & Wright, M. C. (in press). Effective use of graduate peer teaching consultants: Recruitment, training, supervision, and evaluation. In K. Brinko (Ed.), *Practically speaking: A sourcebook for instructional consultants in higher education* (2nd ed.). Stillwater, OK: New Forums Press.

Meizlish, D. S., & Wright, M. C. (2009). Preparing advocates for faculty development: Expanding the meaning of "growing our own." In L. B. Nilson & J. E. Miller (Eds.), *To improve the academy: Resources for faculty, institutional, and organizational development, Vol. 27* (pp. 385–400). San Francisco: Jossey-Bass.

Menges, R. J., & Svinicki, M. (1989). Designing program evaluations: A circular model. In S. Kahn (Ed.), *To improve the academy: Resources for faculty, instructional, and organizational development, Vol. 8* (pp. 81–97). Stillwater, OK: New Forums Press and The Professional and Organizational Development Network in Higher Education (POD).

Merriam, S. B. (2009). *Qualitative research: A guide to design and implementation.* San Francisco: Jossey-Bass.

Millis, B. J. (2004). A versatile interactive focus group protocol for qualitative assessments. In C. M. Wehlburg & S. Chadwick-Blossey (Eds.), *To improve the academy: Resources for faculty, instructional, and organizational development, Vol. 22* (pp. 125–141). Stillwater, OK: New Forums Press.

Milloy, P. M., & Brooke, C. (2004). Beyond bean counting: Making faculty development needs assessment more meaningful. In C. M. Wehlburg & S. Chadwick-Blossey (Eds.), *To improve the academy: Resources for faculty, instructional, and organizational development, Vol. 22* (pp. 71–92). Bolton, MA: Anker.

Montgomery, S. (1999). A course on teaching engineering. *Proceedings of the 1999 American Society for Engineering Education Annual Conference and Exposition.* Retrieved from http://soa.asee.org/paper/conference/paper-view.cfm?id=14736

Montgomery, S. M., & Groat, L. N. (1998). *Student learning styles and their implications for teaching.* CRLT Occasional Paper, No. 10. Ann Arbor, MI: Center for Research on Learning and Teaching, University of Michigan.

Morris, R. V. (2003). Acting out history: Students reach across time and space. *International Journal of Social Education, 18*(1), 44–51.

Moser, F. Z. (2007). Faculty adoption of educational technology. Retrieved from http://www.educause.edu/EDUCAUSE+Quarterly/EDUCAUSEQuarterlyMag azineVolum/FacultyAdoptionofEducationalTe/157436

Murray, H. (1985, September). Classroom teaching behaviors related to college teaching effectiveness. In J. G. Donald & A. M. Sullivan (Eds.), *Using research to improve teaching* (pp. 21–34). New Directions for Teaching and Learning, No. 23. San Francisco: Jossey-Bass. doi:10.1002/tl.37219852305

Nagda, A., Gurin, P., Sorensen, N., & Zuniga, X. (2009). Evaluating intergroup dialogue: Engaging diversity for personal and social responsibility. *Diversity & Democracy, 12*(1), 4–6.

National Institute of Education. (1984). *Involvement in learning: Realizing the potential of American higher education.* Washington, DC: Author.

National Science Board. (2004). *Science and engineering indicators, 2004.* (NSB 04-01). Arlington, VA: National Science Foundation, Division of Science Resource Statistics.

National Science Foundation, Division of Science Resources Statistics. (2003). *Women, minorities, and persons with disabilities in science and engineering: 2002.* (NSF 03-312). Arlington, VA: National Science Foundation.

Neal, E., & Peed-Neal, I. (2010). Promoting your program and grounding it in the institution. In K. J. Gillespie, D. L. Robertson, & Associates (Eds.), *A guide to faculty development* (2nd ed., pp. 99–115). San Francisco: Jossey-Bass.

Nicolle, P. S., & Lou, Y. (2008). Technology adoption into teaching and learning by mainstream university faculty: A mixed methodology study revealing the "how, when, why, and why not." *Journal of Educational Computing Research, 39*(3), 235–265. doi:10.2190/EC.39.3.c

Nyquist, J. D., & Sprague, J. (1998). Thinking developmentally about TAs. In M. Marincovich, J. Prostko, & F. Stout (Eds.), *The professional development of graduate teaching assistants* (pp. 61–88). Bolton, MA: Anker.

Nyquist, J. D., & Wulff, D. H. (1988). Consultation using a research perspective. In E. Wadsworth, L. Hilsen, & M. Shea (Eds.), *A handbook for new practitioners* (pp. 81–88). Stillwater, OK: New Forums Press.

O'Neal, C., & Karlin, J. (2004). Graduate student mentors: Meeting the challenges of the ongoing development of graduate student instructors. In C. M. Wehlburg & S. Chadwick-Blossey (Eds.), *To improve the academy: Resources for faculty, instructional, and organizational development, Vol. 22* (pp. 320–332). Bolton, MA: Anker.

O'Neal, C., Meizlish, D., & Kaplan, M. (2007). *Writing a statement of teaching philosophy for the academic job market.* CRLT Occasional Paper, No. 23. Ann Arbor, MI: Center for Research on Learning and Teaching, University of Michigan.

O'Neal, C., & Pinder-Grover, T. (in press). *How can you incorporate active learning into your classroom?* Ann Arbor, MI: Center for Research on Learning and Teaching (CRLT), University of Michigan.

Ouellett, M. (Ed.). (2005). *Teaching inclusively: Resources for course, department and institutional change in higher education.* Stillwater, OK: New Forums Press.

Ouellett, M., & Ortquist-Ahrens, L. (2009, January). *Multicultural Organizational Development Institute,* joint session of the Professional and Organizational Development Network (POD) and Association of American Colleges and Universities (AAC&U). Retrieved from http://www.podnetwork.org/conferences/2009-AACU/index.htm and http://www.podnetwork.org/about/pdf/2009%20MCOD%20Institute%20Report.pdf

Overall, J. U., & Marsh, H. W. (1979). Mid-term feedback from students: Its relationship to instructional improvement and students' cognitive and affective outcomes. *Journal of Educational Psychology, 71*(6), 856–865.

Pace, D. (2004, Summer). Decoding the reading of history: An example of the process. In D. Pace & J. Middendorf (Eds.), *Decoding the disciplines: Helping students learn disciplinary ways of thinking* (pp. 13–21). New Directions for Teaching and Learning, No. 98. San Francisco: Jossey-Bass. doi:10.1002/tl.143

Pace, D., & Middendorf, J. (Eds.). (2004). *Decoding the disciplines: Helping students learn disciplinary ways of thinking.* New Directions for Teaching and Learning, No. 98. San Francisco: Jossey-Bass.

Park, P. (1999). People, knowledge, and change in participatory research. *Management Learning, 30*(2), 141–157.

Patton, M. Q. (2002). *Qualitative research and evaluation methods* (3rd ed.). Thousand Oaks, CA: Sage.

Pchenitchnaia, L., & Cole, B. R. (2009). Essential faculty development programs for teaching and learning centers in research extensive universities. In L. B. Nilson & J. E. Miller (Eds.), *To improve the academy: Resources for faculty, instructional, and organizational development, Vol. 27* (pp. 287–307). San Francisco: Jossey-Bass.

Penny, A. R., & Coe, R. (2004). Effectiveness of consultation on student ratings feedback: A meta analysis. *Review of Educational Research, 74*(2), 215–253.

Perlman, B., Gueths, J., & Weber, D. A. (1988). *The academic intrapreneur: Strategy, innovation and management in higher education.* New York: Praeger.

Pinder, T. (2007). Teaching practice: Emphasis on active learning. In C. Ross & J. Dunphy (Eds.), *Strategies for teaching assistant and international teaching assistant development* (pp. 76–79). San Francisco: Jossey-Bass.

Pinder-Grover, T., & Groscurth, C. (2009). *Principles for teaching the millennial generation: Innovative practices of U-M faculty.* CRLT Occasional Paper, No. 26. Ann Arbor, MI: Center for Research on Learning and Teaching, University of Michigan. Retrieved from http://www.crlt.umich.edu/publinks/occasional.php

Pinder-Grover, T., Milkova, S., & Hershock, C. (in press). Training TAs as consultants at the University of Michigan: Workshop series for peer mentors. In K. Brinko (Ed.), *Practically speaking: A sourcebook for instructional consultants in higher education* (2nd ed.) Stillwater, OK: New Forums Press.

Pinder-Grover, T., Millunchick, J., & Bierwert, C. (2008). Using screencasts to enhance student learning in a large lecture material science and engineering course. *Proceedings of the 38th IEEE/ASEE Frontiers in Education Conference*, Saratoga Springs, NY. Retrieved from http://fie-conference.org/fie2008/papers/1362.pdf

Pinder-Grover, T., Root, S., & Cagin, E. (2008, June). Preparing graduate students to be successful as teaching mentors and as future professionals. *Proceedings of the 2008 American Society for Engineering Education Annual Conference and Exposition*, Pittsburgh, PA. Retrieved from http://soa.asee.org/paper/conference/paperview.cfm?id=8379

Plank, K. M., & Kalish, A. (2010). Program assessment for faculty development. In K. J. Gillespie, D. L. Robertson, & Associates (Eds.), *A guide to faculty development* (2nd ed., pp. 135–149). San Francisco: Jossey-Bass.

Plank, K. M., Kalish, A., Rohdieck, S. V., & Harper, K. A. (2005). A vision beyond measurement: Creating an integrated data system for teaching centers. In S. Chadwick-Blossey & D. R. Robertson (Eds.), *To improve the academy: Resources for faculty, instructional, and organizational development, Vol. 23* (pp. 173–190). Bolton, MA: Anker.

Polanyi, M., & Cockburn, L. (2003). Opportunities and pitfalls of community-based research: A case study. *Michigan Journal of Community Service Learning, 9*(3), 16–25.

Reason, P. (1999). Integrating action and reflection through co-operative inquiry. *Management Learning, 30*(2), 207–226.

Redmond, M. V., & Clark, D. J. (1982, February). Small group instructional diagnosis: A practical approach to improving teaching. *AAHE Bulletin, 34*(6), 8–10.

Rhodes, T. (2002). Could it be that it does make sense? A program review process for integrating activities. In D. Lieberman & C. Wehlburg (Eds.), *To improve the academy: Resources for faculty, instructional, and organizational development, Vol. 20* (pp. 49–61). Bolton, MA: Anker.

Ringstaff, C., & Kelley, L. (2002). *The learning return on our educational technology investment: A review of findings from research.* San Francisco: WestEd RTEC. Retrieved from http://www.wested.org/online_pubs/learning_return.pdf

Rogers, E. M. (2003). *Diffusion of innovations* (5th ed.). New York: Free Press.

Schneider, A. (1999, February 19). When revising a curriculum, strategy may trump pedagogy: How Duke pulled off an overhaul while Rice saw its plans collapse. *The Chronicle of Higher Education*, p. A14.

Schön, D. (1983). *The reflective practitioner.* New York: Basic Books.

Schön, D. (1987). *Educating the reflective practitioner.* San Francisco: Jossey-Bass.

Schroeder, C. M., & Associates. (2010). *Coming in from the margins: Faculty development's emerging organizational development role in institutional change.* Sterling, VA: Stylus.

The Secretary of Education's Commission on the Future of Higher Education. (2006). *A test of leadership: Charting the future of U.S. higher education—A report of the Commission appointed by Secretary of Education Margaret Spellings.* Washington, DC: U.S. Department of Education.

Seldin, P. (1997). Using student feedback to improve teaching. In D. DeZure & M. Kaplan (Eds.), *To improve the academy: Resources for faculty, instructional, and organizational development, Vol. 16* (pp. 335–345). Stillwater, OK: New Forums Press.

Selingo, J. (2005, October 14). U.S. spends billions to encourage math and science students, but it's unclear if programs work, report says. *The Chronicle of Higher Education.* Retrieved from http://chronicle.com/daily/2005/10/2005101402n.htm

Senge, P. M. (1990). *The fifth discipline.* New York: Doubleday.

Senge, P. M. (2000). The academy as learning community: Contradiction in terms or realizable future? In A. F. Lucas & Associates (Eds.), *Leading academic change: Essential roles for academic change* (pp. 275–300). San Francisco: Jossey-Bass.

Seymour, E. (2001). Tracking the processes of change in U.S. undergraduate education in science, mathematics, engineering and technology. *Science Education*, *86*(1), 79–105. doi:10.1002/sce.1044

Seymour, E., & Hewitt, N. M. (1997). *Talking about leaving: Why undergraduates leave the sciences.* Boulder, CO: Westview.

Seymour, E., Melton, G., Wiese, D., & Pedersen-Gallegos, L. (2005). *Partners in innovation: Teaching assistants in college science courses.* Lanham, MD: Rowman & Littlefield.

Shavelson, R. J. (2010). *Measuring college learning responsibly: Accountability in a new era.* Stanford, CA: Stanford University Press.

Shulman, L. S. (1986). Those who understand: Knowledge growth in teaching. *Educational Researcher*, *15*(2), 4–14. doi:10.3102/0013189X015002004

Small, S. (1995). Action-oriented research: Models and methods. *Journal of Marriage and the Family*, *57*(4), 941–955.

Smith, C. (2008). Building effectiveness in teaching through targeted evaluation and response: Connecting evaluation to teaching improvement in higher education. *Assessment & Evaluation in Higher Education*, *33*(5), 517–533.

Smith, K. S. (2003). Assessing and reinvigorating a teaching assistant support program: The intersections of institutional, regional, and national needs for preparing future faculty. In C. M. Wehlburg & S. Chadwick-Blossey (Eds.), *To improve the academy: Resources for faculty, instructional, and organizational development, Vol. 21* (pp. 143–159). Bolton, MA: Anker.

Smith, M. K., Wood, W. B., Adams, W. K., Wieman, C., Knight, J. K., Guild, N., & Su, T. T. (2009). Why peer discussion improves student performance on in-class concept questions. *Science*, *323*(5910), 122–124.

Smith, P. (2009). *Taking back the tower: Simple solutions for saving higher education.* Westport, CT: Praeger.

Snooks, M. K., Neeley, S. E., & Revere, L. (2007). Mid-term student feedback: Results of a pilot study. *Journal of Excellence in College Teaching*, *18*(3), 55–73.

Sorcinelli, M. D. (1991, Fall). Research findings on seven principles. In A. W. Chickering & Z. F. Gamson (Eds.), *Applying the seven principles for good practice in undergraduate education* (pp. 13–25). New Directions for Teaching and Learning, No. 47. San Francisco: Jossey-Bass. doi:10.1002/tl.37219914704

Sorcinelli, M. D. (2002). Ten principles of good practice in creating and sustaining teaching and learning centers. In K. H. Gillespie, L. R. Hilsen, & E. C. Wadsworth (Eds.), *A guide to faculty development: Practical advice, examples and resources* (pp. 9–23). Bolton, MA: Anker.

Sorcinelli, M. D., Austin, A. E., Eddy, P. L., & Beach, A. L. (2006). *Creating the future of faculty development: Learning from the past, understanding the present.* Bolton, MA: Anker.

Sorcinelli, M. D., & Yun, J. (2007, November/December). From mentor to mentoring networks: Mentoring in the New Academy. *Change: The Magazine of Higher Learning, 39*(6), 58–61. doi:10.3200/CHNG.39.6.58-C4

Sorenson, D. L., & Bothell, T. W. (2004). Triangulating faculty needs for the assessment of student learning. In C. M. Wehlburg & S. Chadwick-Blossey (Eds.), *To improve the academy: Resources for faculty, instructional, and organizational development, Vol. 22* (pp. 23–40). Bolton, MA: Anker.

Spolin, V. (1963). *Improvisation for the theater: A handbook of teaching and directing techniques.* Evanston, IL: Northwestern University Press.

Spolin, V. (1986). *Theater games for the classroom: A teacher's handbook.* Evanston, IL: Northwestern University Press.

Stanley, C. (Ed.). (2006). *Faculty of color: Teaching in predominantly white colleges and universities.* Bolton, MA: Anker.

Stanley, C. A. (2001). The faculty development portfolio: A framework for documenting the professional development of faculty developers. *Innovative Higher Education, 26*(1), 23–35.

Stark, J. S., Lowther, M. A., Bentley, R. J., Ryan, M. P., Genthon, M. L., Martens, G. G., & Wren, P. A. (1990). *Planning introductory college courses: Influences on faculty.* Ann Arbor, MI: University of Michigan, National Center for Research to Improve Postsecondary Teaching and Learning.

Steele, C., & Aronson, J. (1995). Stereotype threat and the intellectual test performance of African-Americans. *Journal of Personality and Social Psychology, 69*(5), 797–811.

St. John, E. P., McKinney, J. S., & Tuttle, T. (2006, Summer). Using action inquiry to address critical challenges. In E. P. St. John & M. Wilkerson (Eds.), *Reframing persistence research to improve academic success* (pp. 63–76). New Directions for Institutional Research, No. 130. San Francisco: Jossey-Bass. doi:10.1002/ir.180

Strand, K., Marullo, S., Cutforth, N., Stoecker, R., & Donohue, P. (2003). Principles of best practice for community-based research. *Michigan Journal of Community Service Learning, 9*(3), 5–15.

Streitwieser, B., Light, G., & Pazos, P. (2010, May/June). Entering the community of practitioners: A science research workshop model. *Change: The Magazine of Higher Learning, 42*(3), 17–23. doi:10.1080/00091381003704867

Strenta, A., Elliot, R., Adair, R., Matier, M., & Scott, J. (1994). Choosing and leaving science in highly selective institutions. *Research in Higher Education, 35*(5), 513–547.

Stringer, E. T. (1999). *Action research* (2nd ed.). Thousand Oaks, CA: Sage.

Svinicki, M. D. (1999, Winter). New directions in learning and motivation. In M. D. Svinicki (Ed.), *Teaching and learning on the edge of the millennium: Building on what we have learned* (pp. 5–27). New Directions for Teaching and Learning, No. 80. San Francisco: Jossey-Bass. doi:10.1002/tl.8001

Svinicki, M., & McKeachie, W. J. (2011). *McKeachie's teaching tips: Strategies, research, and theory for college and university teachers* (13th ed.). Belmont, CA: Wadsworth Cengage Learning.

Tiberius, R., Tipping, J., & Smith, R. (1997). Developmental stages of an educational consultant: Theoretical perspective. In K. T. Brinko & R. J. Menges (Eds.), *Practically speaking: A sourcebook for instructional consultants in higher education* (pp. 217–221). Stillwater, OK: New Forums Press.

Tobias, S. (1990). *They're not dumb, they're different: Stalking the second tier*. Tucson, AZ: Research Corporation.

Travis, J. E., Hursh, D., Lankewicz, G., & Tang, L. (1996). Monitoring the pulse of the faculty: Needs assessment in faculty development programs. In L. Richlin & D. DeZure (Eds.), *To improve the academy: Resources for faculty, instructional, and organizational development, Vol. 15* (pp. 95–113). Stillwater, OK: New Forums Press.

Turner, C., & Myers, S. (2000). *Faculty of color in academe: Bittersweet success*. Boston, MA: Allyn & Bacon.

University of Michigan. (2001). [UMIT Survey]. Unpublished data.

University of Michigan. (2005). [UMIT Survey]. Unpublished data.

University of Michigan. (2007). *Diversity blueprints task force final report*. Retrieved from http://www.diversity.umich.edu/about/bp-summary.php

University of Michigan. (2010a). Accreditation 2010: University of Michigan: An institution of global learning, knowledge and engagement. Retrieved from http://www.accreditation.umich.edu/reports/Accreditation%20Report%20Final.pdf

University of Michigan. (2010b, May 21). How laptops can enhance learning in college classrooms. *ScienceDaily*. Retrieved from http://www.sciencedaily.com/releases/2010/05/100520161950.htm

Usability, Support, and Evaluation Lab, University of Michigan. (2008). [CTools usage data]. Unpublished data.

Usability, Support, and Evaluation Lab, University of Michigan. (2009). [CTools usage data]. Unpublished data.

Von Hoene, L., Bo-Linn, C., Border, L., Johnston, K. M., Ronkowski, S., Pingree, A., & Stanton, K. (2006, October). *Differences in common: Graduate student teaching certificate programs*. Presentation at the annual conference of the Professional and Organizational Development Network in Higher Education (POD), Portland, OR.

Wankat, P. C. (2002). *The effective, efficient professor: Teaching, scholarship and service*. Boston, MA: Allyn & Bacon.

Way, D. G., Carlson, V. M., & Piliero, S. C. (2002). Evaluating teaching workshops: Beyond the satisfaction survey. In D. Lieberman & C. M. Wehlburg (Eds.), *To improve the academy: Resources for faculty, instructional, and organizational development, Vol. 20* (pp. 94–106). Bolton, MA: Anker.

Wehlburg, C. (2008). *Promoting integrated and transformative assessment*. San Francisco: Jossey-Bass.

Weick, K. E. (1984). Small wins: Redefining the scale of social problems. *American Psychologist, 39*(1), 40–49.

Weimer, M. (2002). Reading lists. In *Learner-centered teaching: Five key changes to practice*. San Francisco: Jossey-Bass.

Wellman, N., & Spreitzer, G. (2010). Crafting scholarly life: Strategies for creating meaning in academic careers. *Journal of Organizational Behavior*. Advance online publication. doi:10.1002/job.708

Welsh, J. F., & Metcalf, J. (2003a). Cultivating faculty support for institutional effectiveness activities: Benchmarking best practices. *Assessment & Evaluation in Higher Education, 28*(1), 33–46.

Welsh, J. F., & Metcalf, J. (2003b). Faculty and administrative support for institutional effectiveness activities. A bridge across the chasm? *The Journal of Higher Education, 74*(4), 445–468.

Whetten, D. A. (2007). Principles of effective course design: What I wish I had known about learning-centered teaching 30 years ago. *Journal of Management Education, 31*(3), 339–357. doi:10.1177/1052562906298445

Wiggins, G., & McTighe, J. (1998). *Understanding by design*. Alexandria, VA: Association for Supervision and Curriculum Development.

Williams, D., Berger, J., & McClendon, S. (2005). *Toward a model of inclusive excellence and change and postsecondary institutions*. American Association of Colleges and Universities. Retrieved from http://www.aacu.org/inclusive_excellence/documents/Williams_et_al.pdf

Wright, D. L. (2000). Faculty development centers in research universities: A study of resources and programs. In M. Kaplan & D. Lieberman (Eds.), *To improve the academy: Resources for faculty, instructional, and organizational development, Vol. 18* (pp. 291–301). Bolton, MA: Anker.

Wright, M. C. (2010). *The growing importance of teaching at the University of Michigan, 1996–2010*. CRLT Occasional Paper, No. 28. Ann Arbor, MI: Center for Research on Learning and Teaching, University of Michigan.

Wright, M. C., & Bogart, P. (2006, October). *Mutual benefits: Developing intercultural learners and ITAs*. Presentation at the annual conference of the Professional and Organizational Development Network in Higher Education (POD), Portland, OR.

Wright, M. C., Cook, C. E., & O'Neal, C. (2009). The role of a teaching center in administrative training: A developmental model for academic leadership preparation. In L. B. Nilson & J. E. Miller (Eds.), *To improve the academy: Resources for faculty, instructional, and organizational development, Vol. 27* (pp. 278–291). San Francisco: Jossey-Bass.

Wright, M. C., Cook, C. E., & O'Neal, C. (2010). Developing and renewing department chair leadership. In L. B. Nilson & J. E. Miller (Eds.), *To improve the academy: Resources for faculty, instructional, and organizational development, Vol. 28* (pp. 278–291). San Francisco: Jossey-Bass.

Wright, M. C., Finelli, C. J., Meizlish, D., & Bergom, I. (2011). Facilitating the scholarship of teaching and learning at a research university. *Change, 43*(2), 50–56.

Wright, M. C., & Kaplan, M. (Eds.). (2007). *Handbook on departmental GSI development.* Ann Arbor, MI: Center for Research on Learning and Teaching (CRLT), University of Michigan. Available from http://www.crlt.umich.edu/gsis/dept gsidevelopment.php

Wright, M. C., Purkiss, J., O'Neal, C., & Cook, C. E. (2008). International teaching assistants and student retention in the sciences. *Studies in Graduate and Professional Student Development, 11*(1), 109–120.

Wright, W. A., & O'Neill, W. M. (1995). Teaching improvement practices: International perspectives. In W. A. Wright & Associates (Eds.), *Teaching improvement practices: Successful strategies for higher education* (pp. 1–57). Bolton, MA: Anker.

Wrzesniewski, A., & Dutton, J. E. (2001). Crafting a job: Revisioning employees as active crafters of their work. *Academy of Management Review, 26*(2), 179–201.

Wulff, D. H., & Nyquist, J. D. (1986). Using qualitative methods to generate data for instructional improvement. In M. Svinicki, J. Kurfiss, & J. Stone (Eds.), *To improve the academy: Resources for faculty, instructional, and organizational development, Vol. 5* (pp. 37–46). The Professional and Organizational Development Network in Higher Education (POD) and The National Council for Staff, Program and Organizational Development. Stillwater, OK: New Forums Press.

Xie, Y., & Shauman, K. A. (2003). *Women in science: Career processes and outcomes.* Cambridge, MA: Harvard University Press.

Yazisi, H. J. (2004). Student perceptions of collaborative learning in operations management classes. *Journal of Education for Business, 80*(2), 110–118.

Young, R. E. (1987, Winter). Evaluating faculty development programs: Program goals first. In J. F. Wergin & L. A. Braskamp (Eds.) (pp. 71–82). *New Directions for Institutional Research,* No. 56. San Francisco: Jossey-Bass. doi:10.1002/ir.37019875609

Zhu, E. (2007). *Teaching with clickers.* CRLT Occasional Paper, No. 22. Ann Arbor, MI: Center for Research on Learning and Teaching, University of Michigan.

Zhu, E., & Bergom, I. (2010). *Lecture capture: A guide for effective use.* CRLT Occasional Paper, No. 26. Ann Arbor, MI: Center for Research on Learning and Teaching, University of Michigan.

Zhu, E., Groscurth, C., Bergom, I., & Hershock, C. (2010). Assessing and meeting TAs' instructional technology training needs: Research and practice. *Journal of Faculty Development, 24*(3), 37–43.

Zuber-Skerrit, O. (1992). *Action research in higher education: Examples and reflections.* London, UK: Kogan Page.

Zuelke, D. C., & Nichols, T. M. (1995, November). *Collaborative school climate action research for school improvement: Part II.* Paper presented at the Annual Meeting of the Mid-South Education Research Association, Biloxi, MS.

# ABOUT THE EDITORS AND CONTRIBUTORS

## Editors

**Constance E. Cook** has served as executive director of CRLT since 1993, and she was named associate vice provost for academic affairs in 2006. Prior to becoming the director of CRLT, Connie was executive assistant to the president of the University of Michigan, and from 1987 to 1990, she coordinated the FIPSE (Fund for the Improvement of Postsecondary Education) Comprehensive Program at the U.S. Department of Education. Before going to Washington, D.C., Connie was an associate professor at Albion College, where she chaired the political science department. At CRLT, her focus is on institutional transformation (i.e., creating a culture of teaching at a research university), a topic on which she has been writing and lecturing for more than a decade. Her scholarship concerns strategies for pedagogical improvement (e.g., action research, the scholarship of teaching and learning, curricular reform, and multicultural teaching and learning). As executive director, Connie coordinates new initiatives at CRLT and represents both CRLT and the broader university community on teaching and learning issues. She also coordinates professional development programs for international higher education leaders. Connie is clinical professor of higher education at the Center for the Study of Higher and Postsecondary Education as well as adjunct associate professor of political science. She received her BA from Barnard College, her MA from The Pennsylvania State University, and her PhD from Boston University—all in political science. Her two books concern American political interest groups: *Lobbying for Higher Education: How Colleges and Universities Influence Federal Policy* (Vanderbilt University Press, 1998) and *Nuclear Power and Legal Advocacy: The Environmentalists and the Courts* (D.C. Heath/Lexington Books, 1980). See also http://sitemaker.soe.umich .edu/soe/faculty&mode=single&recordID=50749.

**Matthew Kaplan**, CRLT's managing director, runs the day-to-day operations of the center, including oversight of budget, publications and publicity, and CRLT's seminar series. He collaborates with the artistic director of the CRLT Players on theatre projects and with CRLT's professional staff on meeting the needs of the university's instructional community. He also co-directs the LSA Teaching Academy and oversees the Thurnau competition, the university's highest undergraduate teaching award. Matt received his PhD in comparative literature from the University of North Carolina at Chapel Hill, where he worked at UNC's Center for Teaching and Learning for three years before joining CRLT in 1994. He has published articles on the academic hiring process, the use of interactive theatre as a faculty development tool, and the evaluation of teaching, and he co-authored a chapter of *McKeachie's Teaching Tips* on technology and teaching. He co-edited *The Scholarship of Multicultural Teaching and Learning* (Jossey-Bass, 2007), a volume of New Directions for Teaching and Learning, and edited two volumes of *To Improve the Academy* (New Forums Press, 1998, 1999). He was a member of POD's Core Committee from 1998 to 2001.

## Foreword Author

**Lester P. Monts** is the University of Michigan's senior vice provost for academic affairs; senior counselor to the president for the arts, diversity, and undergraduate affairs; and an Arthur F. Thurnau professor of music. He works with the provost and executive vice president for academic affairs on matters related to budget, tenure and promotion, enrollment, and a broad range of academic issues. He oversees the operations of 13 academic units, ranging from teaching improvement to undergraduate admissions and financial aid. Dr. Monts is a former chair of the College Board's Board of Trustees, and currently serves on the Board of the Association of American Colleges and Universities. He received a bachelor's in music education from Arkansas Polytechnic College, a master's degree in trumpet performance from the University of Nebraska–Lincoln, and a doctorate in musicology from the University of Minnesota.

## CRLT Contributors

**Crisca Bierwert,** CRLT's associate director and coordinator of multicultural teaching and learning, provides workshops and consultations for departments and programs, consults with individual faculty members and TAs, and leads programs to promote diversity and social justice efforts at the university. She also does research on student learning outcomes, supports interdisciplinary teaching, and provides multicultural training. She participates in university-wide diversity initiatives and currently chairs the President's Diversity Council. Before coming to CRLT in 2000, she obtained her PhD in cultural anthropology from the University of Washington, worked in the Native educational programs of the Coqualeetza Centre (Sardis, B.C.), and taught at the University of Michigan. Her major publications in anthropology and Native American studies focus on text analysis, cultural politics, and environmental issues; they include *Lushootseed Texts: An Introduction to Puget Salish Narrative Aesthetics* (University of Nebraska Press, 1996) and *Brushed by Cedar, Living by the River: Coast Salish Figures of Power* (University of Arizona Press, 1999).

**Cynthia J. Finelli** is director of CRLT in Engineering, which serves the UM College of Engineering. She earned her BSEE, MSEE, and PhD from UM in 1988, 1989, and 1993, respectively. She holds a joint appointment in the College of Engineering and CRLT and is research associate professor of engineering education at UM. Before joining CRLT in April 2003, she was the Richard L. Terrell Professor of Excellence in Teaching, founding director of the Center for Excellence in Teaching and Learning, and associate professor of electrical engineering at Kettering University. Cynthia is a strong advocate of active, team-based learning in the classroom and is engaged in several engineering education research projects. She is also a past chair of the Educational Research and Methods Division of the American Society for Engineering Education.

**Chad Hershock,** an assistant director at CRLT, coordinates CRLT's sciences and health sciences projects and works on instructional technology initiatives, consults with faculty and TAs on teaching and course design, participates in research and evaluation projects, and facilitates customized workshops on teaching methods. He also created and directs the UM Graduate Teacher Certificate Program and UM Postdoctoral Short-Course on College Teaching in Science and Engineering. Chad's training includes a BS in biology from the University Scholars Program at The Pennsylvania State University and a PhD in biology from UM, where he also completed a postdoctoral fellowship in ecology and evolutionary biology. Prior to joining CRLT in 2005, he worked as a research scientist and project manager at BioMedware, Inc., and as a lecturer at UM's Ann Arbor, Dearborn, and Biological Station campuses. He has been teaching at UM since 1994.

**Deborah S. Meizlish,** an assistant director at CRLT, consults with administrators, faculty, and TAs on course and curricular issues, including assessment; plans university-wide programs on teaching, learning, and academic leadership; and conducts seminars on a wide variety of pedagogical topics.

Deborah co-directs the LSA Teaching Academy and is co–principal investigator on "The Impact of Mega-Cognitive Strategies Within Writing in the Disciplines: Experiments to Improve Writing and Critical Thinking," funded by the Teagle and Spencer foundations. Deborah's research and writing focus on the scholarship of teaching and learning, academic hiring, preparing future faculty developers, and academic integrity. She has a PhD in political science from UM.

**Stiliana Milkova** has a PhD in comparative literature from UC Berkeley and an AB from Brown University. Before coming to CRLT, Stiliana taught comparative literature at Berkeley, where she also mentored TAs. As an assistant director at CRLT, she coordinates the one-day Preparing Future Faculty Conference and the Graduate Teaching Consultant program, and she co-directs the courses for prospective TAs educated in languages other than English. She also consults with faculty and TAs, provides workshops on teaching and learning, and conducts midterm student feedback sessions.

**Tershia Pinder-Grover** received a BS in fire protection engineering from the University of Maryland and went on to earn her MS and PhD in mechanical engineering from UM. In August 2005, she joined CRLT, where she is an assistant director responsible for planning teacher training for new engineering TAs, overseeing the Engineering Graduate Student Mentor (EGSM) Program, co-directing the Rackham-CRLT Preparing Future Faculty Seminar, coordinating the Rackham CRLT Intercampus Mentorship Program, and developing pedagogical workshops. Tershia also consults with faculty and TAs on a variety of teaching and learning issues and participates in engineering education research initiatives.

**Jeffrey Steiger** has been working in theatre and with interactive theatre techniques for over 20 years. His career as an actor and director centers on the idea of theatre as a compelling agent for social change. As artistic director of the CRLT Theatre Program and an artist in residence at CRLT, he creates original scripts, facilitates interactive performances and workshops, collaborates with academic units to apply theatre to their faculty development needs, and consults with faculty and teaching assistants on voice and communication issues. Under his direction, the CRLT Theatre Program has become a national resource, performing at campuses and conferences around the country. In addition to his work with the CRLT Players, Jeffrey writes, directs, and produces original work for the stage. He also has experience in the classroom, having taught courses on performance art, comedy, and acting for non-actors both at UM and in the Ann Arbor community.

**Mary C. Wright** is assistant director for evaluation and an assistant research scientist at CRLT. In this capacity, she works with UM's faculty and academic units on assessment of student learning, evaluation of educational initiatives, and the scholarship of teaching and learning. She also is involved with CRLT's Preparing Future Faculty initiatives. Her research and teaching interests include teaching cultures, graduate student professional development, undergraduate retention in the sciences, and qualitative research and evaluation methods. Her book, *Always at Odds?: Creating Alignment Between Faculty and Administrative Values*, was published in 2008 by SUNY Press. Outside CRLT, Mary has served as an external evaluator for several NSF grants, and she chairs the Professional and Organizational Development Network in Higher Education Graduate and Professional Student Development Committee. Mary earned an AB in sociology from Princeton University, an MA and a PhD in sociology from UM, and an MA in higher education administration from the Center for the Study of Higher and Post-secondary Education at UM.

**Erping Zhu**, who earned a PhD in instructional systems technology from Indiana University, is an assistant director for instructional technology initiatives at CRLT, where she consults with faculty about integrating technology into their teaching and developing courses that incorporate instructional technology. She collaborates with colleagues from UM technology units to provide services and programs to faculty through the Enriching Scholarship program. She also coordinates the Teaching Innovation Prize and directs the Teaching with Technology Institute. She has authored and co-authored chapters in books and encyclopedias, and articles in academic journals. Her research focuses on technology and teaching, scholarship of teaching, and online learning and instruction, and she coordinates CRLT's China initiatives.

## Contributors From Other Institutions

**Terry Aladjem**, executive director, Derek Bok Center, Harvard University

**Lori Breslow**, director, Teaching and Learning Laboratory, Massachusetts Institute of Technology

**Susanna Calkins**, associate director, Searle Center for Teaching Excellence, Northwestern University

**Charles Dershimer**, coordinator of the Woodrow Wilson/Kellogg Foundation/Noyce Secondary Mathematics and Science Teacher Education Programs, School of Education, University of Michigan (CRLT assistant director, 2009–2010)

**Deborah DeZure**, assistant provost for faculty and organizational development, Office of Faculty and Organizational Development, Michigan State University

**Robyn Dunbar**, senior associate director, Center for Teaching and Learning, Stanford University

**Jean C. Florman**, director, Center for Teaching, University of Iowa

**Christopher R. Groscurth,** senior consultant for culture transformation and change leadership at Trinity Health (CRLT instructional consultant, 2008–2010)

**Marne Helgesen**, director, Center for Instructional Excellence, Purdue University

**Alan Kalish**, director, University Center for the Advancement of Teaching, The Ohio State University

**David Langley**, director, Center for Teaching and Learning, University of Minnesota

**Gregory Light**, director, Searle Center for Teaching Excellence, Northwestern University

**Angela Linse**, executive director, Schreyer Institute for Teaching Excellence, The Pennsylvania State University

**Michele Marincovich**, director, Center for Teaching and Learning, Stanford University

**Joan Middendorf**, associate director, Center for Innovative Teaching and Learning, Indiana University

**Christopher O'Neal**, associate director, Teaching, Learning, and Technology Center, University of California, Irvine (CRLT assistant director, 1999–2008)

**Allison Pingree**, director, Center for Teaching, Vanderbilt University

**William C. Rando**, assistant dean and director, Graduate Teaching Center, Graduate School of Arts and Sciences, Yale University

**Mary Deane Sorcinelli**, associate provost for faculty development, Office of Faculty Development, University of Massachusetts Amherst

**Kathy Takayama**, director, Harriet W. Sheridan Center for Teaching & Learning, Brown University

**Pratibha Varma-Nelson**, executive director, Center for Teaching and Learning, Indiana University-Purdue University Indianapolis

**Suzanne Weinstein**, director of instructional consulting, research, and assessment, Schreyer Institute for Teaching Excellence, The Pennsylvania State University

**Mary-Ann Winkelmes**, campus coordinator for programs on learning and teaching, University of Illinois at Urbana-Champaign

AAC&U *see* Association of American Colleges and Universities
ABET, 32
Abbott, R. D., 65
academic job search
    conference for, 102–104
    Graduate Teacher Certificate Program for, 107–109
    mentorship program for, 104–105
    seminar for, 101–102
    teaching course for, 105–107
academic leaders. *see* administrators
accountability, 32, 34, 38
accreditation, 35–36, 58, 129, 134
achievement gaps, 139, 140, 149
action research
    challenges related to, 171–172
    common type of, 170–171
    at CRLT, 174–180
    description of, 168, 169
    and retention in scientific fields, 172–174
    stages and steps, 173
    staying involved in, 180–182
    variants of, 170
active learning
    clicker technology for, 164
    incorporating, 70, 71
    and postdoc short-course, 106, 110
    promoting, 155
    and TA training, 99
    and theatre program, 185
activism, 144
actors
    role-plays using, 187–188
    role-plays without, 191–194
Adair, R., 172
Adams, M., 145
administrative leadership program, 46

administrative support, 27, 131
administrators
    and action research, 181
    being visible to, 59–60
    commitment to teaching by, 114
    and curricular reform, 123–127, 132–134
    forging alliances with, 146–147
    obtaining support of, 176–177
    offering opportunities to, 60–62
    recommendations for, 109–112
ADVANCE program, 142–143, 183, 185
advertising for hiring staff members, 23
advisory committees, 58, 111
Agee, A. S., 151
Ajjan, H., 152
Aladjem, Terry, 203
Albright, M. J., 63
Allan, D., 60
alliance building, 146–147
Allison, D. H., 151
Anselmi, K., 187
antiracist teaching, 187
Armstrong, F., 170
Armstrong, P., 98
Aronson, J., 140
assessment
    of student learning, 14, 15, 30, 171
    services, 35–36, 39, 46, 60–63, 121–136, 140, 145–146, 181, 204–206
Associates in Teaching (AT) Program, 211
Association of American Colleges and Universities (AAC&U), 8, 28, 97, 148
Astin, A. W., 172
Astin, H. S., 172
attrition and retention in sciences, 172–174, 176
Austin, A. E., 6, 19, 57

Bain, Ken, 203
Baldwin, R., 210
Banta, T. W., 122, 123, 124
Baron, L., 35, 51, 58
Bartlett, T., 2
Bass, Randy, 205
Baumal, R., 187
Baxter Magolda, M. B., 146
Beach, A. L., 6, 19, 168
beats, 189
Beebe, S. A., 6
Bell, L., 145
Bellows, L., 98, 171
Benbassat, J., 187
benchmarking, 46, 60, 180
Bennett, W. J., 2
Bensimon, E. M., 140
Benson, L., 170
Bentley College, 206
Berg, J. M., 25
Berge, Z. L., 165
Berger, J., 148
Bergom, I., 44, 154
Bernstein, D. J., 6, 51
Bierwert, C., 141
Bishop, R., 171
Bjork, R. A., 140
Black, B., 65, 73, 171
Black, K. E., 122
Blackburn, R. T., 52, 56
blended and online teaching, 107, 197, 204
blogs, 154
Blumberg, P., 51
Boal, Augusto, 186
Bogart, P., 100
Boice, R., 56, 110
Bok, D. *see also* Derek Bok Center at Harvard University, 2, 56, 122
Border, L., 80
Bothell, T. W., 39, 46
Brandsford, J., 140
breakout sessions, 103, 107, 139
Breneman, D. W., 2
Breslow, Lori, 210
Brinko, K. T., 77, 170, 193
Brooke, C., 39, 46

Brookfield, S., 140
Brown, A., 140
Brown, Donald, 4
budget issues
    CRLT in Engineering, 31–32
    development and fund-raising, 31
    fee-for-service approach, 30–31
    foundation grants, 31

Cagin, E., 45
Calkins, S., 39, 204, 205
Callan, P. M., 2
Cameron, K., 21
Camp, J. S., 151
Campbell, P. B., 172
Campus Leadership Program, 43, 59, 60, 188
campus visits, 104, 105
Canales, J., 6
capstone, 99–100, 107
Career stages, addressing specific, 209–210
Carlson, V. M., 39
Carnegie Foundation for the Advancement
    of Teaching, 8
Celsi, R. L., 152
Center for Research on Learning and Teach-
    ing (CRLT)
    50th anniversary of, 1
    action research project at, 174–180
    assessment projects, 35–36
    changing roles of, 3–5
    creation of, 3
    current profile, 5
    directors of, 4
    evaluation matrix, 40–47
    faculty issues, 14
    graduate students at, 5, 14, 27, 42
    grant competitions by, 20, 30, 35
    mission of, 13, 87
    MSF process at, 7
    vs. other teaching centers, 5–8
    overview of, 13–16
    PTC program at, 80–81
    publicity efforts by, 52–53
    purpose of, 1
    research agenda, 3–4, 29, 56
    services provided by, 13

special emphasis of, 14
staff members, 5, 13
support for, 2–3
Center for Teaching at the University of
    Massachusetts at Amherst, 150
Centra, J. A., 38, 39
centralized peer consultant program, 81
change agencies, 51, 122, 132
Change Magazine, 184
Chesler, M. A., 186
Chesler, N. C., 171, 186
Chickering, A., 71, 164
Chism, N. V. N., 19, 42, 43
Chronicle of Higher Education, The, 23, 125
CIC. *see* Committee on Institutional
    Cooperation
civic engagement, 125
Clark, D. J., 65
classroom
    climate, 68, 99, 114, 148, 179
    communication, 99
    discussion, guidelines for, 143
    dynamics, 15, 70, 74, 139, 144
    observations, 76, 84, 93, 117
clearinghouse, 6, 64
Clerici-Arias, M., 83
clickers
    description of, 163
    evaluation of, 163–164
    use of, 155
coaching, 158–159
Cockburn, L., 171
Cocking, R., 140
Coe, R., 65
cognitive crafting, 27
cognitive development, 27, 146
cognitive psychology, 211
Cohen, M. D., 34
Cohen, P., 65
Colbeck, C. L., 97
Cole, B. R., 6, 51, 63
Cole, J., 154
College of Engineering, 7, 8, 13, 29, 31
College of Literature, Science, and the Arts
    (LSA), 45, 81, 82

Colloquium on the Science of Learning, 145,
    146
Colloquium on the Science of Multicultural
    Teaching and Learning, 46
Committee on Institutional Cooperation
    (CIC), 196
communication
    of evaluation data, 47–48
    of study results, 177–178
    strategies, 179
    with teaching assistants, 178–179
community colleges, 1, 101
community engagement, 206
conference(s)
    for PFF program, 102–104
    for staff members, 28
    technology, 158
Connolly, M. R., 39, 97
consultants
    CRLT in Engineering, 32
    faculty perceptions of, 72
    hiring issues, 21–25, 191–192
    and in-house programs, 28
    and instructional technology, 154
    and MSF process, 66–67
    research data for guiding, 70–73
    surveys by, 74–75
consultation
    about role playing, 192
    assessing impact of, 70–71
    with chairs and deans, 142
    for curricular reform, 131–132
    on diversity training, 147
    with faculty, 144, 194–195
    individual, 141, 143, 156–157, 205
    for multicultural teaching, 142
    for student learning, 135
    on teaching philosophy statements, 113
    training for, 192–194
    for TTI process, 161
Cook, C. E., 19, 45, 46
course management system, 152, 157
Cox, A., 141
CRLT Annual Report
    communication through, 48, 133

and research agenda, 29
UM clients data in, 42
CRLT in Engineering
   as branch of CRLT, 31
   creation of, 32
   PTC program in, 82
   TA orientation in, 99
CRLT *Occasional Papers*, 4, 53, 56, 155,
   181–182
cross-disciplinary exchange, 144
Cross, K. P., 170
curricular reform and assessment
   and action research, 181
   conducting, 128
   consultation for, 131–132
   and faculty involvement, 123–127
   grants for, 130–131
   introduction to, 121
   and outcome measures, 127–130
   research on, 122–123
   sample survey for, 129
Curriculum Enhancement Grant, 208
Cutforth, N., 170

Dalkey, N. C., 73
Damsker, J. I., 187
data collection
   about curriculum review, 127–128
   research for, 60–61
   on science TAs, 174
   for student learning, 135
deans. *see also* administrators
   addressing priorities of, 61–62
   consultation with, 142
   curricular reform initiative by, 124–127
   meeting needs of, 62–63
DeBlois, P. B., 151
decision making process, 23–25
Deerman, A., 140
Delphi technique, 73
Denman, M., 83
D'Eon, M., 44
department-based peer consultant program,
   81
department chairs. *see* administrators

Derek Bok Center at Harvard University,
   203, 239
Dewey, B. I., 151
deWinstanley, P. A., 140
Dey, E., 140
DeZure, D., 140, 209, 210
Diamond, M. R., 65
Diamond, R. M., 51, 101, 122
Diaz, A., 205
directors, list of CRLT, 4
disciplinary backgrounds
   diversity issues, 102
   for hiring staff members, 22
   and PFF conference, 103
discipline-specific programming, 207–209
diversity. *see also* multicultural teaching and
   learning
   and clientele, 7, 11, 15, 56–57, 110
   and disciplinary backgrounds, 102
   and faculty issues, 57, 141–143
   hiring issues, 23
   impact of, 15, 147–150
   and student success and retention, 140–141
   and theatre program, 7
doctoral students, teaching opportunities for,
   210–211
Donohue, P., 170
Dotson, W. H., 6, 51
dramatic techniques, 189–191
Drane, D., 39, 205
Dreifus, C., 2
Dunbar, Robyn, 201
Dutton, J. E., 25, 26

early adopters, 152
Eble, K. E., 42, 57
Eddy. P. L., 6, 19, 168
EDUCAUSE, 23, 151, 213, 216, 218, 222, 226
Edwards, P. M., 39
Elden, M., 171
Elliot, R., 172
*Engaging the Whole of Service Learning,
   Diversity, and Learning Communities*,
   145
Engineering Graduate Student Mentor
   (EGSM) program
   creation of, 82

evaluation of, 84–86
impact of, 86–87
English Language Institute, 100, 107, 142, 146, 178
enriching scholarship, 158, 239
environmental justice, 194–195
e-portfolios, 131
Erb, S., 187
Ericksen, Stanford C., 3
evaluation data
 communication of, 48
 internal use of, 47
evaluation forms, 43
evaluation research, 7, 26, 34, 169
Ewell, P. T., 2
experimental design, 48–49, 130
external grants, 30, 31, 32, 156

F2P2 program, 200
faculty. *see also* preparing future faculty (PFF) program
 and action research, 181–182
 being visible to, 52–53
 and community engagement, 206
 and consultants, 72, 74, 75
 creating relationship with, 52–54, 56–58, 181
 at CRLT, 14
 and curricular reform, 123–127
 customized programs for, 57
 engaging, in teaching, 202–205
 geographic dispersion issues, 204
 grant competitions for, 7, 14, 54–55
 guidelines for, 143–144
 individual consultation for, 156–157
 international, 15, 57, 142
 mentors, 105
 mid-career, 209–210
 and MSF process, 67–68, 70
 network opportunities for, 57
 obtaining support of, 176–177
 offering opportunities to, 53–54, 56
 opinion leaders, 57, 58
 orientation. *see* New Faculty Orientation
 and PFF program, 113–114
 publicizing accomplishments of, 54

research on, 123
responding to needs of, 56–58
and role playing, 187–191, 194–195
seminars for, 145
strengths of, 67–68
and student learning–based perspective, 205–206
success of, 141–143
suggestions for, 69
support for, 198–199
and teaching innovation, 151–152
technology training for, 158–159
tenure and promotion, xi, 4–5
TTI use by, 159–162
workshops for, 4
Faculty Advisory Board, 57, 58, 209
Faculty Communities Hub, 204
faculty development/developers. *see also* teaching center
 and action research, 169–172
 and alliance building, 147
 and China initiative, 36
 defined, 50
 discipline-specific, 208–209
 effectiveness of, 51
 evaluation of, 39
 hiring people with, 22
 and institutional needs, 197–198
 literature on, 122
 long-term transfer issues, 45
 and multicultural teaching and learning, 138, 148–150
 recommendations for, 109–112
 role-playing in, 186–187
 and university initiatives, 33
federal agency, 31, 172
feedback
 about courses, 170
 about workshops, 42–44
 from advisory committees, 111
 during MSFs, 70, 78–79
 other ways to get, 73–76
 TA training, 85–86
 on teaching, 106, 107
fee-for-service approach, 30–31
Felten, P., 98

Fendrich, L., 124
Ferren, A., 39, 42
Finelli, C. J., 44, 70, 74
first-year seminars, 57, 197
Fishman, B., 154
focus groups. *see* interviews and focus groups
foundation grants, 31
Frantz, A. C., 6, 39, 57
Freirie, Paulo, 186
Freisem, K., 39
Fried, C., 140
funding
    from academic units, 30
    measuring impact of, 44
Future Faculty Preparation Program (F2P2),
    200

Gaddy, C. D., 172
Gaff, J., 122
Galura, J., 145
*Games for Actors and Non-Actors*, 186
Gamson, Z., 71, 164
garbage can model of policymaking, 34–35
Gardner, S. K., 104
gateway courses
    and action research, 174
    description of, 174
    designing, 177
    problems with, 180
    and research agenda, 29
    survey for, 140, 174
Geltner, B. B., 170
gender
    and authority, 142–143
    dynamics of, 143, 186
general education requirements, assessing,
    127–128
genetic counseling, 194
"Getting Ready for an Academic Career"
    conference, 102
Gillespie, K. J., 1, 6, 19
Glenn, D., 2, 54
Good, C., 140
Google Analytics, 42
Gordon, H., 81
Gottfried, A. C., 70

Gouldner, A. W., 176
grading, 99–100, 116, 132, 157, 179.
Graduate School
    and course on teaching, 105–107
    and Graduate Teacher Certificate Pro-
        gram, 107–109
    and mentorship program, 104–105
    and PFF program, 100–104
graduate students. *see also* peer teaching con-
        sultants (PTCs); preparing future fac-
        ulty (PFF) program
    at CRLT, 5, 14, 27, 42
    IMP for, 104–105
    international, 103
    mentors, 29, 98, 180
    surveys, 45, 47, 85
Graduate Teacher Certificate Program, 44,
    107–109, 116–117
Graduate Teaching Consultant (GTC)
        Program
    creation of, 81–82
    evaluation of, 84–86
    impact of, 86–87
    syllabus, 91–94
grants
    for curricular reforms, 130–131
    external, 30, 31, 32, 156
    foundation, 31
    instructional, 44, 134
    for multicultural learning, 138
    by Schreyer Institute, 204
    for student learning, 135
    for technology, 155–156, 163
grant competitions
    by CRLT, 20, 30, 35
    for faculty, 7, 14, 54–55
Greenwood, D. J., 171
Griffin, P., 145
Groat, L. N., 172
Grooters, S., 39
Groscurth, C., 47
GSI (Graduate Student Instructor). *see also*
        TA training
GSI mentor program, 95–96
Guest Lecture series, 208
Gueths, J., 51

Gurin, G., 140
Gurin, P., 102, 140

Ha, L., 156
Hacker, A., 2
Hagner, P. R., 156
Hake, R. R., 71
Halaby, C. N., 127
Halperin, D., 187
Halstead, D. K., 169
Harkavy, I., 170
Harper, K. A., 40
Harriet W. Sheridan Center for Teaching &
     Learning at Brown University, 207, 241
Harrison, A., 44
Hartshorne, R., 152
Harvard University, 124, 203, 239
Hativa, N., 59
Helgesen, Marne, 202
Helmer, O., 73
Henderson, T., 39
Herschbach, Dudley, 203
Hersh, R. H., 124
Hershock, C., 47, 70, 82
Heru, A. M., 187
Hess, C. W., 65
Hewitt, N. M., 172, 174
Higher Ed. *see* Inside Higher Ed
Hines, S. R., 39
hiring
     and advertising, 23
     criteria, 23–25
     and role playing, 191–192
     staff members, 21–25
     and theatre program, 184
Hoey, L., 172
Holland, P. E., 152
Holstrom, E. I., 172
Horii, C. V., 80, 83
Horvath, V. S., 6
hot moments, 144
Howard, J., 145
Howland, J., 156
Hugentobler, M. K., 171
humanities, 68, 70, 103, 139, 159
human resources offices, 28

human subjects approval, 49
humor, 139, 184
Hunt, N., 65, 73
Huntzinger, M., 80, 81
Hursh, D., 39
Hurtado, S., 140
Hussey, T., 2
Hutchings, Pat, 64, 122
Huwe, J. M., 104
hybrid course. *see* blended and online
     teaching

IGR. *see* Program on Intergroup Relations
*Improvisation for the Theatre*, 186
IMP. *see* Intercampus Mentorship Program
individual consultations, 141, 143, 156–157,
     205
individualized learning, 156
Ingerman, B. L., 151
in-class engagement, 154
inclusive teaching, x, 15, 116, 138–140
in-house programs, 28
innovation issues
     and faculty needs, 54, 56
     and multicultural teaching and learning,
          138, 140
     and TA training, 87
     technology related, 151, 152
inquiry-based learning, 107
Inside Higher Ed, 23
institutional problems
     feedback about, 44
     solving, 34–35
     and teaching centers, 197–202
institutional review board (IRB), 49, 131, 174
instructional consultants. *see* consultants
instructional development
     and curricular reform, 122
     custom designed solutions for, 62–63
     defined, 50
instructional grants, 44, 134
instructional improvement. *see* teaching
     improvement
instructional technology (IT)
     collaborative approach for, 164–165
     conclusion about, 165–166

at CRLT, 6
evaluation of, 129–130, 162–164
grants for, 155–156, 163
integration of, 151
promoting effective use of, 152–156
PTC program for, 83
support for, 156–162
surveys about, 47
and teaching innovation, 151–152
instructional theme, 154
instructors. *see* faculty
intensive training, 158–159
interactive lecturing, 69, 99, 140
Intercampus Mentorship Program (IMP),
   104–105
interdisciplinary degree programs, 130
international faculty, 15, 57, 142
International Society for the Scholarship of
   Teaching and Learning (ISSOTL), 28,
   92
interviews and focus groups
   for instructional changes, 44
   for MSF sessions, 67
   for multicultural teaching, 128
   and role playing, 187–188
   use of, 43
intrapreneurial leadership, 51, 64
Investigating Student Learning Grant, 15, 44,
   163
IRB. *see* institutional review board
Israel, B. A., 171
IT, *see* instructional technology
IT-PTC program, 83, 85, 157–158
Ivy League (Plus) institutions, 6
Ivy League (Plus) Teaching Consortium, 21
Ivy League (Plus) Teaching Center Directors,
   196

Jacobson, W., 39
job crafting
   cognitive crafting, 27
   description of, 25–26
   relational crafting, 26–27
task crafting, 26
Johnson, W. B., 104
Johnston, J., 98

Jolly, E., 172
Jones, C., 187
Jones, D., 2
just-in-time training, 158

Kalish, A., 40, 43, 49, 198
Kaplan, Matthew, 9, 45, 47
Karlin, J., 82
Keller, G., 21
Kelley, L., 162
Kendall Brown, M., 110, 182
King, Patricia, 146
Kodotchigova, M. A., 187
Krogh, L., 170
Kucsera, J. V., 49
Kuhlenschmidt, S., 1, 6, 51
Kulik, James, 3, 4, 56

laboratory course, 107, 185
laggards, 152
Langley, D., 40, 199
Lankewicz, G., 39
large lectures, 15, 63, 110, 155, 164
late adopters, 152, 155, 156
Lattuca, L. R., 122
La-Vaque-Manty, D., 184, 185, 186
Lawrence, J. H., 52, 56
leadership
   and budget issues, 30–32
   development of, 210
   and director's role, 19–21
   and finding and nurturing staff, 21–25
   and operational principles, 32–37
   and professional development, 27–29
   and workload issues, 25–27
leading discussion, 100, 139
learning bottleneck, 205–206
learning communities, 39, 81, 145, 198, 206
learning outcomes, 2, 131, 133–134, 138, 144,
   161, 163, 199, 236
learning styles, 179, 207
learning and teaching commons, 197
*Lecture Capture: A Guide for Effective Use*, 155
LectureTools, 129, 130
Lee, J., 139
Levin, M., 171

Lewin, K., 169, 172, 180
Lewis, K. J., 72, 77, 81
LGBT students, 147
liberal arts, college of, 30–31, 57–61, 143, 176
Liebowitz, J., 187
"Life After the PhD: Adjusting to a New
    Institutional Context," 103
Light, G., 39, 204, 205
Likert scale, 43, 76
Lin, C., 156
Linse, Angela, 203
living-learning programs, 4
Lonn, S., 152
Lou, Y., 154, 156
Lovitts, B., 104
Luna, M., 39
Lund, J. P., 122

Mann, B. D., 187
March, J. G., 34
Marincovich, M., 56, 59, 81, 201
Marsh, H. W., 65
Marullo, S., 170
Massachusetts Institute of Technology
    (MIT), 6, 124, 210, 239,
Massy, W., 152
mathematics. *see also* STEM, 11, 60–61, 208
Matier, M., 172
matrix model of evaluation, 39
McClendon, S., 148
McDonald, J., 88
McGregor, J., 187
McKeachie, Wilbert, 3, 42, 57
*McKeachie's Teaching Tips*, 3
McKinney, J. S., 169
McPherron, P., 80
medical schools, 1, 58
Meizlish, D., 44, 45, 84
Melton, G., 174
*Memo to the Faculty*, 4
Menges, R. J., 39, 77
mentors/mentorship
    graduate students, 29, 80, 95–96, 180
    intercampus, 104–105
    postdoctoral, 106
    and PTC program, 87

for staff members, 27
Merriam, S. B., 3
Metcalf, J., 123, 124, 127
Michigan-China University Leadership
    Forum, 8, 36, 45–46
Michigan State University, 209, 239
microteaching sessions, 99, 100
Middendorf, Joan, 205
midterm student feedbacks (MSFs)
    common themes related to, 67
    conducting, 66–67
    at CRLT, 7
    feedback on, 67–68, 70, 85–86
    form for, 78–79
    *see also* Small Group Instructional
        Diagnosis
Milkova, S., 82
Millar, S. B., 39
Miller, A. T., 138
Millis, B. J., 65
Milloy, P. M., 39, 46
Millunchick, J., 141
minority students. *see* diversity
mission drift, 198
MIT *see* Massachusetts Institute of
    Technology
Montgomery, S. M., 82, 172
Moore, M., 170
Moreno, Jacob, 186
Moretto, K., 210
Morgan, S., 6
Morris, R. V., 187
MSFs. *see* midterm student feedbacks
multicultural teaching and learning
    addressing, 128–129
    consultation for, 142
    focus on, 7
    in general program, 138–140
    grants for, 138
    supporting, 143–146
multimedia elements, 155, 157, 183
Murray, H., 67, 71, 76
Mussell, K., 39, 42
Myers, S., 141

Nagda, A., 102
Nation, J., 44

National Center for Institutional Diversity, 63, 146
National Conference for Race & Ethnicity in Higher Education (NCORE), 28
national Initiatives, 8
National Science Foundation (NSF), 114, 156, 172
Neal, E., 51
needs assessment
　conducting, 63, 110–111
　models, 39
　for planning initiatives, 46
Neeley, S. E., 65
new faculty. *see also* faculty
　orientation for, 14, 41, 53, 139
　reception for, 57
Nichols, T. M., 170
Nicolle, P. S., 154, 156
Nidiffer, J., 47
Nielan, B. A., 187
Nieman, L. Z., 187
Nyquist, J. D., 65, 97, 170

*Occasional Papers. see* CRLT *Occasional Papers*
Oblander, F. W., 122
Office of Academic Multicultural Initiatives, 147
Office of Faculty and Organizational Development, Michigan State University, 209, 239
Office of Faculty Development, University of Massachusetts, 197, 241
Ohio State University, 40
Olsen, J. P., 34
on-campus professional development, 28
O'Neal, C., 47, 60, 70
O'Neill, W. M., 170
online learning. *see* online and blended teaching
operational principles, 8, 9, 19, 32–37, 51
organizational action research, 169
organizational development, defined, 50
orientation
　for new faculty, 14, 41, 53, 139
　teaching, 98–100, 114

teaching assistants, 139, 178–179
　and trigger vignette development, 188–189
Ott, M., 70
Ouellett, M., 138
*Our Underachieving Colleges*, 122
outcome measures, analysis of, 127–130
Overall, J. U., 65
overview of CRLT. *see* CRLT

Pace, D., 140, 205
Park, P., 170
participant narratives, 43
partnerships, 88, 101, 181, 183, 202, 208
Pasque, P., 145
Pazos, P., 205
Pchenitchnaia, L., 6, 51, 63
pedagogy. *see* teaching
Pedersen-Gallegos, L., 174
Peed-Neal, I., 51
peer teaching consultants (PTCs)
　CRLT program for, 80–81
　description of, 83–84
　emergence of, 81–83
　evaluation of, 84–87
　graduate students as, 45, 80
　GTC and EGSM programs impact on, 86–87
　implications of, 87–88
　program coordinators for, 84
　selection of, 84
　workshops for, 83, 89–90
Penny, A. R., 65
People of Color Environmental Summit, 194
Perlman, B., 51
Perlman, L. K., 172
PFF. *see* preparing future faculty program.
PhD students, teaching opportunities for, 211
Piliero, S. C., 39
Pinder-Grover, T., 45, 74, 82
Pingree, A., 98, 197, 200
Plank, K. M., 40, 43, 49
plenary sessions, 103, 138, 139
POD. *see* Professional & Organizational Development Network in Higher Education
podcasts, 15, 28, 106–107, 141, 155

Polanyi, M., 171
postdocs
  as facilitators, 100
  IMP for, 104
  teaching course for, 105–107, 110
postdoctoral science scholars, 29
poster fairs, 59, 131, 136, 163
Povlacs, J. T., 72, 77
power, privilege, and oppression, 145
Power, Eugene, 3
practice teaching sessions, 89, 107, 114, 178
preparing future faculty (PFF) program. *see
    also* faculty
  conclusion about, 114–115
  conference for, 102–104
  courses for, 29, 105–107
  faculty's role in, 113–114
  influence of, 112–113
  intercampus mentorship program,
    104–105
  models for, 98
  piloting and evaluating, 111–112
  requirements of, 114
  seminar for, 100–102
  surveys about, 47
  teacher orientations, 98–100
  UM Graduate Teacher Certificate,
    107–109
preparing actors, 195
private foundations, 31
procedures manuals, 26–27
Professional and Organizational Develop-
    ment Network in Higher Education
    (POD), 22, 50, 92, 210
professional development
  China initiative for, 36
  for graduate students, 108
  needs, addressing, 200–201
  and PTC program, 83
  for staff members, 27–29
  and trigger vignette development, 188–189
professional schools, 58, 131, 132, 136
professional staff members. *see* staff members
Program on Intergroup Relations (IGR), 145
project staff, hiring of, 25
Prostko, J., 97

provost
  and budget issues, 30
  campus leadership program, 43, 59, 60, 188
  and CRLT initiatives, 33
  and curricular reform, 133
  and faculty orientation, 53
  meeting needs of, 62
  seminars on teaching, 37, 43, 124
  and teaching awards, 54
PTCs. *see* peer teaching consultants
publicity efforts
  by CRLT, 52–53
  for faculty's accomplishments, 54
  for showcasing technology's use, 154–155
publishing. *see* research.
Purkiss, J., 100

qualitative evaluation, 75, 112
quality control issues, 34
quantitative evaluation, 89, 112
quantitative reasoning (QR) requirement,
    127–128
Quick Course Diagnoses, 65

race, 57, 141, 191
reaccreditation, 35–36
*Rainbow of Desire, The*, 186
Rajagopal, M., 80
Rando, William C., 211
RCM. *see* Responsibility-Centered
    Management
Reason, P., 170
Redmond, M. V., 65
relational crafting, 26–27
research
  assessment and evaluation, 7
  at CRLT, 3–4, 29, 56
  on curricular reform, 122–123
  for data collection, 60–61
  on faculty, 123
  and grant writing, 204–205
  for guiding consultants, 70–73
  for improving student learning, 15–16
  publication of, 4–5, 7, 159
  on teaching and learning, 101, 110

research universities, 2–3, 6, 9, 20, 28, 45, 51–52, 54–59, 67, 80, 130, 196–212
Responsibility-Centered Management (RCM), 30
retention
and faculty success, 141–143
in scientific fields, 172–174, 176
and student success, 140–141
retention and transfer, 211
retrospective data, 44
return on investment, 39
Revere, L., 65
reward system, 52
Ringstaff, C., 162
risk management process, 200
Robert Menges Award for Outstanding Research in Faculty Development, 210
Robertson, D. L., 1, 6, 51
Rogers, E. M., 152
Rohdieck, S. V., 40
role-playing
benefits of, 195
consultation about, 194–195
in faculty development, 186–187
and faculty-staff relations, 188–191
using actors, 187–188
without actors, 191–194
Root, S., 45
Ropp, V. A., 65
roundtables for instructional technology, 153–154
Rovito, M. A., 187
rubrics, 90, 92, 101, 108, 130, 132, 145

Sachdeva, A. K., 187
Sadownik, L., 44
Saturday Night Live, 186
Schneebeck, C. A., 156
Schneider, A., 124
Schoem, D., 145
Scholarship of Teaching and Learning (SoTL) projects
determining effectiveness of, 44
for instructional improvement, 131
promotion of, 56
and research agenda, 29

Schön, D., 24, 170
school of social work, 195
Schreyer Institute of Teaching Excellence, The Pennsylvania State University, 81, 203–204, 240, 241
Schurman, S. J., 171
science faculty, 174, 207
Science Fridays (SciFri), 207
science of learning, 15, 93, 99, 140, 145
Science, Technology, Engineering, and Mathematics (STEM), 103, 105–106, 131, 145, 173, 207, 208
Scott, J., 172
Searle Center for Teaching Excellence, Northwestern University, 204, 239, 240
Second City, 186
Seldin, P., 170
self-reports, 44, 45
Selingo, J., 172
seminars. see also workshops
for academic job search, 101–102
for active learning, 106
for instructional technology, 153–154
by IT-GTCs, 156–157
longer-term, 145
for PFF program, 100–102
on teaching, 37
Service-Learning Course Design Workbook, 145
service-learning courses, 206
service orientation, 32–33
Seymour, E., 172, 174
SGID. see Small Group Instructional Diagnosis
Shavelson, R. J., 2
Shaw, A., 210
Shopkow, L., 205
Shulman, T. S., 57
Shuman, K. A., 172
Singer, R., 156
sketches for theatre program, 143, 183, 184, 185
Small, S., 170
Small Group Instructional Diagnosis (SGID), 65, 81, 170
Smith, K. S., 97
Smith, P., 2, 110

Smith, R., 23
Snooks, M. K., 65
social work, 195
Sorcinelli, M. D., 6, 19, 33, 197
Sorensen, N., 102
Sorenson, D. L., 39, 46
Spolin, Viola, 186
Sprague, J., 97
Spreitzer, G., 26
staff members. *see also* consultants
    at CRLT, 5, 13
    desired skills for, 23–24
    hiring, 21–25
    professional development for, 27–29
    staff retreat for, 28
    support for, 26–27
    workload issues, 25–27
Stanford University, v, 6, 80, 201, 240
Stanley, C., 141
Stark, J. S., 122
State of Michigan's Distinguished Professor
    Award, 54
Steadman, M. H., 170
Steele, C., 140
Steiger, J., 45, 184
STEM disciplines, 106, 131, 207, 208
Stewart, A. J., 184
St. John, E. P., 169
Stoecker, R., 170
Stout, F., 97
Strand, K., 170
Streitwieser, B., 205
Strenta, A., 172
Stringer, E. T., 170
student feedback. *see* feedback
student learning
    assessment of, 15, 106, 121, 126, 134
    collaboration for, 63–64
    consultation for, 135–136
    CRLT in Engineering for, 32
    data collection for, 135
    facilitating, 99
    grants competitions for, 54
    improvement of, 3, 13, 15–16
    research in, 101

technology for, 129–130
and theatre program, 184–185
student ratings
    and CRLT services, 44
    gains in, 71
    for teaching improvement, 76
student(s). *see also* graduate students; teach-
        ing assistants
    diversity issues, 99, 138, 139
    success and retention, 140–141
surveys
    about courses, 140, 170, 174, 180
    about instructional technology, 47
    about PFF program, 47
    of audiences, 44
    by consultants, 74–75
    faculty development professionals, 39, 42
    of grantees, 44
    of students, 29, 45, 47, 70–71, 85
Svinicki, Marilla, 3, 39, 49
Swee, D. E., 6
Sweetland Center for Writing, 63
"switch" technique, 190–191
Szabó, B., 42, 43, 54

Takayama, Kathy, 207
Tang, L., 39
task crafting, 26
*Task Force on Testing and Training Prospective
        Graduate Student Instructors*, 178
TA training
    at CRLT, 29, 32
    department-based, 82, 201
    EGSM program for, 82
    feedback issues, 85–86
    improvement of, 178–180
    IT-GTC program for, 83
    and orientation issues, 98–100, 114, 139,
        178–179
    and PTC program, 87–88
teaching
    awards, 37, 54, 56, 58
    changes in practice of, 71–72
    commitment to, 114
    engaging faculty in discussion about,
        203–205

excellence, promoting, 112–115
feedback on, 106
graduate assistant development in, 201
innovation issues, 140, 151–152, 170
and learning perspective, 205–206
orientations, 98–100, 114
philosophy statement, 90, 101, 108, 113
technology for, 162–164
workshops related to, 83
Teaching Academy program, 41, 45, 60, 209
Teaching and Learning Laboratory, Massachusetts Institute of Technology, 210, 239
teaching assistants. *see also* action research; TA training
communication issues, 178–179
at CRLT, 6, 13
international, 99
and multicultural teaching and learning, 138–139
orientation, 139, 178–179
and retention in scientific fields, 172–174, 176
seminars for, 145
suggestions for, 69
teaching experience as, 22
teaching center. *see also* Center for Research on Learning and Teaching (CRLT)
and action research, 170–171
appropriate involvement of, 199–200
budget issues, 30–32
challenges for, 132–134
checks and balance system for, 198
clients served by, 42
collaboration efforts by, 63–64, 111
conclusion about, 48–49, 212
demand for, 202
development of, 1–2
director's role at, 19–21, 37
and discipline-specific programming, 207–212
evaluation matrix, 39–47
and faculty engagement, 202–206
hiring issues for, 21–25
and institutional-level challenges, 197–202
leveraging experience of, 110

literature on, 122
mission of, 175–176
operational principles, 32–37
opportunistic nature of, 35–36
professional development issues, 27–29
promoting faculty use of, 52
purpose, 1
workload issues, 25–27
Teaching Certificate program, 200, 201
teaching experience
and CRLT services, 43
hiring people with, 22
lack of, 106
as professional development, 29
*Teaching for Diversity and Social Justice*, 145
teaching improvement
consultants' role in, 72
director's role in, 19
grants for, 4, 54
and SoTL projects, 131
student ratings for, 76
teaching opportunities
for doctoral students, 210–211
for PhD students, 211
*Teaching with Clickers*, 155
Teaching with Technology Institute (TTI), 41, 46, 159–162
Teagle Foundation, 203
Teasley, S. D., 152
technology. *see* instructional technology
*Theatre Games for the Classroom: A Teacher's Handbook*, 186
*Theatre of the Oppressed*, 186
theatre program
and ADVANCE program, 142–143, 183
at CRLT, 7, 14
evaluation model, 44–45
and faculty-staff relations, 188–191
impact of, 185–186
reasons for success of, 184–185
and role playing, 186–187, 191–195
and trigger vignettes, 187–188
Thurnau Professorships, 14, 54
Tiberius, R., 23, 27, 28
"time-out/time-in" technique, 189–190

Tipping, J., 23
Tobias, S., 172
training
    for consultation, 192–194
    intensive, 158–159
    just-in-time, 158
    of science TAs, 175
Travis, J. E., 39, 46
trigger vignettes, 187–190, 195
Turkle, Sherry, 203
Turner, C., 141
Tuttle, T., 169
Two-Survey Method (TSM), 73–75

Undergraduate Research Opportunities Program, 63
Unit Liaisons, 204
University Center for the Advancement of Teaching, The Ohio State University, 198, 240
university diversity council, 147
university initiatives
    and CRLT initiatives, 33
    curricular reform, 123–130
    grants for, 54, 130–131
    Michigan-China University Leadership Forum, 36
University of Chicago, 6
University of Illinois at Urbana-Champaign, 208, 241
University of Michigan
    assessing need for new services at, 46–47
    CRLT creation by, 3
    Graduate Teacher Certificate Program, 107–109, 116–117
University of Minnesota, 40
University of Washington, 150
University of Wisconsin, 127
university reaccreditation, 35
upper-level writing requirement, 131
U. S. Professor of the Year, 14, 54

Van Horne, V. V., 172
Varma-Nelson, Pratibha, 207
video podcasts, 106, 107, 129

vignette development, 187–191
von Hoene, L., 80, 107

Wankat, P. C., 56
Way, D. G., 39, 45
Weaver, S., 6
Weber, D. A., 51
Wedman, J. A., 156
Wehlburg, C., 122, 132
Weick, K. E., 35, 126
Weinstein, Suzanne, 203
Weissinger, E., 98, 171
Wellman, N., 26
Welsh, J. F., 123, 124, 127
"What's Working in TA Training", 201
Whetten, D. A., 101
Wieman, Carl, 203, 208
Wiese, D., 174
wikis, 35, 84, 152, 154
Williams, D., 148
Winkelmes, Mary-Ann, 208
Wolfinbarger, M., 152
workload issues
    cognitive crafting, 27
    description of, 25–26
    relational crafting, 26–27
    task crafting, 26
workshops
    for consultation, 192–193
    for curricular review, 132
    customized, 145, 146, 182
    for doctoral students, 210–211
    facilitators for, 100
    for faculty, 4
    feedback about, 42–44
    for instructional development, 63
    on multicultural teaching, 139, 142, 144, 148
    by prospective candidates, 23–24
    for PTC program, 83, 89–90
    and role playing, 193–194
    for student learning, 135
    teaching related, 83
Wright, D. L., 6, 51, 130
Wright, M. C., 44, 45, 47, 188
Wright, W. A., 170

Wright Dunbar, R., 83
writing centers, 63, 131, 132
Wrzesniewski, A., 25, 26
Wulff, D. H., 39, 65, 170

Xie, Y., 172

Yang, C., 151
Yazisi, H. J., 187
Young, R. E., 39

Yun, J., 104

Zemsky, R., 152
Zhu, E., 47, 154, 161
Zimmerman, C. M., 172
Zlotkowski, Edward, 206
Zuber-Skerrit, O., 171, 172
Zuelke, D. C., 170
Zuniga, X., 102

# Also available from Stylus

**Coming in From the Margins**
*Faculty Development's Emerging Organizational Development Role in Institutional Change*
Connie Schroeder
With Phyllis Blumberg, Nancy Van Note Chism, Catherine E. Frerichs, Susan Gano-Phillips, Devorah Lieberman, Diana G. Pace, and Tamara Rosier

"No doubt about it, we have entered a new era in faculty development. As our institutions face a myriad of changes, faculty developers will increasingly need to look beyond traditional instructional development boundaries to emerging organizational development roles. The pressures put on faculty developers during this time of flux are immense. Luckily, this important new book, based on original research and state-of-the-art practice, provides a cogent range of insights into what we are all experiencing. This book is an indispensable and timely addition to the field that takes a hard look at where we are right now, and provides a road map for the future." —*Mary Deane Sorcinelli, Associate Provost for Faculty Development, and Professor, Educational Policy, Research and Administration, University of Massachusetts Amherst*

Recognizing that a necessary and significant role change is underway in faculty development, this book calls for centers to merge their traditional responsibilities and services with a leadership role as organizational developers. Failing to define and outline the dimensions and expertise of this new role puts centers at risk of not only marginalization, but of dissolution.

Proposing a newly defined *organizational development* role for academic and faculty developers, and directors of teaching and learning centers, the authors explain how significant involvement in broader institutional change initiatives is becoming a critical aspect of this work.

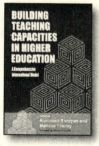

**Building Teaching Capacities in Higher Education**
*A Comprehensive International Model*
Edited by Alenoush Saroyan and Mariane Frenay
Foreword by James E. Groccia

This book is the culmination of three years' work by teams from eight institutions in five different European and North American countries interested in developing and disseminating a more profound understanding of university-level pedagogy. The purpose of the project was, first, to conceptualize what an internationally-appropriate, formal academic program for faculty development in higher education might look like, taking into account differing national contexts in Belgium, Canada, Denmark, France, and Switzerland.

The second purpose was to define a common curriculum, or core course with common foundations, for faculty and graduate students, based on a distributed learning model. This book offers practitioners around the world a framework and model of educational development that can serve a number of purposes including professional development, monitoring, and assessment of effectiveness, and research, as they seek to meet increasing demands for public accountability.

**Rethinking Teaching in Higher Education**
*From a Course Design Workshop to a Faculty Development Framework*
Edited by Alenoush Saroyan and Cheryl Amundsen

"If one could write the shortest review I would write: 'read this book.' It is a well-designed and structured description of how to provide an environment conducive to reflection through meaningful dialogues and relevant and informative workshops [for faculty development]. This book is highly readable, informative and engaging. It is a good text to have on the shelf, when pondering: what to do, why do I do this and what can I do to change others' practice." —*Quality Assurance in Education (Australia)*

Sty/us

22883 Quicksilver Drive
Sterling, VA 20166-2102

Subscribe to our e-mail alerts: www.Styluspub.com